HOLY MURDER

Abraham, Isaac, and the Rhetoric of Sacrifice

Larry Powell

William R. Self

University Press of America,® Inc.
Lanham · Boulder · New York · Toronto · Plymouth, UK

I would like to express my appreciation to my wife, Clarine, for her love, patience and understanding during the development of this study. Special thanks must also go to my father, Harold Powell, who is himself an ardent student of the Bible and its teachings.

Larry Powell

Dr. Larry Powell has been a pleasure to work with on this effort. The most important person who inspired me to write my portions of the book is Tani Self, the best wife in the world. I also thank Laura Elizabeth Self, my daughter for her presence in my life. My mother, Katharine Self is responsible for most of my verbal abilities. She and I are living proof that reading to children at early ages provides them with verbal tools and literary skills. To Mark Hickson, Jean Bodon, and others who advised me, I thank you sincerely.

William R. Self

Table of Contents

SECTION I

AN ORIENTATION

Chapter 1
Introduction

The sun rising over the desert illuminated a busy scene. Servants scurried around the owner's elaborate campsite, preparing for an unexpected journey.

Their master's intentions caught them by surprise, for he had only learned of the trip himself the night before. He arose early that morning, gave his servants instructions, then proceeded to awaken his son.

His son was an obedient child, the joy of his life. The master would do practically anything for the youngster who was slated to inherit all of his worldly riches, as well as continue his line into perpetuity.

And he knew his son was just as devoted to him, the father. His son would do whatever he asked.

This day he would ask the child to join him on a three-day journey. The father knew the child would comply. In all likelihood, the child would agree even if he knew what his father planned to do. But his father would not tell him that. At least not now. That was too painful to speak of, even to himself.

After all, he planned to kill his own son.

The Voice had told him to do it. Not just any voice, but The Voice. The One that spoke to him like God.

"Go to the mountains," The Voice had said. And sacrifice his son. His only son. Who he loved.

He dared not disobey. Regardless of how much he loved his son, he must obey The Voice.

The servants were preparing for the trip now. He would summon his son himself.

And, three days later, he would be poised to kill him.

That scene, recounted briefly in Genesis 22:3, opens one of the most intriguing and controversial stories in the Bible—the *akedah*, or sacrifice of Isaac. The original story covers 14 verses (Gen. 22:1-14) credited to the mysterious Genesis writer who scholars call "E" (Marks, 1983). It starts with Abraham's awakening early one morning and concludes three days later when the Patriarch climbed a mountain with Isaac, intent on sacrificing his son to the God who commanded the act.

Today, more than 3,000 years later, the story continues to evoke controversy. As Bill Moyers (1996) wrote, "No story in Genesis asks harder questions. Would God make an unethical demand? Should we consider pious or crazy or both the father who puts a knife to the throat of his son because he's heard the voice of God telling him to do so?" (p. 219). Feiler (2001) noted that "Because of this story's drama and its potential chilling consequences for history, the *akedah* has been one of the most discussed chapters of the Bible" (p. 90). Marks (1983) called it "a literary masterpiece" (p. 49). Theologian Robert Alter (1996) said "The abrupt beginning and stark, emotion-fraught development of this troubling story have led many critics to celebrate it as one of the peaks of ancient narrative" (p. 103).

It has had an impact on three great religions—Judaism, Christianity, and Islam—each with a different interpretation. It has inspired religious fundamentalists, biblical theologians, philosophers, and songwriters—each with different insights. Even among adherents of a common faith, interpretations of the passage differ. It has been used to support both free-will and deterministic theologies, liberal and conservative views, traditional and feminist interpretations. Even more disturbing, the story has been used to justify a range of questionable behaviors ranging from baby killings, mass murder, and suicide bombings.

Regardless of which interpretation is favored, the story creates a moral dilemma that makes most readers "feel extremely ill at ease when faced with the task of decoding" the story (Keller, 1980, p. 438.). As Joseph Telushkin noted, "Abraham's readiness to obey God's command shows him to be ethically deficient by later standards" (p. 38). Folk-rock singer Bob Dylan expressed a similar sentiment when he sang, "God said to Abraham, 'Go kill me a son.' Abe said, 'Man, you must be puttin' me on.'" Yet Abraham continued, and the specifics of his story offer modern man a chance to examine a diverse range of moral, theological, and rhetorical dilemmas.

The passage attracts the reader by its sheer repulsiveness, depicting a potential act so despicable, so alien to modern morality that it invites moral uncertainty. Davis (1999) noted, "To many people, it has always seemed an unnecessarily cruel test of faith" (p. 77). Phyllis Trible (as cited in Moyers, 1996, p. 226) said, "this story is terrifying precisely because it is God Who sets up the test." Cahill (1998) wrote:

> I doubt that anyone has ever read this story. . .without being transfixed. Many who heard the story as children and know perfectly well how it will end . . . cannot bring themselves to look at it again or consider seriously 'the monster god of the Old Testament,' as one woman called him with a shudder. (p. 82)

Similarly, Karen Armstrong (1993) argued that "to modern ears, this is a horrible story: it depicts God as a despotic and capricious sadist, and it is not surprising that many people today who have heard this tale as children reject such a deity" (p. 67). Marks (1983) described the story as "a literary masterpiece," but added that the story is "bearable only because the reader knows the situation is a trial" (p. 49).

Erich Fromm (1967, p. 47) noted that the story is psychologically uncomfortable to modern readers. "The human attitude behind [that story] is profoundly different from that behind Abraham's readiness to sacrifice Isaac," he wrote. Fox (1995) described it as "a story which is so stark as to be almost unbearable" (p. 92). Telushkin (1997, p. 38) agreed when he wrote that the story:

> provokes an intense moral conflict in modern readers. On the one hand, Jews and Christians see Abraham as the first Patriarch, a man to be admired and emulated. But how can moral people admire a man who is prepared to commit an act for which moral people might wish to see him executed, imprisoned for life, or consigned permanently to an asylum? (p. 38)

Feilor (2001) noted that the story is also:

> the first time that God explicitly challenges Abraham, or anyone else in the Bible. Up to now, God has created the world; he has formed the Garden of Eden, then banished Adam and Eve; he has flooded the world, then salvaged Noah; he has commanded Abraham to "go forth." But here he openly tests Abraham's faith, and, by extension, the faith of the readers. The *akedah* is the first truly interactive moment in the Bible, the first time the reader is forced to ask: "What would I do in this situation?" (p. 91)

Davis (1999) called the story "a central moment in the Bible" (p. 77). McGee (1999) described the single chapter that recounts the tale as "one of the ten greatest chapters in the Bible" (p.66). Miles (1996) called the story "one of the boldest, deepest fables in the Bible . . . [that] is rightly admired as a masterpiece of economy, psychology, and artistic subtlety" (p. 58). It is God's seventh and final recorded appearance to Abraham, and begins the Patriarch's final test. "After this, there is nothing more that God could ask Abraham to do," McGee (1999, p. 66) concluded.

The story begins with an explanatory sentence telling the reader about the test, i.e., "that God did tempt Abraham" (Gen. 22:1). Abraham was not provided with that information in advance, but his answer was nonetheless simple, indicating a willingness to obey even though he had not yet received the instructions: "Behold, here I am."

Then God gave his instructions. "Take now thy son, thine only son Isaac, whom though lovest, and get thee into the land of Moriah; and offer him there for a burnt offering upon one of the mountains which I will tell thee of" (Gen. 22:2). He arose early the next morning, saddled his donkey, and embarked on a three-day journey with Isaac and two servants (v. 3). Their destination—the mountains of Moriah. After three days of travel (v. 4), when the caravan could see their destination, they stopped and established a camp.

With the two servants remaining in the camp, Abraham and Isaac went up the mountain to worship, promising the men that he and the son would go "and come again to you" (v. 5). Abraham had Isaac carry the wood for the burnt-offering, while he carried the fire and the knife. Isaac, by now, had deduced that the purpose of the trip was to make a sacrifice to God, but he was confused by the absence of an offering. When he raised the issue, Abraham responded, "God will provide himself a lamb for a burnt offering" (22:8).

That is the last conversation between the two characters recorded in Genesis. They continued the climb, reaching a spot that has a large rock that could serve as a natural altar, "the place which God had told him of" (v. 9).

Abraham and Isaac built an altar and gathered the wood for the fire, after which Abraham bound his son in preparation for the sacrificial ritual. As he raised his knife to plunge it into the boy, though, he was stopped by the voice of an angel that "called unto him out of heaven" (v. 11).

Abraham's response is almost identical to his initial response to God's instructions: "Here am I" (v. 11). Isaac was not to be killed, because the angel said, "Now I know that thou fearest God" (v. 12).

Looking up, Abraham spotted a ram caught in a thicket by his horns. He removed Isaac from the altar, offering the ram as "a burnt offering in the stead of his son" (v. 13).

Questions

Even in a simple retelling, it's a chilling story that raises a number of disturbing questions (Davis, 1999): Is that kind of obedience to a divine call acceptable? Would Abraham actually have gone through with the sacrifice? What kind of God would ask a parent to do this?

The latter question so disturbed 12th century commentator Rashi that he painted Abraham as a religious zealot who insisted on the sacrifice himself even when God relented. As Goldstein (1998) noted, "Rashi was disturbed, as many modern readers are, by the idea that God would need or want such a sacrifice in the first place" (pp. 20-21). Such questions nag at those who seek a God who fits into a logical human framework, but they have no easy answers.

Purpose of the Book

The happy ending does little to alleviate the moral questions raised by the story. Instead, that is handled by the beliefs, faith, or rationalizations of those who are interested in the story. Most answers, though, are still unsatisfying. Most raise as many questions as they are intended to answer. The purpose of this book is not to answer those questions so much as to examine them and to understand how different people might incorporate those explanations as rhetorical devices for their personal belief systems (i.e., how some individuals and cultures use the story as the basis for a *rhetoric of sacrifice*). As Dershowitz (2000) noted:

> No one can read the story of the *akeidah* literally and accept it as a clear guide for human action. It cries out for explication, for disagreement, for reflection, and for concern. It provides no answers, only eternally unanswerable questions, and in that

respect it is the perfect tool for teaching the realities, limitations and imperfections of both divine and human justice. (p. 129)

We will review some of the theological interpretations but make no attempt to resolve the disagreements that still exist. Philosophers, theologians and other scholars have addressed the questions for years, often with no definitive answers. The authors have little to add to that debate. What can be addressed, from the perspective of communication scholars, are the rhetorical implications of the story. Hick (1957) observed that a people's religious beliefs serve as fundamental standards by which they interpret their experiences. Thus the goal is to examine those interpretations in terms of the rhetorical implications of the passage, rather than try to explain its theological implications.

Given Aristotle's definition of rhetoric as discovering, in any given situation, all of the "available means of persuasion," two avenues of study are available. The first is argument from justification, i.e., interpreting the elements of the story in such a manner as to support an existing belief. Scholars who engage in this form of interpretation argue in reverse. Standard deductive logic takes a series of logical premises and uses those to reach a logically consistent conclusion. Justification development, though, starts with an accepted conclusion and works the argument backward by constructing premises that support that conclusion. Unfortunately, the predetermined conclusion typically influences the justification drawn by that scholar. That is the limitation of any biased interpretation, whether it be St. Augustine who uses the story to support his belief in God or the atheist who argues that such a god could not exist. Both interpretations are limited by the fact that the critics have decided in advance what the conclusion of the argument will be. Such arguments are still important to the communication scholar, though, because justifications provide insight into the rhetorical theories of the individual making those judgments. Those justifications will be studied, as such, in this book.

The second rhetorical implication of the story is the use of the story as a rhetorical device. The story of Abraham and Isaac has provided fodder for a number of rhetorical arguments ranging from literary inspiration to political rhetoric. In terms of literary allusions, John Steinbeck looked in Genesis for the inspiration of *East of Eden*. He retold the book by following the lives of several generations of a family that lived in Salinas Valley. In the political arena, Alabama voters defeated a proposed amendment for a state lottery to finance college scholarships in 1999, a defeat commonly attributed to anti-gambling opposition from churches. After the defeat, one pro-lottery commentator compared the churches' opposition to God's instructions to Abraham to kill his son, arguing that preachers were asking people to sacrifice the education of their children: "If God speaks to you and tells you to sacrifice your children (either in His name or in the name of politics), it might be time to start making your own decisions for a change (Butler, 1999)."

The scene has even found its way to popular culture. An episode of NBC's *"The Pretender"* included a story line in which a man kidnaps young boys to mold them into his own sons; those that were found unacceptable were killed. When cornered, the villain said, "I am the father. He is the son. I am Abraham. He is Isaac." Although this was a fictional story, it's not unrealistic. Mentally ill criminals often proclaim themselves to be biblical characters.

While many rhetorical examples are from the secular world, the story has also provided inspiration for thousands of pulpit sermons on a variety of topics—some of which have drawn contradictory conclusions. This study will examine some of those arguments. In doing so, the various theological approaches to the story will be examined, but those "answers" will be studied in terms of what they say about the rhetorical uses of the story by believers of the three great religions more than what they say about God. Those arguments that one uses in an attempt to persuade others are usually those arguments that the source of the message has found personally persuasive. Again, the authors will not attempt to look at each of these individual rhetorical efforts. Instead, the goal will be to examine the story in terms of the rhetorical devices available for the rhetor to use. The rhetorical implications of such analyses can provide further insight into the story and its theological implications.

One theory of Bible study is that thorough examination of any passage in the Bible will eventually lead to a study of the entire Bible. While that will not be totally accurate for this particular passage, it will lead to a number of other areas of biblical, theological and philosophical study. As Feiler (2001) discovered, the story of Abraham and Isaac is a "crystal" through which you can look "and see a hundred different angles" (p. 92). That crystal spreads light on a number of other theological issues that are discussed elsewhere in both the Old and New Testament.

In looking through this crystal, hopefully some rhetorical insight will be revealed. Questions may not be fully answered, but perhaps they can be better understood.

Chapter 2
The Story: Verse by Verse

The Judeo-Christian version of Abraham's sacrifice of Isaac is told in 19 verses in the 22nd chapter of Genesis. Before examining some of the issues raised by the story, it will be instructive to look at each verse individually. Those verses, which are presented here in the King James Version, have much to offer.

1. **And it came to pass after these things, that God did tempt Abraham, and said unto him, Abraham: and he said, Behold, here I am.**

And it came to pass after these things . . . This phrase could also be translated as "some time afterward," a reference to the events recorded in the preceding chapter. That indicates the timing was important. "The supreme crisis in Abraham's life," as Thomas (1985, p. 49) called it, came after the birth of Isaac (Gen. 21:1-8), the exile of Hagar and Ishmael (Gen. 21:9-21), and Abimelech's covenant with Abraham at Beersheba (Gen. 21:22-34). The birth of Isaac fulfilled God's promise to Abraham and Isaac, with Isaac becoming the most important person in Abraham's life. The exile of Hagar and Ishmael further intensified the importance of Isaac as Abraham's only remaining son at home. Meanwhile, Abraham met with Abimelech, a meeting that expanded Abraham's understanding of God. That meeting prompted the Patriarch to dig a well and plant a grove of trees at Beersheba. And, Beersheba would be the place to which Abraham would return after the crisis at Moriah had passed.

The phrase also affects calculations regarding Isaac's age. The verse does not say "immediately after these things," so some period of time had passed. The fact that Isaac could carry on a conversation with his father means that he was beyond young childhood. In other words, several years had passed between the beginnings of chapters 21 and 22.

. . . *that God did tempt Abraham* . . . The idea that God tempts people is associated with the problem of evil, an issue discussed later in this book. Most theologians (e.g., Cahill, 1998, pp. 82-84) argue that God never tempts anyone to do evil. That concept is supported by the Book of James, in which the author wrote, "God cannot be tempted with evil, neither tempteth he any man" (James 1:13). But, the word "tempt" in the context of this story, can be translated as "to test" or "to prove," and that has been the most common interpretation (Spiegel,

1993). One common interpretation of the entire story, in fact, is that it was Abraham's final test before the covenant with God was sealed. It was, as Spiegel (1993) called it, "The Last Trial" (p. 1). The anti-climatic remainder of Abraham's life is described in the following chapter, but nothing he does ever reaches the level of tension and suspense that is created by the *akedah.*

But why tell us that? As Telushkin (1997) noted, this "uncharacteristic, explanatory sentence" gives the reader "important information that is being withheld from Abraham" (p. 37). Cahill (1998) argued that "the narrator, knowing that poor human readers could never bear the suspense, tells us that this will be a 'test,' so we know that Yitzhak [Isaac] will not actually be sacrificed" (p. 82). Otherwise, the story might be too painful to read. Indeed, Marks (1983) added, the passage is "bearable only because the reader knows the situation is a trial" (p. 49).

. . . *and said unto him, Abraham:* . . . God addresses Abraham by name, which illustrates the unique relationship between the Patriarch and Jehovah. Abraham would become, after all, the founder of God's chosen people. But there may have been a more immediate reason for including Abraham's name in this verse. Baldwin (1986) argued that God's use of Abraham's name emphasized that the approaching test was both a personal and lonely test for Abraham, one that he was not "to share with the mother of an only son. Abraham . . .bore the full force of the instruction" (p. 90).

. . . *and he said, Behold, here I am.* Abraham's response to God's call has been the topic of numerous sermons that talk of his readiness to do God's will. This phrase frequently appears in the Bible as a term used to convey readiness. In the New Testament, for example, when God speaks in a dream to Ananias of Damascus, Ananias says, "Behold, I am here, Lord" (Acts 9:10). But the implications of the response are broader. Within the Hebrew culture, the term was usually a reply that someone would make after being addressed by superior or someone of higher social status (Fox, 1995, p. 93). Thus Abraham's response indicated both a readiness to obey and recognition of being in the presence of a Superior Being.

2. And He said, Take now thy son, thine only son Isaac, whom thou lovest, and get thee into the land of Moriah; and offer him there for a burnt offering upon one of the mountains which I will tell thee of.

And He said, Take now thy son, thine only son Isaac, whom thou lovest . . . Baldwin (1986) said "The threefold description rules out any possibility of misunderstanding" (p. 90). Fox (1995) noted that the name of the child "is left until the end of the phrase, to heighten tension" (p. 93). Telushkin (1997) said that "The language . . .is deliberately intended to magnify the pain the command raises" (p. 38). Alter (1996) wrote that "The Hebrew syntactic chain is exquisitely forged to carry a dramatic burden . . ." (p. 103). Each phrase, each word is carefully chosen to intensify the pain of the approaching command. For example, some scholars prefer the phrase "favored one" instead of "thine only son," but Alter argued that this interpretation misses the point that Isaac is Abraham's only son by his legitimate wife. Further, this phrase returns as a thematic refrain later in the story, in verses 12 and 16.

Although Abraham never speaks, Atler (1996) offered a possible implied conversation: "Your son (I have two sons), your only one (this one is an only one to his mother and this one is an only one to his mother), whom you love (I love both of them), Isaac" (p. 103). While the dialogue is hypothetical, it illustrates how each phrase is increasingly more intimidating to Abraham.

Fox (1995) also noted an interesting parallel with the triplet in this passage and with God's earlier instructions to Abraham to leave his father and homeland. In Genesis 12:1, God instructed Abraham to migrate to Canaan with the instruction to depart "From your land, from your kindred, from your father's house." The difference, he noted is that "There he had been asked to give up the past (his father); here, the future (his son)" (p. 92). Between the two events, Abraham has an active life in which he communicates with God. This instruction from God, though, is the last he will receive. After this, God never speaks to him again.

. . . *and get thee into the land of Moriah* . . . The traditional English translation of Abraham's destination is "Moriah." It can also be translated as "Moriyya," which is typically interpreted as "seeing" or "Yahweh sees." By the fourth century BC the most common interpretation identified the location as Mount Moriah, primarily based on a reference in II Chronicles 3:1 that identifies it as the place where Solomon's Temple was built (Armstrong, 1996b). Others believe it might refer to Mount Moreh, which is near Sheechem. Tradition identifies it as "Abraham's Rock," the peak of Mount Moriah that currently lies beneath the Islamic Dome of the Rock in Jerusalem. This story does not specify exactly where the event occurred, identifying it only as the "land of Moriah." Realistically, though, the actual location remains in doubt (Alter, 1996, p. 104). As Marks (1998) noted, the Mount Moriah location is inconsistent with the Genesis story, which indicates that there are several mountains in the area. Further, Genesis depicts the event as occurring in an isolated area, while the area around Jerusalem was likely already occupied at the time Abraham and Isaac began to climb the mountain. Regardless, the consequence of designating Jerusalem as the location is that the city has become the center of disagreements and fighting between the Jewish, Islamic, and Christian populations of the area. Those conflicts over the location provided a major source of rhetoric of sacrifice, as members of all three great religions have sought to possess or occupy the land at some point in history.

. . . *and offer him there for a burnt offering* . . . McGee (1991) noted that this part of the instruction represented "the first time human sacrifice is even suggested" in the Bible (p. 66). In fact, it's only the second time that Abraham engages in any form of sacrifice. Hammer (1994) observed that "Abraham erected altars wherever he wandered in Canaan and 'invoked the Lord by name' (Gen. 12:8), but there is no mention of him bringing offerings" (p. 42). The only other instance in which Abraham offered a sacrifice was when God specifically commanded him to do so as part of a covenant ceremony (Gen. 15:9-21). Since the *akedah* represents the final sealing of the Covenant between God and Israel, this incident has some parallels to that ceremony. Specifically, the number three plays an important role in the sacrifice (15:9), the sacrifice includes a ram (v. 9), and God spoke to Abraham while he was in a "deep sleep" (15:12). Regardless, though, sacrifice apparently remained a little-used ritual for the Patriarchs. Hammer also noted that neither Isaac nor Jacob is depicted in subsequent biblical passages as ever offering sacrifices (p. 42).

Another unusual aspect of this part of the command is that it is somewhat ambiguous. It commands Abraham only to "offer" Isaac for a burnt offering, not to actually complete the deed. Some theologians argue that the ambiguity is deliberate, because God would never order anyone to sacrifice their own child. Haley (1992) argued that, because of that ambiguity, Abraham misinterpreted the command and thought it implied the actual slaying of his son (p. 238). Still, it is reasonable to assume that Abraham, a man who was accustomed to hearing God speak, would follow God's most recent orders to the letter. That is, he took all actions short of actually sacrificing Isaac. Indeed, he "offered" Isaac for sacrifice and went so far as to raise his knife—ready, willing and able to sacrifice the son he loved.

. . . upon one of the mountains which I will tell thee of. As noted earlier, this verse refers to the Moriah region which has several mountains—not just one. God gives Abraham rather precise instructions, with one exception—the specific mountain to be used will be revealed later. Interestingly, that never occurs in the story itself. At some point, Abraham comes to realize they have reached their destination, but the reader is never told how Abraham received this knowledge. Perhaps he traveled past all of the mountains in that region and, having reached the final one with no explicit instructions, assumed that it was the one that God intended. In any event, this is one of many examples of the story omitting details surrounding the *akedah*

3. And Abraham rose up early in the morning, and saddled his ass, and took two of his young men with him, and Isaac his son, and clave the wood for the burnt offering, and rose up, and went unto the place of which God had told him.

And Abraham rose up early in the morning . . . Why does Genesis note that Abraham departs from his house "early?" Two factors may be operating here—the timing of God's command and Abraham's desire to leave. Apparently, the message from God came to Abraham the night before. In the Islamic version of the story, the command came in the form of a dream, and this interpretation would be consistent with the Genesis version. God might have used a more direct means of addressing Abraham; if so, though, one would expect that Abraham would have spent a sleepless night—something that the narrator would likely have reported. However, such details are omitted from the story.

Regardless of how the message was received, it was important enough that Abraham wanted to address it immediately the next day.

Telushkin (1997) offered another explanation: Abraham wanted to leave while Sarah was still asleep. As Telushkin noted, "there is every indication within the text that Abraham never discusses with his wife the divine decree he intends to carry out" (p. 39). Given Sarah's nagging about previous events in their married life, Abraham would likely have found little support for his plan if he had confided in Sarah. She had already insisted that he get rid of his handmaiden Hagar and son Ishmael. He probably concluded that it was better to leave early and not have to explain where he was going and what he was going to do.

. . . *and saddled his ass, and took two of his young men with him,* . . . Abraham's reliance on a burro as their means of transportation would be historically accurate. Camels had not yet been introduced into the area as beasts of burden. The two young men who went with him would be two servants, loyal to their master for he provided them security in a rough land. A wealthy nomad like Abraham would have had several servants who would be available for such duty.

. . . *and Isaac his son,* . . . The reference to Isaac is delayed until the end of the list of preparations, thus intensifying the drama of the story. Again, the dramatic effect intensifies the reader's concern.

. . . *and clave the wood for the burnt offering,* . . . Abraham may have had servants available for such manual labor. For some reason, though, he chose to split the wood needed for the offering himself. By doing so, Abraham takes responsibility for all of the details of the deed that is to come. As Atler (1996) wrote, "In a narrative famous for its rigorous economy in reporting physical details, this act of Abraham, wielding an axe and cutting things apart is ominously singled out for attention" (p. 104). The reader can visualize Abraham frantically cutting the wood with all the force he could muster, the sound of the ax striking the tree, hiding his sobbing but not his tears.

. . . *and rose up, and went unto the place of which God had told him.* The simple writing of this phrase emphasizes Abraham's obedience to the command. In fact, the most amazing aspect of it is Abraham's protracted silence throughout this section and the rest of the journey. As Baldwin (1986) noted, "Abraham stifles all questions and comments, and simply does as he is told" (p. 90). Similarly, Fox (1996) wrote that the most noticeable feature of the story is Abraham's "silence, his mute acceptance of, and acting on, God's command. We are told of no sleepless night, nor does he ever say a word to God. Instead, he is described with a series of verbs: starting early, saddling, taking, splitting, arising, going" (p. 92).

Telushkin (1997) pointed out that Abraham's silence "is even more surprising considering that Abraham previously has not been silent when he disagreed with God" (p. 38). Indeed, in the 18th chapter of Genesis, Abraham had argued with God over the destruction of Sodom and Gomorrah, with Abraham taking the moral side, arguing for mercy on behalf of the innocents in the city. As Fox (1996) noted, Abraham "the bargainer," the man so willing to negotiate "with relations (Ch. 13), allies (Chap. 14), local princes (Chap. 20), and even God himself (Chap. 18) here falls completely silent" (p. 92).

4. Then on the third day Abraham lifted up his eyes, and saw the place afar off.

Then on the third day . . . It's about 45 to 50 miles from Beersheba to Mount Moriah. Such a trip could reasonably take three days (McGee, 1992). Baldwin (1986) noted that, "Even with an early start it would indeed be the third day before their destination came in sight" (p. 90). But a man in a hurry could have done it quicker.

Why did it take so long? Telushkin (1997) suggested that the extended time was used to "underscore the magnitude of the test." "In a moment of religious enthusiasm," Telushkin added:

> Abraham might readily fulfill the divine command. Now, however, he is forced to journey with Isaac a full seventy-two hours. When the sacrifice occurs, it will not be a spontaneous action; by imposing on Abraham a three-day trek, God is forcing him to act in a premeditated and deliberate way. (p. 39)

Baldwin (1986) represented the Christian view, that the three-day journey is a symbolic prophecy of Jesus. In this perspective, the three-day journey is analogous to the three days that separated the crucifixion and the resurrection of Jesus.

Either way, three days is a long time for a father and son to go without talking to each other. Surely such conversations occurred, but Genesis provides no details about the journey. We are told nothing of campsites, and no conversation between Abraham and Isaac is reported. Of course, a report of such conversations would have to come from either Abraham or Isaac. Isaac rarely speaks of anything after this incident, and Abraham would likely be reluctant to discuss it either. Still, the omission is bothersome.

. . . *Abraham lifted up his eyes* . . . We can imagine a weary Abraham, tired and saddened from a three-day journey and its purpose, slowly pacing forward with his eyes on the ground or the terrain immediately ahead. To see his goal, though, required a longer view. To see where he was going, Abraham had to look toward the heavens. And perhaps he was looking up, hoping to see a sign of a reprieve.

. . . *and saw the place afar off.* The travelers were still some distance away from their destination, but at least they knew the location of the destination. In verse two, God had given Abraham vague directions, saying that he would tell him later which mountain would be their specific destination. Perhaps, at the moment that he "lifted up his eyes," Abraham realized that the mountain he saw was the one God had chosen.

5. And Abraham said unto his young men, Abide ye here with the ass; and I and the lad will go yonder and worship, and come again to you.

And Abraham said unto his young men, Abide ye here with the ass; . . . Popular images often view the servants as waiting at the base of the mountain while Abraham and Isaac climb to the top. That's not exactly what Genesis reports. Instead, Abraham spots the place "afar off" and tells his servants to "Abide ye here with the ass."

. . . and I and the lad will go yonder and worship, and come again to you. Why would a man, on his way to kill his son, make such a statement? Was it merely a way of reassuring the two servants and Isaac? Was it a "white lie" to make everybody feel better? Or did Abraham actually believe he was telling the truth, i.e., that somehow—despite the impending death of his child—that Isaac would survive the ordeal?

Baldwin (1986) supported the latter position when he wrote that "when Abraham told his servants that he and the lad would go to worship while they looked after the ass, there was nothing remarkable in his statement." However, Baldwin added, "To us . . ., who know what was at stake, having been let into the secret of God's command, Abraham's words here reveal faith's certainty" (p. 90). Similarly, Gibson (1999) said, "Abraham had no doubt that he and Isaac would both return" (p. 178).

However, the King James Version may not fully capture the nuance of this phrase. Atler (1996) noted that a more accurate translation of the beginning of this phrase is "let me and the lad" (p. 104). That translation is based on the conjugation of the verbs in Hebrew. In the original Hebrew, the statement does not involve a direct declaration of future actions. Thus, a comparable English phrasing of the final phrase might be stated as "and we *can* return to you." Atler also noted that the Hebrew structure of the verse has "an ironic divergence of meanings" (p. 104), with the first portion of the verse devoted to the young men who are his servants or slaves as compared to his own young son whom he has been directed to kill.

And don't overlook the role of the second verb—"worship." Abraham doesn't simply say that they will "go yonder and come again to you," but distinctly says that they will "worship" while they are there. Abraham's form of worship was different from that of modern day church-goers in that it was primarily a solitary or family activity. Still, the wording of the phrase implies that without the worship, the two of them may not "come again to you."

6. And Abraham took the wood of the burnt offering, and laid it upon Isaac his son; and he took the fire in his hand, and a knife; and they went both of them together.

When Abraham and Isaac set out for the mountain, Isaac carried the wood, while Abraham handled the knife and the fire. It's easy to find symbolic elements in their individual responsibilities here. McGee (1991), for example, argued that "The fire here speaks of judgment, and the knife speaks of the execution of judgment and of sacrifice" (p. 70). Even there, the terminology may not be quite right. Alter (1996) noted that the actual cutting instrument that Abraham carried was more likely to be a cleaver, not a knife; a knife might have been used for butchering an animal, but a cleaver was typically used for sacrificial purposes (p. 105). It would have been Abraham's duty, as father of the clan, to take responsibility for such an implement.

Abraham would also have born primary responsibility for the fire. In a time before the invention of matches, it was difficult to start a new fire from scratch. Instead, he would have carried a charcoal ember, wrapped in some sort of protective garment that could be used to start a new fire for the altar. Feiler (2001) wrote that many Bedouin tribes continue this tradition even today: "They have a special plant, a cane, they put the charcoal inside the husk, wrap it in cotton, and it burns slowly all day. At night they break the cane, blow on the charcoal, and start the fire" (p. 90).

But an obvious symbolism is apparent in Isaac's responsibility. The son of Abraham carries the wood much like Jesus carried his own cross to Golgotha. That similarity is not accidental. In addition to the symbolism captured in the analogy, there is a common purpose in each. As Spiegel (1993) noted, "this was common practice, to have the condemned themselves laden with the beams and firewood by which their sentence would be carried out" (pp. 84-85).

7. And Isaac spake unto Abraham his father, and said, My father: and he said, Here am I, my son. And he said, Behold the fire and the wood: but where is the lamb for a burnt offering?

And Isaac spake unto Abraham his father . . . Thomas (1985) wrote that this "conversation between father and son is beautiful, indicating real faith in both of them" (p. 50). The literary quality of the verses is apparent with the first phrase—"And Isaac spake unto Abraham his father." As Alter (1996) noted, "The narrator does not miss a chance in the story to refer to Isaac as 'his son' and Abraham as 'his father,' thus sharpening the edge of anguish that runs through the tale" (p. 104).

. . . *and said, My father:* The phrase "My Father" is a little more complicated in Hebrew than in the English translation. In the Hebrew form, the possessive "My" has an ending that applies to an intimate form of address (Alter, 1996, p. 105).

. . . *and he said, Here am I, my son.* "Here am I" echoes Abraham's response to God in verse 1. Norman Cohen wrote, "When Abraham responds, 'Here I am' to both God and Isaac, he uses the Hebrew word *hineini*, which is the word or response in relationship. . . . Abraham uses the same word of response to the divine that he does to his son" (quoted by Moyers, 1996, p. 222). When this phrase is combined with the intimate reference to "my son," it conveys both a sense of readiness to help and love for the child.

And he said, Behold the fire and the wood: Isaac referred to the wood that he carried and the fire that Abraham carried. But he said nothing about the knife. As Atler (1996) noted, the previous verse had specifically mentioned all three objects—wood, fire, and knife—but, "as Isaac questions his father, he passes in silence over the one object that would have seemed scariest to him, however unwitting he may have been of his father's intention—the sharp-edged butcher knife" (p. 105).

. . . but where is the lamb for a burnt offering? Baldwin (1986) observed that this question " . . . made a painful moment all the more poignant for his father. . ." (p. 92). What makes the question more intriguing, though, is that Isaac asks specifically for a lamb. It was a ram, not a lamb that was eventually substituted for Isaac. Further, according to Hebrew tradition, a ram—not a lamb—was the proper choice for such a sacrifice. The use of a lamb as a sacrifice occurs only a few times in the Old Testament, most notably in the instance of the Passover lamb in Egypt (Baldwin, 1986, p. 92). Isaiah also referred to the lamb led to slaughter (Isaiah 53:7). Such an unusual use of the word "lamb" is one reason that Christian theologians often see this passage as a prophetic message of Jesus as "the Lamb of God" (John 1:29).

8. And Abraham said, My son, God will provide himself a lamb for a burnt offering: so they went both of them together.

And Abraham said, My son, . . . The narrator loves refrains. Here he repeats the refrain of "my son" from the previous verse. Again, the reader can imagine Abraham uttering the words with a heavy heart.

. . . God will provide himself a lamb for a burnt offering. This is the crucial verse for Christians. The concept of God providing a substitute for human suffering was the essence of Christian belief regarding the crucifixion of Jesus.

Structurally, though, there is a hidden analogy in the statement. Alter (1996) contended that the word "provide" is implied by the idiomatic context of the sentence, but is not part of the literal translation. Instead, a more literal translation of the sentence would begin "God will see for himself" (p. 105). This structure is then similar to the same structure that was used in verse 4 when Abraham lifted his eyes and saw the place afar. Thus, the element of extended vision is implied in both sentences. It is particularly important here, since the name of the place is Moriah, or "God sees." As Alter added, "Beyond the tunnel vision of a trajectory toward child slaughter is a promise of true vision" (p. 105).

There is no indication in the narrative that Abraham was told anything regarding a lamb being the animal that would eventually take Isaac's place, particularly since the substitute in the story was a ram. Perhaps Abraham needed an answer and needed it quickly. His reply may have been a simple delaying tactic, or perhaps he saw Isaac as a helpless lamb. A ram, after all, might have resisted while a lamb would have reacted more like Isaac did.

. . . so they went both of them together. Verse six ended with the statement, "and they went both of them together." Now verse eight ends with a similar

statement. Alter (1996) wrote that "The impassive economy of this refrainlike repeated clause is haunting; two people, father and son, together for what threatens to be the last time, together 'in one purpose'. . ., the father to sacrifice the son" (p. 105). Fox (1995) noted that the two statements also serve a framing function in which Abraham deflects Isaac's question about the purpose of the trip while providing a "hint of a happy ending" (p. 94). Still, it also signals the end of any dialogue between the father and child and a return to silence. Abraham is never recorded as speaking to Isaac again.

9. And they came to the place which God had told him of; and Abraham built an altar there, and laid the wood in order, and bound Isaac his son, and laid him on the altar upon the wood.

And they came to the place which God had told him of. . . But the narrator doesn't specifically tell us where it is or how Abraham knew it was the right place. Perhaps those details were lost some time when the story existed merely as part of the Hebrews oral tradition. Perhaps Abraham experienced some sort of insight that was hard to convey in a story. Or perhaps the narrator considered it a detail which was irrelevant to the overall theme of the narrative. Regardless, it seems like a crucial detail has been omitted from the story.

. . . and Abraham built an altar there . . . Abraham was a frequent builder of altars, having previously constructed altars at Sichem (Gen. 12:6-7), on a mountain east of Bethel (Gen. 12:8), and at Hebron (Gen. 13:18). Why, though, does Genesis say that Abraham built the altar, with no mention of Isaac? Spiegel (1993) offered two possible explanations: (1) Isaac did not labor for fear that a stone might fall on him, thus blemishing him and make him unworthy of being sacrificed, and (2) that Isaac only assisted by collecting and handing the stones to Abraham (p. 108). Either way, though, the reader wonders why the narrator did not provide this information.

. . . and laid the wood in order . . . Here the obedient Abraham made a mistake—at least according to Hebrew tradition—but saved Isaac's life in the process. This mistake is simple: He did not light the fire. The Jewish tradition of offering a sacrifice followed a very specific ritual. Abraham was supposed to light the fire on the altar before placing the wood "in order." That procedure is outlined specifically in Leviticus (1:7). However, Abraham was making his sacrifice in the absence of any written procedures, so he may have been improvising. Even so, the change in procedure either saved Isaac's life or at least delayed God's intervention. If Isaac had been placed upon a burning altar, he likely would have died whether Abraham had slaughtered him with the knife or not. Some traditional Jewish views, though, assume that Abraham did follow the proper procedure and that the narrator simply forgot to include it in detail (Spiegel, 1993, pp. 36-37). This view assumes that Isaac did die that day, consumed by the flames, but was resurrected by God after the sacrifice. Such an interpretation, though, disregards the later command from God for Abraham not to harm Isaac.

. . . and bound Isaac his son, . . . This is no young child we're talking about here. Isaac was probably about 30 years old when this event occurred. As McGee (1991), noted, "Isaac is not just a little boy whom Abraham had to tie up. He is a grown man (p. 71)." So, as Telushkin (1997) asked, "Does Isaac protest, try to flee, fight with his father, weep, or submit to God's will (p. 40)? The text doesn't say. But, given that no mention is made of resistance, the assumption here is that Isaac allowed the binding to occur. If so, then this may be a test of obedience for both Abraham and Isaac.

10. And Abraham stretched forth his hand, and took the knife to slay his son.

As Alter (1996) noted, there is a noticeable change in pace by now. "In contrast to the breathless pace of the narrative as a whole, this sequence inscribes a kind of slow motion," (p. 105). Abraham seems to have moved slowly as he reached ("stretched") for the knife, picked it up, and prepared to kill his son. A key point here, though, is the verb translated "slay." The Hebrew version is a specific form that was used to describe animal sacrifice, specifically by slitting the animal's throat (Fox, 1995, p. 94).

Jewish tradition (Spiegle, 1993, p. 45) argues that when Abraham "stretched forth his hand," that he was inspecting the knife. A proper animal sacrifice required that the worshiper go through a 12-point inspection of the knife, to ensure that it is suitable for the ritual, before slaughtering the animal. If Abraham were indeed following that tradition, the time spent inspecting the knife would have provided God with time to evaluate his completion of the test and then to stop it.

11. And the angel of the Lord called unto him out of heaven, and said, Abraham, Abraham: and he said, Here am I.

And the angel of the Lord called unto him out of heaven, . . . Why an Angel? And which angel? Is this an archangel working directly with God, or a mere messenger? Often in the Bible, an angel is presented as a representative of God. The question persists, though, why now? Why didn't the voice of God Himself speak out to stop the deed? God gave the command Himself? Wouldn't it be appropriate for him to speak again at this time? And was it a true angel, or merely a way for the writer to represent Abraham's inner voice—his own conscience—as suggested by Schulweis (1994, p. 124). For whatever reason, though, He sent a substitute at this critical moment. And that substitute is symbolic of change in the relationship between God and Abraham. Never again did God speak directly to the Patriarch.

. . . and said, Abraham, Abraham: The angel called Abraham by name—not once, but twice. The double use of the Patriarch's name seems to indicate an urgency on the part of the angel. The angel speaks twice to be sure he gets Abraham's attention in time to stop the dark deed. The urgency was needed,

because God had waited until just the right moment to make his intervention (Thomas, 1985).

. . . and he said, Here am I. There's that phrase again—"Here am I." It's the third time that Abraham has uttered those words since the story began: First when God first spoke to him to give him the command, then when Isaac asked about the lamb, and finally when the angel intervened to stop the act.

12. And he said, Lay not thine hand upon the lad, neither do thou any thing unto him: for now I know that thou fearest God, seeing thou hast not withheld thy son, thine only son from me.

And he said, Lay not thine hand upon the lad . . . As Abraham raised the knife to slay his son, the angel called out to Abraham, telling him not to harm his son. Sense of relief must have flowed through Abraham as he realized that Isaac was not to be killed.

However, why did the angel refer to the hand and not the knife? After all, it would be the knife that would have inflicted the mortal blow. Modern readers often assume that it was a simple metaphorical phrase, with the hand representing the entire act of slaying. Jewish tradition, though, doesn't treat the word so lightly; in this tradition, the angel speaks of the hand to stop Abraham from doing anything that would harm the child—whether it be by stabbing, strangling, or beating (Spiegel, 1993, p. 45).

. . . neither do thou any thing unto him: There is a sense of reinforcement in this statement. Spiegel (1993) noted that this second phrase emphasizes "that Abraham was categorically and in no uncertain terms forbidden from heaven so much as to touch Isaac with evil intent" (p. 46).

for now I know that thou fearest God, . . . The verb used in this verse is most frequently translated as "afraid," thus the "fearest God" interpretation. Within context, it is frequently understood to have some connotation related to being "in awe of" God. Still, regardless of the translation, this phrase may rank as one of the most controversial statements in the Old Testament—so much so that it will be discussed in more detail later. Marks (1983) offered the standard interpretation that the statement indicates that Abraham had successfully passed the test. But, as Dershowtiz (2001) noted, "This suggests that . . . neither God nor the angels knew what its outcome would be" (p. 114). That raises a series of questions about God's omniscience and the free will of mankind.

. . . seeing thou hast not withheld thy son, thine only son from me. The refrain appears again, this time emphasizing that God understood how difficult this task had been for Abraham. It also sets up some later verses that emphasized Isaac's role in fulfilling God's promise of the covenant.

13. And Abraham lifted up his eyes, and looked, and behold behind him a ram caught in a thicket by his horns: and Abraham went and took the ram, and offered him up for a burnt offering in the stead of his son.

And Abraham lifted up his eyes, and looked . . . Indeed, the narrator loved repetition. Here he repeats a phrase—"lifted up his eyes"—that first appeared in verse 5 when Abraham spotted "the place afar off." Now it's used again, when Abraham is at that very place.

. . . *and behold behind him a ram caught in a thicket by his horns:* Fox (1996) noted that the ancient transcripts of this verse have two different versions, one which speaks of "a ram" and another that is translated "one ram" (p. 95). However, the "a ram" version is the more common translation, even in early texts. When written in Hebrew, the difference is a minor grammatical difference—the use of "bd" for "a" instead of "br" for one. In the original Hebrew writing, the difference is even less—a difference in one stroke of the pen. The theological differences, though, may be major. The use of the "a ram" phrase implies a grander and broader view of the event that could apply the sacrifice to future generations (Spiegel, 1993, p. 98).

Another key point is that it is a ram—*not the lamb* mentioned in verses 8 and 9. Moreover, the ram was the proper choice—at least by Jewish standards. Although not mentioned in the Bible, several different legends about this ram have developed over the centuries (Spiegel, 1993, pp. 38-44). Some believed that other parts of the sacred animal appear in other parts of the Bible—its tendons became the ten strings of David's harp; its skin, Elijah's leather girdle; one of its horns sounded at Mount Sinai. One Jewish writer suggested that an angel fetched the ram from the Garden of Eden, where it had been grazing under the Tree of Life. Another suggested that it was a ram from Abraham's own flock, one that he had named Isaac in honor of his son. Others have suggested it was the same ram that Abel offered in the first recorded sacrifice in the scripture. Interesting, perhaps, but highly speculative.

. . . *and Abraham went and took the ram, and offered him up for a burnt offering in the stead of his son.* Thomas (1985) called this portion of the story "The Triumph." Fox (1996) argued that it "is the midpoint of Genesis," adding that after this point "we can breathe easier, knowing that God will come to the rescue of his chosen ones in the direst of circumstances. At the same time we are left to ponder the difficulties of being a chosen one, subject to such an incredible test" (p. 92).

The sacrificial substitute, of course, is important in both Jewish and Christian theology. In the Jewish tradition, the ram dies for the survival of the Jewish people. Had the ram not be provided instead of Isaac, Isaac would have never had any children and God's covenant and promise could not have been fulfilled. Thus, "since Isaac was redeemed it is as though all Israel had been redeemed" (Spiegel, 1993, p. 38). In Christian theology, Abraham and God established a tradition of substitute sacrifice that culminated in the crucifixion of Jesus for the sins of the world.

14. And Abraham called the name of that place Jehovahjireh: as it is said to this day, In the mount of the Lord it shall be seen.

And Abraham called the name of that place Jehovahjireh: "Jehovah-Jireh" is typically translated as "Jehovah will provide." This interpretation refers back to Abraham's statement in verse 8 that "God will provide the lamb." As Baldwin (1986) noted, "The Lord will provide" has since become a proverbial statement and part of the heritage of the Christian church (p. 91).

. . . as it is said to this day, In the mount of the Lord it shall be seen. While the common interpretation of *Jehovah-jireh* is "Jehovah will provide," the literal interpretation of the phrase in verse 8 is that "God will see to the lamb." That interpretation is reflected in the second half of this verse, in which J*ehovah-jireh* is said to mean "In the mount of the Lord it shall be seen." As Baldwin added, since the Lord had commanded this sacrifice, it was reasonable to suppose that the Lord would see the need (the Hebrew verb *yir'eh* literally means 'see') and meet it, but to answer thus is easier with hindsight than, as in the case of Abraham, without any precedent" (p. 91).

Unfortunately, while the name *Jehovah-jireh* fits with the narrative and explains the story, it does little to help scholars locate the original mountain. No such place name has survived. As Marks noted, the reference to *Jehovah-jireh* "is the best we have, but the name of the cultic center cannot be satisfactorily determined" (p. 50).

15. And the angel of the Lord called unto Abraham out of heaven the second time,

Many readers might notice that verse 14 seems to provide a natural ending to the story, but then the angel prolongs the narrative a bit longer. The change in pace is due to a change in authors. The original story, consisting of verses 1-14, is attributed to the unknown biblical narrator known as E (Marks, 1983). A new narrator—the one biblical scholars call J—picks up the story in verse 15, apparently to reinforce the lessons form the story. Baldwin (1986), for example, said the Angel spoke a second time and thus "the Lord reiterated his blessing on Abraham's descendants and promised them victory over their enemies" (p. 91).

Others, though, have questioned why the angel should have to speak a second time. Spiegel (1993) noted that this verse has created several different interpretations among Jewish theologians. Those interpretations include a second call was needed because (a) Abraham refused to listen the first time and still intended to fulfill the sacrifice, (b) the first call was interrupted before the angel could give Abraham the full message, or (c) it was a way of God expressing his displeasure that Abraham would actually considered carrying out the sacrifice. This latter idea will be discussed in more detail in Chapter 7.

16. And said, By myself have I sworn, saith the Lord, for because thou hast done this thing, and hast not withheld thy son, thine only son:

And said, By myself have I sworn, saith the Lord, . . . The angel began by reminding Abraham that God had made a promise to Abraham. Thomas (1985) referred to these four verses as "The Testimony" and noted that the angel spoke to recognize what Abraham had done and to renew God's promise with another oath.   One phrase used in this verse—"saith the Lord"or "Yahweh's utterance"—is a phrase often found in the books of the prophets (Fox, 1993). The rhetorical effect of the phrase is to bring attention and to increase the credibility of the statement.

. . . for because thou hast done this thing, . . . The angel refers to the act as "this thing," a broad inclusive statement that may refer to the trip, the climbing of the mountain, the ritualistic sacrifice to which it was leading, or all of the above. Regardless, the curious use of an indefinite reference here indicates that either the narrator didn't know how to label the act or couldn't bring himself to directly say, "because you almost killed your son." Given that the statement is made by God's representative, though, it may also indicate that even the Divine was reluctant to directly address the issue of killing the child.

. . . and hast not withheld thy son, thine only son: The new narrator knew a good refrain when he saw one, and he continued to use the phrase "thine only son" for dramatic effect. Christians sometimes interpret this phrase as a reference to Jesus. Buber (1982), for example, saw this verse as making Abraham a spiritual ancestor. As McGee (1991) noted, "Notice how God plays upon that—because He gave His only Son (p. 74)."

17. That in blessing I will bless thee, and in multiplying I will multiply thy seed as the stars of the heaven, and as the sand which is upon the sea shore; and thy seed shall possess the gate of his enemies;

God reaffirmed his promise to Abraham and that Abraham's offspring would "possess the gate of his enemies." Fox (1993) acknowledged that another possible interpretation of this phrase is that they will "Inherit the gate," which implies that they will capture their enemies city (p. 95).

18. And in thy seed shall all the nations of the earth be blessed; because thou hast obeyed my voice.

And in thy seed shall all the nations of the earth be blessed, . . . In an earlier chapter of Genesis, God promised Abraham that "in thee shall all the families of the earth be blessed (12:3)." This verse reiterated that phrase and promise. McGee (1991, p. 75) noted that, in the New Testament, Paul interprets the "seed" of this verse as Jesus Christ (Galatians 3:16). This verse is also Paul's justification (Gal. 3:8) that Abraham's ultimate "inheritance" was that his "seed" would produce Jesus. As Paul wrote, "God gave it (man's inheritance) to Abraham by promise."

. . . because thou hast obeyed my voice. As Fox (1995) noted, Abraham had received blessings and promises before, but never before "because thou has obeyed my voice" (p. 95). This phrase serves to emphasize the general theme of the story as a test of obedience.

This verse ends all dialogue in the story. The angel's words from "the second time" that he speaks are, in essence, a monologue. As Baldwin (1986) observed, "no reaction from Abraham is recorded. The experience was too deep for words" (p. 91). However, the absence of any words from Abraham may also be due to the simple fact that verses 15-18 were written by a different narrator who had something to say—something that could be said by one voice without the other saying a word.

19. So Abraham returned unto his young men, and they rose up and went together to Beersheba; and Abraham dwelt at Beersheba.

So Abraham returned unto his young men, . . . "Abraham returned unto his young men," the passage says. So, where was Isaac. The writer went out of his way in verse 3 to mention both Abraham and Isaac traveling to Moriah. Again, in verse 5, both Abraham and Isaac are mentioned as they prepare to ascend the mountain. So why is Isaac not mentioned in verse 19. In fact, after the reference to "thine only son" in verse 16, "all traces of Isaac . . .disappear" in the story (Spiegel, 1993, p. 3). Spiegel (pp. 3-8) also noted that the omission of Isaac's name in this verse has created a great deal of speculation among Jewish theologians. Among the suggestions:

* It was a symbolic way of treating Isaac as if he had indeed been sacrificed. Maybe, but the doubt raised by such an omission seems unnecessary.

* Isaac may have actually died during the incident, before being brought back to life at a later date. Several different versions of this interpretation have been presented, but they all ignore the literal version of the story which says Isaac was not harmed.

* Isaac's name was omitted because Abraham was the central figure in the story. If so, then why mention Isaac's presence so specifically in verses 3 and 5.

* Isaac may have still been under 13 years of age, and thus still under the direct authority of his father. In that case, his presence could have been implied. That's possible, but not consistent with most theological estimates of Isaac's age. Despite the traditional image of Isaac as still being in childhood, the timing of the story in light of subsequent verses indicates he was probably about 30 years old when the incident occurred.

* Perhaps Abraham had sent him back to Hebron by a different route, so that he could tell Sarah that everything had worked out well. This is a reasonable possibility but, nevertheless, Abraham would still have taken Isaac back down the mountain first. After all, he had promised his servants that both would return before they made additional plans.

. . . and they rose up and went together to Beersheba . . . Notice the recurring use of the phrase "went together." The same reference was made

earlier in terms of Abraham and Isaac walking together. As Norman Cohen wrote, "The irony, of course, is that at the end of the story, when Abraham returns to Beersheba, the line is repeated—but in relation to his servants. Isaac is no longer there, and Abraham is walking together with his two servants. That's all he's left with at the end of the journey" (quoted by Moyers, 1996, p. 222).

. . . *and Abraham dwelt at Beersheba.* The story ends with Abraham returning to Beersheba, the place where Abraham had planted a grove after working out an agreement with Abimelech (Gen. 21:32-33). Conspicuous by its absence, however, is the fact that the passage makes no mention of where Sarah is living. In the following chapter, we learn that Sarah dies in Kirjatharba, or Kiryat Arba (Gen. 23:1), a connection that has caused some commentators to believe that the *akedah* placed a strain on the marriage of Abraham and Sarah, possibly leading to their separation.

Either way, the story quickly draws to a close, but not without leaving apparent scars on the family. While Genesis makes no direct statement on the issue, it appears that Abraham and his family never fully recovered from that three-day trip to Moriah. How did the incident affect Sarah's relationship with Abraham? Given the harshness with which she had engaged him on other issues, it's hard to believe that she would have taken this lightly.

Verse 19 reveals that when Abraham returns from the trip, he stayed in Beersheba. But the next chapter specifically states that Sarah died in Kiryat Arba or Hebron (Genesis 23:2). Abraham wasn't with her when she died, for the same verse says he had to travel there to mourn for her. While the text never directly says it, there is at least an indirect implication that Abraham and Sarah were living apart when she died. Had Sarah moved back to Hebron, one of Abraham's earlier stops, after she heard what had happened? It's at least a possibility.

After Sarah's death, Abraham bought his first piece of property in Canaan so that she will have a tomb. The family—including Isaac and Ishmael—gather for the funeral, but there is no record of any conversation between Abraham and his children.

Isaac seemed to be the one most affected by the whole episode. Armstrong (1996a) called Isaac "The primary casualty of Mount Moriah" (p. 70). He and Abraham never speak to each other again in the Bible, not even at Sarah's funeral. Indeed, Isaac doesn't utter another word in the recorded text of Genesis until he gives his blessing to Jacob on his deathbed. Even there, the trauma of Moriah (Gen. 31:42, 53) emerges, with him referring to God as "The Fear" (Armstrong, 1996a, p. 70).

Abraham, meanwhile, seems isolated from everybody who was once close to him. God is true to his Promise, and makes him the father of a great nation. But God never speaks to him again either.

Still, the Promise is kept. By passing the final test, Abraham sealed the covenant between God and thus established the Hebrews as God's chosen people.

The Islamic Version

The Islamic version of the sacrifice is briefly recounted in eleven verses of the thirty-seventh *Surah* (chapter) in the Koran (*Surah* XXXVII: 101-111). These eleven verses are brief and lack the emotional drama of the Judeo-Christian version. Further, while there are differences in the two narratives, there is a similarity in theme. The following selections were taken from Shakir's (2002) translation.

101. So we gave him the good news of a boy, possessing forbearance.
The Islamic story opens with a happy note—a reference to the Abraham and Sarah receiving a son. The name of the boy is not mentioned in these verses, but Islamic tradition assumes that it is Ishmael. Justification for the assumption comes from verse 112—the verse that immediately follows this story—which reads, "And we gave him the good news of Ishaq [Isaac], a prophet among the good ones." The reference in verse 112 has a parallel structure with that of verse 101, and seems to be referring to a different person. Isaac is viewed by the Koran is "a prophet," while Ishmael is "a boy, possessing forbearance."

102a. And when he attained working with him, he said. O my son! Surely I have seen in a dream that I should sacrifice you; consider then what you see.
And when he attained working with him, he said. O my son! In the Genesis version, Abraham first seeks out his servants so they can prepare for the necessary trip. In this version, Abraham first seeks to talk with his son to share the vision with him. There remains an element of pessimism, because the vision isn't a good one. Still, rather than taking the command from God at face value, as Abraham did in the Genesis story, this Abraham is somewhat confused and needs to talk with someone about the vision.

Surely I have seen in a dream . . . The Koran specifically says that Abraham received his instructions in a dream, but it does not recount the specific words used by God to give the instructions. In fact, in this version, Abraham notes that he had "seen" in a dream that he is to sacrifice his son. A dream might be open to more interpretations than the direct command that Abraham received in Genesis, thus explaining his need to discuss the dream with someone else. The Genesis version doesn't specifically say that God spoke to Abraham in a dream, but that scenario is at least implied by the reference in verse 3 that "Abraham rose up early in the morning" after receiving the instructions.

. . . that I should sacrifice you. On this point, the two stories agree. In both versions, Abraham believes he has been given an instruction to sacrifice his son.

Consider then what you see. What did the son see? The Koran is vague as to the details at this point. Did Ishmael see a worried father who was unsure of what to do? Was Abraham asking his son if he had received a similar vision? Or, more likely, was the father showing the son that he had brought the tools for the sacrifice—the knife, the wood—with him?

102b. He said: O my father! Do what you are commanded; if Allah please, you will find me of the patient ones.

He said: O my father! Whatever he "considered" when he saw his father, the son was not dismayed. He answered his father with a phrase ("O my father!) that was similar to how he was initially addressed ("O my son!").

Do what you are commanded; In the Islamic religion, obedience to God is the major issue of faith. Ishmael tells Abraham that he recognizes that the father must obey the command of God.

If Allah please . . . This is the Islamic equivalent of "God willing," an individual's recognition that they may need assistance from God in obeying God's command.

. . . you will find me of the patient ones. Some translations interpret this in terms of worthiness, i.e., Ishmael is unsure whether he is pure enough to be an acceptable offering. At the very least, he hopes to be submissive ("patient") during the deed. This verse, then, represents a dramatic departure from the Genesis version in which Isaac is an unwitting participant. Until Abraham and Isaac climb the mountain, Isaac is unaware of what is coming. In this Islamic version, though, Ishmael is informed about the purpose and is a willing participant in the impending sacrifice.

103. So when they both submitted and he threw him down upon his forehead.

So when they both submitted . . . Submission to the will of God is a major virtue within the Islamic tradition. Here that concept is emphasized. Again, the key element is that "both"—the father and the son—have submitted to God's will.

. . .and he threw him down upon his forehead. Forget the three day trip to Moriah. The Islamic version moves from decision to action in one verse, with Abraham immediately preparing to sacrifice Ishmael.

104. And We called out to him saying: O Ibrahim [Abraham]!

This translation of the Koran uses uppercase plural pronouns to refer to statements made by Allah, an attempt to convey the similar concept as written in Arabic. Thus "We" is a reference to Allah, or God. This then reflects another difference in the stories. The Genesis version has an angel speaking to Abraham as a messenger from God. The Koran has God speaking directly to Abraham; In fact, the order to stop the sacrifice is more direct than was the use of a dream to issue the command.

105. You have indeed shown the truth of the vision; surely thus do We reward the doers of good;

You have indeed shown the truth of the vision . . . Allah first assures Abraham that his interpretation of the dream was the correct one and that he had responded in the appropriate manner.

. . . surely thus do We reward the doers of good; "You don't have to go any further," Allah is saying, "You've done enough, and We [Allah] will reward you for your obedience."

106. Most surely this is a manifest trial.

Sometimes the Koran—like the Bible—has a gift for understatement. This was arguably more than merely a "manifest trial," but easily the biggest trial in Abraham and Ishmael's lives. It was still, though, arguably less traumatic than what Abraham and Isaac went through in the Genesis version. In the Koran, the issue is addressed and resolved quickly. Abraham had to bear the burden for three days in Genesis.

107. And We ransomed him with a great sacrifice.

Like the Genesis version, there is a reference to a substitute sacrifice. Unlike the Genesis version, there are no details as to the nature of that substitute.

108. And We perpetuated [praise] to him among the later generations.

God's promise to Abraham in Genesis that he would father a great nation has its parallel in Islamic tradition too. After all, the Arabic people also view themselves as the children of Abraham. The nature of the promise in this verse, though, has more to do with recognition and honors that extend to future generations. In that sense, it is comparable to verse 18 of the Genesis story: "And in thy seed shall all the nations of the earth be blessed; because thou hast obeyed my voice."

109. Peace be on Ibrahim [Abraham].

The story closes with Allah making three final statements of Abraham—a statement of comfort, a promise, and praise. First, he attempts to comfort the Patriarch, no doubt recognizing that he has been racked with doubt and stress, when he says, "Peace be on Abraham."

110. Thus do We reward the doers of good.

The second statement is a reiteration of the promise of a reward. Abraham has demonstrated the ultimate in obedience. Allah will ensure that he is rewarded.

111. Surely he was one of Our believing servants.

The story closes with Allah praising Abraham's faith and obedience. This statement is similar to the Judeo-Christian tradition in which Abraham is held up as a paragon of faith.

Summary

We have examined two versions of the same story with some similarities and some differences. Their similarities address similar problems. The name of one character (Isaac or Ishmael) may be different, as well as the time frame for the story (three days or one day?). Some differences might be attributed to different religious traditions, but both address the same moral problem created by the willingness of a father to kill his own son. Further, and even more important to our book, both stories have become the foundation for a rhetoric of sacrifice. On that point, all three religions share a point of commonality.

Chapter 3
Abraham the Patriarch

Those who wish to understand the *akedah* must first understand the story of Abraham. For thousands of years after he first walked on this earth, Abraham still ranks as one of the most important and influential people in the history of the world. Three different religions—Judaism, Islam, and Christianity—revere him.

Yet, much about the man remains a mystery. Spong (1991, p. 57) described him as "a shadowy figure." The Bible depicts him as a 19th century B.C. nomad who lived in a tent, kept great flocks of sheep and roamed the wilderness with his wives, children, and servants. But even the most learned of theologians disagree on who he was, where he came from, and what he did. After all, the written version of his story probably didn't exist until the tenth century B.C. Before then, as Spong (1991) noted, the story of Abraham "existed in solely word-of-mouth narration for some eight hundred to nine hundred years before stories about him achieved written form" (p. 38).

He also remains controversial. Abraham is at the center of the theological controversies that separate the three great religions. Speculation about his role in history has run rampant. Representatives of the three religions assume he had a divine role in God's plan. Skeptics may view him as an entrepreneur who established an agriculturally based nation of heirs.

Theories about the God of Abraham have ranged from the theological to pop culture. On the latter side, a couple of writers have suggested that the "gods" who met and spoke with Abraham were ancient astronauts who were visiting earth. Alan and Sally Landsburg (1974) suggested that alien visitors would explain "the various angels who came out of the sky and paid visits to Abraham" (p. 142), while Erich Von Daniken (1971) argued that Abraham was a witness when visitors from outer space triggered an atomic explosion to destroy the cities of Sodom and Gomorrah (pp. 37-38). One thing is generally agreed upon ☐ Abraham is viewed as a forceful personality. Cahill (1998, p. 162) described him as "a wily character who seemed up to any challenge." Cooper (1997, p. 74) noted that, on occasion, Abraham argued with God until God changed his mind.

Still, if Abraham's actions are to be understood, they must be interpreted in light of the culture and time in which he lived. Unfortunately, both of these factors are in doubt. Alternative explanations have been offered for each, while some question whether he even existed at all. Some critics argue that the entire story of the Patriarchs was merely that—a story developed as a rhetorical device to support Jewish religious thought. In this view, Abraham and the other Patriarchs are merely fictional characters designed to establish a rhetorical tradition for the Hebrews, or, as Price (1997) described it, "campfire accounts that had been passed down through the centuries" (p. 90).

Proving either argument isn't easy, since finding historical evidence about the historicity of Abraham is difficult. Archaeologists have had no trouble finding a person named "Abraham" who lived during the time when the Patriarch reportedly roamed through the Middle East. Quite the contrary, they found too many. "Abraham" was apparently a common name around 4000 years ago (Keller, 1980). To date, archaeologists have been unable to identify one specific person who bore that name and who can be identified as the Abraham of the Bible.

But the name may be relatively unimportant. The nomadic lifestyle that sustained Abraham has been well documented. After that starting point, though, things get a bit confusing. We will start by looking at the controversy surrounding his birthplace.

Abraham's Origins

Ur of the Chaldees. As Dimont (1962, pp. 191-192) noted, modern scholars know nothing about Abraham's early youth. Little is also known of his family history, beyond his father, although a Jewish tradition holds the Abraham shared a common ancestor with the inhabitants of the southeastern Greek city of Sparta (1 Maccabees 12:20). Most students of the Bible assume that Abraham came from Ur, a Sumerian city in Mesopotamia. This conclusion is based on a single Bible reference which notes that Abraham "went forth . . . from Ur of the Chaldes" (Genesis 11:13).

For centuries, the city of Ur was a mystery to biblical scholars. The reference to Chaldes, or Chaldea, pointed to Mesopotamia, but its exact location was unknown until it was discovered in 1922 and subsequently studied by British archaeologist Sir Charles Leonard Wooley (Wooley & Moorey, 1982). Other research revealed that the names of Abraham's closest relatives—great-grandfather Serug, grandfather Nahor, and father Terah—were names that appear in Old Assyrian and Babylonian texts (Price, 1997, p. 95). Subsequent excavations revealed a city that was remarkably advanced for its time and reflected a Sumerian culture that far surpassed those of the surrounding area. As Keller (1980, p. 7) noted, locating Ur led "to the discovery of a civilization which would take us farther into the twilight of prehistoric times than even the oldest races of man which had been found in Egypt."

Ur was probably the capital of the Sumerian empire, for no other Mesopotamian city has been found that was comparable to its architecture and two-story homes. The city's sacred area, the Temple precinct, was apparently used for both worship and governmental duties, with the Temple's priests collecting sacrifices and taxes. The Sumerians were also apparently the world's first literate people, writing both poetry and epic stories. One Sumerian text, which dates from the third millennium B.C., is the oldest known use of sequential sentences (Howard, 1999). Its discovery caused biblical scholars to re-evaluate their image of Abraham as a simple nomad who happened to be favored by God. As Wooley (1954/1982) noted, "We must radically alter our view of the Hebrew Patriarch . . . . He was the citizen of a great city and inherited the traditions of an old and highly organized civilization" (p. 102).

Civilized? Perhaps. But by modern religious standards, it was still a pagan civilization. When Abraham left Ur, he undoubtedly took some of the local religion with him. Not surprisingly, then, many of Abraham's subsequent actions would probably be questioned by modern religious leaders. Cahill (1998) wrote that, "The family of Terah no doubt took with them on their journey the stories of Sumer about the long-lived ancients and the ill-tempered gods" (p. 62). Yancey (1999) agreed: "To found his tribe, God chooses a pagan . . . and puts him through a series of tests, many of which he fails" (p. 31).

When Abraham left the city, Cahill (1998) added, Abraham and his family took their Sumerian view of life with them. "However much of a discontinuity with the past this journey would come to represent, [they] were people of Sumer and could no more escape the mind-set of their culture than we can escape ours," he wrote (p. 60). For one thing, Abraham obviously adhered to Sumerian ideas about the importance of business, for the narrator specifically mentions that they took with them all the wealth they had accumulated during their stay in Haran. The fact that Abraham departed the city with such wealth, while leaving the most advanced culture of the time, makes Abraham's decision to leave the city even more dramatic. As Dimont (1962) noted, the people of the day "would have laughed at Avram's madness (p. 190). It also raises questions about Abraham's profession. Ur had little or no need for sheepherders, causing Dimont to suggest that Abraham was likely a merchant whom the Bible identified as a sheepherder (p. 190).

The Astronaut Theory

Perhaps the most unusual implication of Abraham's Sumerian roots is its role in the ancient astronaut theory. Erich Von Daniken (1971) has been the major proponent of the theory that many stories in the Bible represent primitive interpretations of visits to earth by ancient astronauts. The "God" with whom Abraham had face-to-face conversations, according to this theory, was really an ancient space traveler who seemed like a god to the simple nomad. "Today we still do not know where [the people who talked with Abraham] came from," Von Daniken (1971) wrote. "But we know that the Sumerians brought with them a superior advanced culture which they forced upon the still semi barbaric Semites. We also know that they always sought their gods on mountain peaks and that if there were no peaks in the regions they inhabited they erected artificial ▯mountains' on the plains" (p. 24).

Von Daniken (1971) also observed that the Apocryphal Book of Abraham has a description of a vehicle that sounds like a rocket-powered space craft: "Behind the being I saw a chariot which had wheels of fire, and every wheel was full of eyes all around, and on the wheels was a throne and this was covered with fire that flowed around it" (Apocryphal Book of Abraham, 18:11-12). Cuneiform texts and tablets found in Ur have a number of references to "'gods' who rode in the heavens in ships, or 'gods' who came from the stars, possessed terrible weapons, and returned to the stars" (Von Daniken, 1971, p. 24).

Landsburg (1974) agreed with Von Daniken's speculations: "Where do the Sumerians of Mesopotamia come from?" he asked. "They pop up like some devilish jack-in-the-box around 3000 B.C., fully equipped with the first written language. Sophisticated mathematics, a knowledge of chemistry, physics and medicine" (p. 87).

If Abraham came from a culture founded by ancient astronauts, and one which sought to expand its reach to a broader area of earth, then the "god's" instructions for the Patriarch to leave Ur could be interpreted as an attempt by the astronauts to explore or expand their control to a larger area. While the astronaut theory provides fodder for speculation, it fails to persuade or even lead to meaningful conclusions. Interesting speculation, perhaps, but little else.

The Other Cities of Abraham's Youth

Nahor. Abraham's supposed ties to the city of Ur have influenced a number of interpretations about the man and his personality. Von Daniken's (1971) ancient astronaut theory is rooted in the Sumerian connection, as is Dimont's (1962) conclusion that Abraham was a merchant instead of a sheepherder. Those theories evaporate, though, if Abraham was—as some people believe—a native of a different city. As noted earlier, support for the Ur hypothesis is based on its inclusion in a single Bible verse (Gen.. 11:13), albeit one that is frequently read in Sunday School lessons. However, the city of Ur is not mentioned in many early Greek translations of the Bible, which refer to Abraham's home only as the "Land of the Chaldees"—a broader reference to Mesopotamia.

The first known dissenter of the Ur hypothesis was Abraham himself. While Genesis 11:13 claimed he came from Ur, Abraham insisted that he was a native of a different Mesopotamian city—Nahor (Keller, 1980). When Abraham sent a servant to seek a wife for his son Isaac, he sent the faithful servant to Nahor. He described this city as his "country" (Gen. 24:4), his "father's house" and "the land of my kindred" (Gen. 24:7).

The next person to support the Nahor theory was another biblical hero, Joshua. In the 24th chapter of Joshua (v. 2), the Israelite leader referred to the home of Abraham and Abraham's father. Joshua noted that they "dwelt on the other side of the flood (i.e., the Euphrates)." Ur was located on the south ("this side") of the Euphrates, but Nahor was located north of the Euphrates.

As Keller (1980) concluded:

Painstaking research . . . makes it almost certain that Abraham cannot ever have been a citizen of the Sumerian metropolis (Ur). It would conflict with all the descriptions which the Old Testament gives of the kind of life lived by the Patriarch: Abraham is a tent dweller, he moves with his flocks from pasture to pasture and from well to well. He does not live like a citizen of a great city ☐ he lives the life of a typical nomad. (p. 20)

Haran. Regardless of Abraham's birthplace, scholars agree that he spent some of his young adult life in the city of Haran. The actual location of the city remained hidden from biblical scholars until 1933 when it was discovered near the small town of Abu Kemal in Turkey, in the Balikh Valley between Damascus and Mosul (Keller, 1980). Archaeological dating of the site indicated that it was an active community around 1900 B.C., the approximate time that biblical dating put Abraham in the area (Keller, p. 50). Price (1997) noted that it had been a major commercial center during the time of Abraham, but remained unoccupied from about 1800 BC to 800 BC. At the time, Abraham was merely one member of a family clan that included his father Terah, his wife Sarai, and his nephew (Terah's grandson) Lot (Gen. 11:31). Abraham apparently did well, financially, in Haran and was financially secure enough to put together a caravan after receiving God's instructions to leave the city (Gen. 12:1).

In the birthplace debate between Ur and Nahor, Abraham's residence in Haran gives a little more credence to the Nahor side of the argument. Culturally, Haram was similar to Nahor, a region in which Abraham would have been more comfortable as a sheepherder. Keller (1980) noted that the family's ultimate destination—the Land of Canaan—was an odd choice for a native of Ur, but a natural one for someone from Haran and Nahor. The Sumerian's of Ur viewed the people of Canaan as a backward culture of people who "ate their meat raw and didn't even know how to bury their dead. No one whose family was established at Ur would have thought to leave it except for a similar city" (Keller, 1980, p. 59). Conversely, if Abraham were a native of Nahor, then the migration to Canaan would represent a partial (and understandable) return to Abram's homeland, not an entirely new county. His route to Canaan, which followed one of the great trade routes of the Middle East, would have taken him through Nahor.

Abraham's Family

In Abraham's time, the basic social organization of the community was the family (Miller & Miller, 1996). The father was the undisputed leader over the lives of his sons, their wives and children, his daughters (until they were married), and any slaves that each might have. The father remained in full control until his death, at which time leadership of the family was passed on to the eldest son (Abramovitch, 1994). The decision to move from Nahor (or Ur) to Haran would have been that of Abraham's father, Terah. As the family Patriarch, it would have been his decision—not Abraham's—to make such a move. And, despite God's instructions to migrate to Canaan, Abraham would have been helpless to do so while his father was alive. The death of his father freed him to migrate.

In a nomadic family, the father's control of the family was total. There were no governmental agencies that granted approval, nor a police department that would punish misdeeds. Those roles were filled by the father, who was not only parental leader but also the political and judicial decision maker. As Miller and Miller (1996) noted, "Within his own family the father was a mini-dictator whose word was law. The other side of the coin was the protection, the security, the father of a nomadic family gave to his own" (p. 134).

This dictatorial-type role of the father is a crucial element in the planned sacrifice of Isaac. The father served as arbitor of family disputes. His power included the right to make life-and-death decisions that affected family members. Thus, the father—if he chose to do so—could kill his own son. And, if he made such a decision, it was his right to do so without consulting his wife or other family members (Abramovitch, 1994).

Sarah. The second most important person in the family hierarchy was the mother of the eldest son. Although the Bible disagrees about Abraham's birthplace, it identifies Sarai as a native of Nahor. She was Abraham's half-sister on his father's side of the family (another indication that Abraham probably came from Nahor, too), and the two married before their move to Haran

Sarah (as she was subsequently renamed by God) had a volatile and grouchy personality, was subject to fits of jealousy and depression, and was occasionally mean and vindictive. Telushkin (1997) politely said that "Sarah has a strong personality" (p. 40). Thomas (1985) described her as "not quite of his (Abraham's) own spiritual stature, but evidently for sixty years his true and loyal wife" (p. 50). Gomes (1996) more bluntly described her as a "conniving wife" (p. 129).

Some of her obstinacy was probably justified, at least by modern standards. The dictatorial Abraham often left her out of his plans and sometimes used her as a pawn in negotiations. He misrepresented to people in Egypt that Sarah was his sister. He did the same before the court of King Abimelech in Gerar. Cahill (1998, p. 70) noted that Abraham even hid God's promise of a son from her.

The family's trips to Egypt (Gen. 12:9) and Gerar (Gen. 20:1) must have been particularly galling to Sarah. One argument is that the reason he pretended to be her brother was to avoid falling victim to the local custom that one could kill a foreigner to take his wife (Gruen, 1997, pp. 471-472). Maybe, but Abraham made a profit on the deal. In Egypt, he sold her to the Pharaoh, receiving in exchange sheep, oxen, donkeys, camels, servants and maids (Gen. 12:16). The Bible gives no information about Sarah's feelings about the trade, but God wasn't pleased. He sent a series of great plagues to Egypt until the Egyptians returned Sarah to Abraham. Abraham, though, got to keep the goods he obtained in trade and even became wealthy from the deal. As the Bible notes, when Abraham returned from Egypt, he "was very rich in cattle, in silver, and in gold" (Gen. 13:2). Abraham's actions, and his subsequent financial gain, caused Yancey (1999) to compare Abraham unfavorably to his Egyptian business associates: "In Egypt," he wrote, "Abraham demonstrates a morality inferior to that of the sun worshipers" (p. 31). Keller (1980, p. 80), by the way, believes that these two stories refer to the same incident, with the details confused about the site and individuals involved. Whether it happened once or twice, though, made little difference to Sarah. Either way, she was likely to have been angry over the incident.

Sources outside the Bible paint an even bleaker picture of Sarah. According to the apocryphal story of Tobit, Sarah was married eight times before she married Abraham, and each of her first seven husbands was killed in their bridal chamber by a demon. The story has her contemplating suicide, but backing out because of the grief it would cause her father (Gruen, 1997, p. 472). Even if such stories are untrue, they at least reflect a portrait of a woman who had suffered and whose personality was likely to be influenced by that suffering. On the outside, Sarah did those things that culture demanded that she do. Inside, though, she did not always like doing them.

The case of Hagar fits that scenario perfectly. According to the customs of the time, if a wife was unable to provide a male heir to her husband, she was required to find a surrogate wife for her husband to handle that duty. Faithful to the custom, Sarah offered her maid Hagar to Abraham as a maternal surrogate (Cahill, 1998, p. 70). Later, however, she grew jealous and demanded that Abraham exile Hagar and her son Ishmael from the family. As Hamada (1990) noted:

> One does not need to possess a prolific imagination in order to see Sarah ruminating a great deal over memories of Hagar's romantic involvement with Abraham. . . . Sarah was forced to repress her feelings and conquer her wrath for more than sixteen years by bringing them reluctantly under mental and emotional subjection (p. 98).

Keller (1980, p. 52) notes that archaeological evidence supports the tradition of the surrogate concubine. The Nuzi tablets of the Mitanni culture, found in Yorgan Tepe of the Mitanni Kingdom, are consistent with that custom. In Genesis 15:2, Abraham worries that he will die without a son and that his servant Eliezer will inherit from him. The Nuzi tablets indicated that it was customary for a childless couple to adopt a "son" who would look after them and inherit their estate, but the arrangement could be changed if a natural son was born to the couple. Further, if a marriage remained childless, the wife was supposed to provide a "substitute wife," as Sarah did when she presented Hagar to Abraham (Gen. 16:2). The Nuzi tablets create one problem for scholars, though. They have been identified as part of the Mitanni culture and dated to the 15th century BC. That puts them five centuries later than the traditional dating of Abraham in the 20th century B.C.

Sarah is remarkably silent during the entire story of the *akedah* (Humphreys, 1998). There is no indication that Abraham consults with her or even tells her of his intentions. That omission has generated a great deal of speculation about their relationship, particularly following this incident.

Hagar. Although not a major player in the sacrifice of Isaac, the role of Hagar in Abraham's family was a pivotal one. Hamada (1990) described Hagar's story as "a haunting one" (p. 101) that itself leaves the reader troubled. We know that Hagar was Sarah's maid and was likely obtained in the trade with the Egyptians. After Hagar gave birth to Abraham's son Ishmael, Sarah had two reasons to resent the woman. Hagar had provided Abraham with a son (something Sarah had failed to do), and Abraham had once traded Sarah to the Egyptians for the maid (along with a lot of cash).

By the time of the binding of Isaac, both Hagar and Ishmael had been exiled from the camp to wander in the wilderness alone. But tension in the family had been building for years. Prior to the exile, Hagar had once tried to run away from Sarah only to be commanded by God to return to Abraham. When she finally left, it was Sarah's decision—not her own. Hagar took her son Ishmael with her. By the time of this story, Abraham's only remaining son was Isaac—his child with Sarah.

Isaac. Isaac, the child God promised Abraham and Sarah, was born when Abraham was 99 and Sarah was 90 years old. When God first told the couple that a son was on the way, both laughed—with Sarah laughing the hardest (apparently she did have a sense of humor). Isaac was to be no ordinary baby, though, for God had promised that he would be the heir and father of God's chosen people (Alter, 1996, pp. 103-104).

God's command for Abraham to sacrifice Isaac came after the Patriarch had exiled Hagar and their son Ishmael. With Ishmael gone, Isaac was his sole heir and the only one who could fulfill God's promise of making Abraham's descendants a great nation. God's instructions to Abraham were a double blow—not only was he being asked to kill his son, but also the "child of promise" that God had given him. Thus MacArtney (1997) noted that Abraham's shock at hearing the command was an emotional one that went beyond his love for Isaac, because "Isaac was the child of the promise," and ". . . it was through him and through him alone that the great blessings to mankind in future ages were to flow. . . . Why had the Lord given them this child in their old age if he was to be offered up and taken from them" (p. 59)?

Isaac remains something of a mystery to Bible scholars. Other passages in the Bible speak of him in referential terms. He is often included in references to the three great Patriarchs of the Bible, with God often referred to as the "God of Abraham, of Isaac, and of Jacob" (Exodus 3:6; 3:15-16; 4:5; Matthew 22:32; Mark 12:26; Luke 20:37; Acts 3:13, 7:32; The book of Exodus also specifically mentions him as God's "servant" (Exodus 32:13). Nevertheless, little is known about him outside of this story. He is born, is subjected to the sacrifice by his father, gets married, has an encounter with Abimelech (Gen. 26), shows up at his mother's funeral, and blesses Jacob instead of Esau (Gen. 27). There are some references to physical disabilities; for example, he can't see well when he mistakenly passes his blessings to Jacob. Other than presiding over a somewhat dysfunctional family, there is little information that can be used to attribute any moral or personality attributes to Isaac as an adult (Kugel, 1997, p. 173).

Lot. Abraham's nephew Lot seems to have been the "Dennis the Menace" of his day, constantly getting in trouble and having to be bailed out by his uncle. The conflicting information—good and bad—about Lot caused Kugel (1997) to note that it's "hard for interpreters to know what to make of Lot" (p. 181). After their return from Egypt, the strife between the two became irritating enough that Abraham and Lot parted ways (Cahill, 1998, p. 67). The final straw came when trouble developed—apparently over grazing lands—between the men herding Abraham's cattle and those in charge of Lot's livestock. Abraham suggested the separation (Gen. 13:6-9), but left the choice of which direction each would go to Lot (Keller, 1980, p. 72). Lot chose the best area, a garden-like spot near the Jordan River (Gen. 13:10) and close to a city called Sodom.

Away from his uncle's protection, Lot's problems only increased. A war broke out in the area and Lot was captured by one of the attackers. Abraham gathered his men and chased after the victorious army. Although he had too few men to attack the invading king, he trailed them for days and waited for an opportunity. Finally, when the enemy reached the city of Dan in north Palestine, Abraham attacked the camp's rear guard at night. In the resulting confusion, Lot was freed (Genesis 14:12-16), although exactly how that was done is not mentioned (Keller, 1980, p. 73).

This episode paints a picture of Abraham that bears little similarity to his contemporary image. Modern readers often envision Abraham as an old, bearded man—one much like Charlton Heston's portrayal of Moses in the movie *The Ten Commandments*. This episode depicts Abraham more like John Wayne, a man of action and wealth who commands others to join him in the fight, and who used his ingenuity and won the fight despite overwhelming odds (Cahill, 1998, p. 69).

When Lot returned to Sodom, more trouble developed. The city and its neighboring city of Gomorrah had become so sinful that God vowed to destroy both. Abraham, told of the plan, had the audacity to argue with God, and he negotiated a deal in which the cities were to be sparred if enough righteous people could be found. Further, he won the argument—a rarity in religious literature (Eisen, 2000). Unfortunately, the cities suffered their deadly fate anyway (although Lot was spared), but the two incidents have augmented our image of Abraham. The man who would deal with God was a self-confident fighter who had forged a fortune out of the wilderness. He had the nerve to oppose anyone—including God Himself—if he believed he was right. This man was later willing to sacrifice his son. As Kirsch (1998) noted:

> Abraham, we should not forget, is the same man who had boldly confronted God over his plan to destroy the vile and despicable Sodomites, the man who has haggled at length with the Almighty to spare the ten righteous ones who might be killed along with the sinners. But when it comes to the life of his own

son, Abraham falls silent. Meekly and wordlessly, Abraham sets off toward the killing ground with his sweetly befuddled son in tow (p. 175).

Abraham's argument with God over Sodom and Gomorrah may also have played another crucial role in the subsequent aborted sacrifice of Isaac. True, Abraham had already had a debate with God over the justice of killing the innocent. While Abraham had won the argument, Sodom and Gomorrah had still been destroyed. That discussion should have made it conceivable to him that God was serious about the death of Isaac. Sodom and Gomorrah were proof: in that instance, He was not bluffing.

Abraham's Destination

In 1900 B.C., the land of Canaan was a thinly populated agrarian area. There were some scattered cities and towns that were actually walled fortresses. The walls of the cities provided places of refuge should the areas were attacked by nomadic tribes or by the soldiers of another city (Keller, 1980, p. 66). The tribal chiefs (called "kings," in the Bible), who led each town, maintained their authority by sheer power while often fighting feuds with other tribal chiefs to retain their power or expand their influence. They also had to deal with a primitive version of the Old West range wars, as endless fights erupted between the sheepherding nomads and the farmers who plowed the lands near the towns. Compared to the urban life in Sumer, Canaan was indeed a wilderness—a place to which few urban dwellers would have wanted to go.

But, then, Abraham might not have known where he was going. As Cahill (1998) noted, the Bible's indication of Canaan as Abraham's destination "does not necessarily indicate that this destination was actually known to Avram when he started out. There is no reason to think that (Abram) knew where he was going or anything more than what his god had told him ☐ that he was to 'go forth'" (p. 62). Abraham is, Cahill added, "a man who does not know where he is going but goes forth into the unknown wilderness under the prompting of his god" (p. 63). If so, then Abram's decision to lead was bold indeed.

Summary

The man who would become the founder of the world's three great religions set out from a pagan land to roam in an unknown wilderness. He would face turmoil, a host of family problems, and occasional personal failure. On more than one occasion, his own behavior was morally questionable. He was a documented liar (Gen. 20:1) and willing to let his wife commit adultery in return for money and his own safety. Nevertheless, he was poised to do something great—develop the idea that the spiritual world was controlled by one God and only one God—his God.

SECTION II

SOURCES OF CONFLICT

Chapter 4
Abraham's Relationship with God

The God of Abraham had asked him to embark on a courageous journey. In the end, the trek would be both an arduous physical sojourn and a trying spiritual journey—one that would engender a unique relationship between deity and a human.

Abraham's Relationship with God
MacArtney (1997) noted that:

> Abraham is revered by more people of different faith and race than any other man in the Bible. The Jews venerate him as the ⊔Father of the Faithful,' the Moslems venerate him as their ancestor through his son Ishmael, and the Christians venerate him as the friend of God and the type of redeeming faith in Christ, for Christ said that Abraham rejoiced to see His day. (p. 56)

Such reverence comes because of Abraham's relationship with God. Theirs was a relationship that is hard for the average person of religion to appreciate fully the attitudinal and cultural values that he had to overcome in the process. Abraham, after all, was one of the world's first monotheists—one of the first people to believe in a single god. The Bible portrays the post-Garden period of history as one in which polytheism prevailed. Between the expulsion of Adam and Eve from the Garden of Eden and until the arrival of Abraham, the heroes of the Bible were lonely figures who believed in God but had trouble convincing their neighbors to do the same. Conflict at the Tower of Babel left people unable to communicate with each other, while Noah built an ark as a refuge from the flood that destroyed his neighbors. The implication is that, despite the monotheistic beginning of the Garden of Eden, the people of the land quickly moved toward polytheistic religious beliefs. By the time of Abraham, monotheism was a rare theological principle.

Thus Abraham was not the very first monotheist, but he was the first to establish a religion around a belief in one God. As Donin (1991) noted, "unlike others whose monotheism was like an oasis in a spiritual wilderness that dried up and disappeared with their deaths, Abraham devoted himself to the propagation of the faith. He succeeded in passing this faith on to his son" (p. 19).

It is unlikely that Abraham began life as a monotheist. As Cahill (1998) noted:

> We can be certain that (Abraham) began, . . . like all human beings before him . . ., as a polytheist . . . . It is highly unlikely that Avraham became during the course of his life a strict monotheist, but what we can say is that Avraham's relationship to God became the matrix of his life, the great shaping experience. (p. 85)

It is that relationship with God that leads to his religious maturation and a religious view that was unique for its time. Abraham, some would argue, stood out among his times as a man who listened to God and became "the Bible's most outstanding example of faith" (Trimiew, 1999, p. 277).

How did the relationship develop? The instigator, it appears, was God. According to the Bible, it was a matter of God seeking Abraham, rather than Abraham seeking God. Had God sought out others before Abraham? We don't really know. However, many readers interpret the Bible's silence on the subject as evidence that the omitted actions never occurred. Regardless, Abraham's greatness came not in seeking God, but in recognizing the call of God and responding to it.

What makes Abraham's relationship with God even more remarkable is that he had no cultural or social support for his beliefs. This God had no temples or churches. The pagan religions of Sumer had their temples, as did others in the area. Abraham was left to worship God on a makeshift basis. Miller and Miller (1996), for example, noted that "At the time of the biblical Patriarchs (c. 1800 B.C.) there was no official priesthood. The various acts of worship, such as prayer, the giving and receiving of blessings, and in particular the offering of sacrifices, were the responsibility of the head of the family or clan (Gen.22; 31:54; 46:1)" (p. 191). With the absence of designated holy sites, the nomadic Abraham identified sacred places by an "hierophany," i.e., an event, sign, or manifestation that served to indicate the holiness of the spot (Eliade, 1957, p. 27). When God manifested himself to Abraham, the Patriarch built an altar there to designate it as a sacred spot. For example, when Abraham reached Canaan, stopping at Shekkem, he built "a small altar by an oak tree where he could offer animal sacrifices to his god" (Cahill, 1998, p. 65). Such altars, scattered around the countryside, were the only "temples" available to the Patriarch.

The lack of such social support proved to be a fatal flaw in the theology of another early monotheist. Akhenaten, the pharaoh who ruled Egypt during the second quarter of the fourteenth century B.C., broke with the polytheistic religious traditions of his predecessors and established a national religion which worshiped a single deity—the sun god Aten (Wiegall, 2000: Hornung, 2001; Redford, 1987). In some ways, Akhenaten's religious views were more advanced than Abraham's, causing one observer to describe it as the first attempt in history that tried to explain the world on the basis of a single principle (Hornung, 2001). Akhenaten's religion was so intriguing that it caused Sigmund Freud (1987) to speculate that the pharaoh was a mentor to Moses and perhaps the true founder of the Israelite religion. Others see him as an early version of Jesus, an Egyptian forerunner of the Christian religion (Redford, 1987). But Akhenaten's religious reforms lacked popular support and died with him, and subsequent Egyptian rulers returned to their polytheistic beliefs for centuries. Why did his views fail? Why did Abraham's expand to three great religions? Two reasons are more frequently considered. First, although it was monotheistic in nature, Akhenaten's views were not comparable to modern views of God; his was simply a focus on a single deity from Egypt's past religious tradition (Aldred, 1991). Others have suggested that Akhenaten's religious reforms were instituted to enhance his own political power, rather than making advances in theology (Reeves & Reeves, 2001). Indeed, a crucial part of Akhenaten's reforms was to eliminate the power of the Egyptian priesthood and naming himself as the only human intermediary who could communicate with Aten.

Abraham appears to have had no such motives. While he knew of God's promises, in many passages he seems to doubt that they will ever occur. He was particularly skeptical about the promise of a child when he and Sarah were at an advanced age. But, despite such skepticism, Abraham continued to believe and developed a singular relationship with his God. The idea of a "relationship" with the Supreme Being implies a developmental process in which the Patriarch gradually learns with Whom he is dealing. As Cahill (1998) noted, initially "the god" was "little more than . . . a good luck charm" for Abraham (p. 84). He likely viewed "his god" as his personal god, i.e., a guardian spirit or angel who was "charged with taking special care of him" (Cahill, 1998, pp. 60-61). Such an attitude toward "gods" was common in the Mideast at the time. The same attitude continues today, with may people viewing God as their personal protector or their team's protector.

Eventually, though, Abraham's faith in his God supercedes superstition. The Bible notes that Abram "trusted in" God and God recognized this trust as "righteousness" on the part of the Patriarch. As Cahill (1998) noted, "For this trust we are given no reason other than Avram's insight; this self-reliant man relies on his own judgment to interpret correctly what is going on" (p. 70). By this time, Abraham is no longer a Sumerian; he is an individual, for "without Abram's highly colored sense of himself—of his own individuality—there could hardly be any relationship . . . , (and) we may almost say that individuality (with its consequent possibility of an interpersonal relationship) is the flip side of monotheism" (Cahill, 1998, pp. 70-71).

The Nature of the Covenant

God's covenant with Abraham was not His first, nor would it be His last. The first covenant was made with Noah (Gen. 6:18; 9:8-17), and later He established another covenant with Moses. What makes His treaty with Abraham so distinctive, though, is its corresponding promise to make his heirs a great nation. This time, the covenant would extend to generations of descendants. This forms the basis of the Jewish belief of their national destiny, although other interpretations have also been offered. Pilzer (1995), for example, views the covenant as the origin of economic evangelism, i.e., the "God-will-make-you-rich" theology, so popular in many evangelical Christian churches today.

Kelly (1977, p. 92) noted that the Hebrew word for covenant (*berith*) appears more than 286 times in the Hebrew text of the Old Testament. Its literal interpretation ("bond" or "fetter") refers to a contract or treaty that binds two parties together. The parties involved could be two individuals (e.g., David and Jonathan, 1 Samuel 18:1-4) or two kingdoms (e.g., the Israelites and the Gibeonites, Joshua 9). In addition, two different types of covenants are recorded in the Bible—those between individuals who were social equals (parity covenants) and those between parties of different status (known as vassal, suzerainty, or ruler covenants. Parity covenants imposed mutual obligations on both parties, but covenants between unequals did not bind the parties equally.

God's covenant with Abraham was of the second type, and it carried with it special obligations on the part of both participants. While the higher status party had obligations to protect the lower-status party, the lower status party was required to repay that protection with loyalty and allegiance to the person of higher power. Further, this was no standard level of allegiance. As Kelly (1977) noted, "The Old Testament had a special word for the personal commitment expected of a covenant partner. It was the word *hesed*, a word which cannot be translated adequately by any single word in English. It combines the ideas of love, loyalty, and ready response to need" (p. 93). Failing to perform the promise of the covenant could trigger major retribution.

Kelly (1977) noted that the verb frequently used to describe the pact could be interpreted as "cutting a covenant" (p. 93). If so, perhaps the phrase was a reference to sacrificing an animal and cutting it into pieces. The parties in the agreement might then be required to walk amid the pieces of flesh (Gen. 15:9-21; Jeremiah 34:18-20), a ritual that symbolized that either party would be killed—like the lamb—if they failed to live up to their side of the agreement. Understanding this aspect of the covenant places the sacrifice of Isaac into a more understandable cultural context. A sacrifice was an expected way to seal the covenant, and—if the sacrifice was commanded—the servant could not refuse.

Another unusual aspect of this covenant is that the suggestion for the treaty was initiated by God. Frequently in covenants between unequal parties, the lower status person would be the one who initiated the request for a contract. The person with lower status, understandably, was usually the one who was more in need of the protection or power that could be provided by the higher status party. Not so with God and Abraham. As Dimont (1962) noted, "it is God who proposes a covenant to the Patriarch . . . . If Abraham will follow the commandments of God, the He, in His turn will make the descendants of Abraham His Chosen People and place them under His protection" (p. 31).

Except for the proposed rewards to Abraham, the proposed covenant from God was not that unusual. Tribal chieftains in the area often formed such covenants with each other, creating alliances that could be mutually beneficial (Cahill, 1998, p. 71). By joining forces, those chieftains became less vulnerable to attack from others. The difference was that the fellow chieftains were making their alliances with other humans. Abraham was asked to ally himself with a disembodied Voice or an Entity that only occasionally made His presence known (Cahill, 1998, p. 70). Still, somewhat remarkably, he accepted the offer. "Out of an age of tall tales of warriors and kings, all so like one another that they are hard to tell apart, comes this story of a skeptical, worldly Patriarch's trust in a disembodied voice," Cahill (1980, p. 70) wrote. But, as Cahill added, "if the relationship is to last, Avraham requires education; and this he receives in a series of manifestation in which 'the god' gradually reveals himself as God—not just a divinity but the only God that counts" (p. 84).

Abraham's Controversies

As with many ancient texts, the story of Abraham is filled with inconsistencies and contradictions. As already noted, two locations are named as Abraham's hometown, and he may have tried to pass off Sarah as his sister either once or twice. Other contradictions exist, but most are outside the scope of this book. Four elements, however, should be mentioned.

Abraham's Angels. Not all of Abraham's encounters with God were with the Supreme Being Himself. Sometimes the interactions were with surrogates— apparently angels. The presence of these angelic beings in the story of Abraham is one basis for the "ancient astronaut" theory. Writers such as Erich Von Daniken (1971) contend that these "angels" were really ancient space travelers. The writings that record their visits, this theory posits, are the writings of a primitive people who have no other words for describing visitors from the heavens. Von Daniken correctly notes that the Bible is not the only ancient text that describes such visitors. Cahill (1998) observed that references to angels are also found in Sumerian literature, where they "are seen as manifestations of God, often hardly distinguishable from him" (p. 75). Von Daniken, though, sees the references to angels in other cultures as further evidence for his ancient astronaut theory.

Melchizedek. Although there were few places to worship God, the ancient Middle East apparently had at least one priest. Abraham ran into this unusual and controversial character in Canaan—a holy leader named Melchizedek. Melchizedek is described by the Bible as the king of Salem and a priest of God (Gen. 14:18-20). Howard (1999) described him as "a shadowy figure" (p. 296), while Kugel (1997) called him "something of an enigma in the Bible" (p. 151). Gruen (1997) noted that "His mysterious appearance and disappearance as a friend of Abraham and fellow worshiper of God has led to considerable speculation about Melchizedek's origins" (p. 366). The New Testament book of Hebrews (Heb. 5:5-10; 6:19-7:17) depicts him as a supernatural figure of unknown origins and possibly possessing eternal life—a description that resembles Jesus in some aspects. Some biblical interpreters see a similar supernatural reference in Psalms, where the psalmist addresses an unknown person and says, "You are a priest forever, after the line of Melchizedek" (Psalms 101:4). Although he is mentioned only briefly in the story of Genesis, it was enough for Everett (1991) to consider him the only man in the Old Testament greater than Abraham (p. 3). Everett's conclusion is based on a simple line of argument: since the priest had the power to provide a blessing to Abraham and Abraham presented offerings to the priest. Melchizedek's greatness must have exceeded that of Abraham. Together, Melchizedek and Abraham, Everett added, "represent the greatest spiritual leadership in the earth at that time" (p. 3). Other Hebrew scholars concluded that he wasn't a real priest (because he didn't follow the proper Jewish procedure when he blessed Abraham before blessing God) or that "Melchizedek" was merely a title and that his real name was Shem, one of Noah's sons (Kugel, 1997, pp. 160-161).

Regardless, Abraham met the priest-king in the valley of Shaveh, and the two formed an immediate mutual admiration society. Melchizedek treated Abram to bread and wine, while Abram—who had just won a battle over Chedorlaomer and his allies (the group who had kidnapped Lot)—gave Melchizedek part of the bounty won in the battle (Miller & Miller, 1996). This tithe is often interpreted as further evidence that Abraham recognized Melchizedek as a holy figure, although it could also be simply an elaborate exchange of gifts between two leaders.

The presence of Melchizedek creates other possible interpretations of Abraham and his role in history. One option, suggested by Spong (1991) is that Abraham may have been working for the holy man. Spong argued that there "is a strong possibility that Abraham, Isaac, and Jacob, far from being the founding ancestors of Israel, were in fact Canaanite holy men, connected with the religious shrines at Hebron, Beersheba, and Bethel" (p. 42). If so, the stories of these Patriarchs might be a Hebrew adaptation of earlier stories that occurred after the Hebrews conquered Canaan, with Abraham becoming a Patriarchal figure that could be used to legitimize their invasion and conquest of Canaan.

Such theological and historical arguments aside, though, the story of Isaac is still riveting, and Melchizedek may have had an indirect role in it. First, in some New Testament writers' views, Melchizedek represented eternal life. That symbolism establishes Melchizedek as a priest-king who prefigured Jesus as Messiah, just as the sacrifice of Isaac is seen as prefiguring the sacrifice of Jesus (Everett, 1991). Second, many authorities believe that Salem—the area that encompassed Melchizedek's kingdom—was associated with modern day Jerusalem (Smith, 1948). Salem, they note, is an early spelling of Jerusalem (Howard, 1999, p. 296). Realistically, there is probably no way to be sure that Salem and Jerusalem constituted the same area, but—if they were—it would explain why the mountains of Moriah were chosen as the spot of the planned sacrifice. The modern day Mount Moriah is located in Jerusalem. Abraham would have been returning to the area controlled by the king-priest he most admired.

Abraham's Camels. The Bible says that Abraham and his people traveled with camels, at least some of which were obtained in the trade with the Egyptians (Gen. 12:16). When Abraham's servant went to Nahor in search of a wife for Isaac, he and Rebekkah returned on camels (Gen. 24:63-64). The problem that this creates for biblical scholars is that the camel was not a domesticated beast in 1900 B.C. Nomadic travel in that century was done with donkeys. As Keller (1980) noted, "The introduction of the camel as a mount and a bearer of burdens was equal to a revolution in the organization of transport in the Ancient East" (p. 81). Camels were more mobile, could travel further, and do both at a lower cost than donkeys, but they apparently were not used during Abrahams's projected time in the Middle East.

At least two possible explanations for the discrepancy exist. First, the estimated timetable of Abraham's journeys may be off; the Patriarch may have made his wanderings in Canaan a few centuries later than has been placed by traditional estimates. Second, the inclusion of the camels may have come from later authors who inserted the animals to emphasize Abraham's wealth. When the camel was first introduced, only the wealthiest of tribal chieftains would have had them. Including them as part of Abraham's possessions would have emphasized the power and riches of the man to later readers.

Camels are important to the sacrifice story because of their absence. Abraham saddled donkeys for the three-day journey that took him to the sacrificial site. There is no mention of camels. If the reference to camels were added by later editors to emphasize Abraham's wealth and power, then their absence from this story may represent a tale from an earlier oral tradition. Finally, their absence from the story may indicate that power and superior worldly possessions are inconsequential when the impending death of a loved one is involved.

Abraham and the Hittites. Abraham camped near the Hittites, i.e., "the Sons of Heth" (Gen. 23:3) near Hebron, where he buried Sarah. To bury his wife, Abraham had to buy his first property in Canaan. His problem, though, was that such purchases in ancient Canaan were not easy for a nomad like the Patriarch (Cahill, 1998, p. 87). The negotiations, as described in the Bible, are highly consistent with known Hittite transactions (Keller, 1980, p. 106). For example, Abraham initially wanted just the cave—not the surrounding land—when he entered the negotiations, but ended up with the cave, the surrounding fields, and "all the trees that were in the field" (Gen. 23:17). Mention of the trees might seem like an unimportant detail, but it was a crucial element in Hittite transactions. Documents detailing Hittite transactions always stated the number of trees on the land (Keller, 1980, p. 106).

Initially, such documents seem to confirm the biblical record of the event, but it also creates a problem. The Hittite empire was not founded until about the sixteenth century B.C.—about 400 years after Abraham supposedly purchased the land; even then, the Hittite empire did not extend that far south into Canaan (Keller, 1980, p. 106). Keller concluded that there were "two kinds of Hittites, with the Biblical version being the children of Heth' (Numbers 13:29-30). As it relates to the story, however, the presence of Hittites in the area raises questions as to exactly when these events were said to have occurred.

Summary

Ultimately, though, such details provide interesting problems for historical scholars, but they take nothing away from the literary and theological implications of the story itself. That story shall be the focus of our attention— the story of a father who is asked by God to kill his only son. A man whose faith had led him to a high level of monotheistic theology was being asked to test that faith with an action that modern people would consider highly immoral. The anguish and agony associated with that story remain the same, regardless of when and where it happened.

Chapter 5:
Different Religions, Different Views

Abraham is arguably the most revered religious figure in the world, honored and respected by the followers of three distinct religions. The reasons for that reverence vary, though, depending upon which religion is being discussed. MacArtney (1997) summarized the differences briefly by noting that:

> The Jews venerate him as the 'Father of the Faithful,' the Moslems venerate him as their ancestor through his son Ishmael, and the Christians venerate him as the friend of God and the type of redeeming faith in Christ, for Christ said that Abraham rejoiced to see His day (p. 56).

Understandably, then, all three religions treat Abraham's sacrifice as a major religious story, but their interpretations of the story vary dramatically. This chapter will look at the sacrifice from the perspective of the Jewish, Islamic and Christian religions.

The Jewish Perspective: "The Binding of Isaac"

The *akedah* has had a bigger impact on the Jewish religious tradition than in the other two great religions. Its importance is evident in the role that it plays in the Jewish holiday *Rosh ha-Shanah*, which celebrates the birthday of the world with a theme of rescue and salvation. The birth of Isaac is the scripture reading for the first day of the celebration, and the binding story is read on the second day (Strassfeld, 1985, p. 100).

The distinctive perspective of the Jewish religion is reflected in the very words used to describe it. Jewish theologians refer to it as the *akedah*, or the "binding of Isaac." Isaac, they point out, was never actually sacrificed to God, so referring to the story as "the sacrifice of Isaac" is inaccurate. Telushkin (1997) argued that referring to the story as "the sacrifice of Isaac" is an error in translation that "distorts the essence of the event, for at the story's end, Isaac is not sacrificed and God makes it clear that He never wants human beings to be sacrificed" (p. 37).

Understanding the Jewish perspective on the binding of Isaac requires an understanding of their views of both Abraham and history. Abraham, of course, is revered as the father of the tribe—the first monotheist and the person whose faith established the Israelites as a distinct and favored nation. That tradition is well documented and fairly well understood by most modern students of history. What may be harder to appreciate for non-Jews is the reverence that the Jewish religion attaches to such history. Smith (1965) noted that "Judaism accounts the memory of the past a priceless treasure. Most historically minded of all the religions, it finds holiness and history inseparable" (p. 284). God is more than just the Ruler of the universe; He is also the Ruler of history, a Being who directly intervenes in the affairs of mankind at critical points in history. This is particularly true for Jewish history, in that the event seals the covenant in which God promises to make Israel a great nation. The story is, in essence, confirmation of the right of Jews to exist as a nation.

Nothing happens by accident. The Jews favored status resulted from God's intervention with Abraham. God intervened to prevent the loss of the tribe when food was needed in Egypt. God intervened to bring the Israelites out of Egypt. When Israel strayed from true belief and service to God, the nation was punished when other nations conquered it. God was in control of all such events. God's role in Jewish history is particularly evident in the early stories of Genesis. As Dimont (1962) noted:

> It is God who proposes a covenant to the Patriarch . . . . If Abraham will follow the commandments of God, then He, in His turn will make the descendants of Abraham His Chosen People and place them under His protection. We must note here that God does not say they shall be better—merely that they shall exist as a separate and distinct entity and be His people. How this is to be brought about is not revealed (p. 31).

Similarly, the binding of Isaac is viewed as an historical event intended to convey a specific message to the Hebrew nation. The exact meaning of that message, though, may depend upon the individual writer. For Guinness (1988), the binding of Isaac served as a "powerful theological symbol" which taught that "The Jew's devotion to God . . . should be modeled on Abraham's unquestioning obedience and Isaac's meek acquiescence" (p. 55). As such, the focus of the message is not on the sacrifice itself, but on Abraham's faith and behavior. Specifically, the binding of Isaac is viewed as a test of Abraham's faith. Not just any test, either, but the third and final test (and also the hardest) that measured whether Abraham was worthy of being the father of a great nation. "Abraham's final test is exactly that—a trial of his devotion to God," Guinness (1988, p. 55) wrote.

Similarly, Kirsch (1998) contended that many Jewish theologians view the bindings "as a test of faith by a compassionate and merciful God who never really intended to permit the sacrifice of a child at the hands of his own father. God is praised by some apologists for miraculously providing a ram to replace Isaac on the altar at the last moment" (p. 176). One factor that made the challenge such a difficult test for Abraham was that it tested both his faith in God and his faith in God's promise. The command to sacrifice Isaac came after Abraham had exiled his elder son Ishmael. With Ishmael gone, Isaac was

Abraham's sole heir. How could God's promise regarding a great nation be fulfilled without Abraham's only heir surviving the Patriarch? Adding to the need for faith was the moral dilemma that the action posed for Abraham. As Telushkin (1997) noted:

> The *akedah* generally provokes an intense moral conflict in modern readers. On the one hand, Jews and Christians see Abraham as the first Patriarch, a man to be admired and emulated. But how can moral people admire a man who is prepared to commit an act for which moral people might wish to see him executed, imprisoned for life, or consigned permanently to an asylum. (p. 38)

"Abraham's readiness to obey God's command shows him to be ethically deficient by later standards, but not by those of his age," Telushkin (1997) added. "Since other contemporary religious believers sacrificed sons to their gods, God, in essence, was asking Abraham if he was as devoted to his God as the pagan idolaters were to theirs" (pp. 38-39). Telushkin argued that the answer to this question was a strong "Yes," but there is room among other Jewish scholars for speculation. Kirsch (1998), for example, quoted a young Jewish rabbi as saying, "The whole of Jewish history might have turned out differently . . . if Abraham had just said, 'No'" (p. 176).

Others have speculated that God had a more immediate message for Abraham that was unrelated to the test, i.e., the action served to express God's opposition to infant sacrifice. Hertz (1981), for example, argued "The story opens the age-long warfare of Israel against the abominations of child sacrifice" (p. 201). Guinness (1988) also recognized this view:

> Bible scholars have . . . (theorized) that the story was meant to show a transition from child sacrifice to animal sacrifice. Yet nowhere in the account is child sacrifice discussed. And later stories in the Bible recount instances of it, which casts doubt on this interpretation. (p. 55)

The Islamic Interpretation: The Participation of Ishmael

A factor sometimes overlooked by amateur Christian theologians is that the Islamic religion has its own version of the story. The Islamic interpretations, not surprisingly, are influenced by Mohammed, the Islamic religious leader. Mohammed remains one of the most influential religious leaders of all time. He was, as Dimont (1962), described him, "one of history's more improbable figures, an Arab imbued with the fervor of Judaism, proclaiming all Arabs descendants of Abraham" (p. 190).

The Islamic version of the story is in the Koran, the book that for Muslims is the infallible Word of God. The printed version is viewed as the transcript of a tablet preserved in heaven and revealed to Mohammed by the Angel Gabriel (Dawood, 1997, p. 1). Except for a few passages, the narrative in the Koran is provided by God speaking in the first person. Smith (1965) summarized the Islamic religion by analyzing its view of the four great stages in which God revealed Himself to man. First, God revealed the concept of monotheism—his oneness—through Abraham. Second, God used Moses to reveal the Ten Commandments. Third, God used Jesus to reveal the Golden Rule that we are to love our neighbors as ourselves. Mohammed provided the fourth great stage—how to love our neighbors (pp. 235-236).

The Participation of the Son. In this context, the Islamic narrative provides a different interpretation of the story, one that gives the child a more active role. Instead of Abraham telling the child and the servants that they will depart for Moriah, the Koran (37:99-110) begins the story with Abraham letting his son in on the command: "My son, I dreamt that I was sacrificing you," Abraham says. "Tell me what you think." "Father, do as you are bidden," Isaac replies. God willing, you shall find me steadfast. "Then the narrator continues: "And when they had both submitted to God, and Abraham had laid down his son prostrate upon his face, We [God] called out to him, saying: 'Abraham, you have fulfilled your vision.' Thus do We reward the righteous. That was indeed a bitter test. We ransomed his son with a noble sacrifice and bestowed on him the praise of later generations. 'Peace be on Abraham!' (37:99-110).

The rhetorical impact of the differences in the story is dramatic. In the Islamic version, there is no need to speculate about the child's silence during the episode, or about his thoughts as the scene unfolded. In the Islamic version, the child is co-conspirator in his own intended sacrifice and thus a partner in its theological message.

The Identification of the Son. The idea that the son was a partner in the story, not a victim, is crucial to Islamic interpretations. After all, perhaps the biggest difference between the Jewish and Islamic versions of the story is the identification of the son chosen for the sacrifice. Moslem tradition considers Ishmael—not Isaac—as the sacrificial child (Guinness, 1988, p. 55). That interpretation is based on tradition, not the text of the Koran itself. The Koran's version does not identify the child by name, but only by the descriptions of "a righteous son" and "a gentle son." Isaac is mentioned immediately after the story ("We gave him Isaac, a saintly prophet, and blessed them both" Koran 37:112), but that's part of a different passage.

Ishmael plays an important role in the Islamic tradition, some of which is reflected in biblical passages in Genesis. The first two believers to participate in the rite of circumcision were Abraham and Ishmael, not Isaac, who was yet to be born. Hamada (1990) sees both sons as fulfilling vital roles in the spread of monotheism, noting "Each one of them was equally loved by God and Abraham" (p. 93). But, he added, God "chose each one of them to play a different role according to His sovereign plan for the human race" (p. 95).

The descriptors of a "righteous" and "gentle" son would be consistent with the Islamic view of Ishmael. Ishmael was Abraham's son by Hagar. Genesis 16 records that mother and son were exiled from Abraham's entourage at Sarah's request (or command, actually). The Koran records a continuing relationship between Abraham and his son after the exile, with the two men joining to build the Kaba, or House of God, in Mecca. Ishmael's descendants subsequently become the Arab nations. Thus much of the Bible and the Koran have similar views of Ishmael. This story, in fact, is one of the major exceptions. As Smith (1965) noted, this story is the "first divergence between the Koranic and Biblical accounts of Abraham" (p. 218).

The Role of the Ram. A third interesting aspect of the Islamic view of the story is the role of the ram provided by God as a replacement for Isaac. In this tradition, the beast that God provides for Abraham is the very same ram that Abel offered in his sacrifice to God—the first ritual sacrifice recorded in the Bible (Girard, 1977, p. 4). The rhetorical impact of this factor is also important. The connection provides a linkage to the tradition of sacrifice, thus increasing the theological significance of the event. And, there is another implicit element in the meaning, that is, the animal being sacrificed has already been sacrificed. The taking of more lives was not necessary.

In that context, the story is one of powerful symbolism for Moslems, a narrative that "plays a pivotal role" in the Islamic religion (Guinness, 1988, p. 55) and essentially summarizes their theological framework. The word "Islam" means "submission" in Arabic, and that is essentially what both Abraham and his son do. Both "submit" to a higher authority—Abraham to his God, and presumably Ishmael to both his father and his God. "Who but a foolish man would renounce the faith of Abraham?" the Koran (2:130-132) asks. "We [God] chose him in this world, and in the world to come he shall abide among the righteous. When his Lord said to him: 'Submit,' he answered; 'I have submitted to the Lord of the Universe.'" Such submission is necessary, Mohammed said, because the Jewish and Christian religions lost sight of God's commandment to worship him. "Having thus gone astray, they must be brought back to the right path, to the true religion preached by Abraham," Dawood (1997) wrote in summarizing the Islamic view. "This was Islam—absolute submission or resignation to the will of God" (p. 2).

The Christian Interpretation: The Symbolism of Isaac

Spiegel (1993), writing from the Jewish perspective, credited Saul (Paul) of Tarsus for adapting the *akedah* to the Christian belief. "It is he (Paul)," Spiegel wrote, "who wove together an entire system of forgiveness without works of the law, from a hybrid mixture of Jewish messianic hopes and pagan notions of gods dying and returning to life in recurring cycles" (pp. 81-82). To do this, Spiegel argued, Paul "placed the *Golgatha Event* at the heart of the new faith" as a "counterpoint to the *Akedah Story*" (p. 82).

Lerch (1950), writing from the Christian perspective, noted that the "description of the binding and sacrifice of Isaac became one of the most pervasive figures of redemption: God, like Abraham, had willingly offered his own first-born Son as a sacrifice." In essence, this approach treats Isaac's sacrifice as "a trial run for God" (Cahill, 1998, p. 80), a pre-test of the eventual sacrifice of Jesus. As Guinness (1988) noted, "Abraham's willingness to sacrifice his son Isaac prefigures God the Father's willingness to let his son Jesus die on the cross for the salvation of all mankind" (pp. 54-55). Similarly,

Cahill (1998) noted that Christians see in Abraham "a type of God, willing to give his 'only son' Jesus as sacrifice for our sins" (p. 83), while Telushkin (1997) described the Christian view as "a foreshadowing of that later 'sacrifice'" (p. 37). McGee (1991) stated the argument more directly: "there on the top of Mount Moriah where Abraham offered Isaac was a picture of the offering and even of the resurrection of Christ" (p. 75).

Pelikan (1985, p. 43) divided the various Christian interpretations into three sub-categories: (1) foreshadowing of the cross, (2) anticipation of the doctrine, and (3) prophecies of the coming of Christ. A fourth option, theological empathy, has been implied in the interpretations of other scholars. We shall look at each of these approaches separately.

Foreshadowing of the Cross. This approach to the *akedah* views the binding of Isaac as more than just a moment in Jewish history, but an event that symbolically represented a form of ancient Christianity (Jensen, 1993). Typical of this approach is the view of McGee (1991, p. 75), who argued that God preached the Christian gospel to Abraham when he called upon him to sacrifice Isaac. The first advocate of this position, though, was Paul. Writing in Galatians (3:16), Paul argued that "the Scripture, foreseeing that God would justify the heathen through faith, preached before the gospel unto Abraham." Rhetorical implications of this approach run the gamut from practical to theological. Strom (1998), for example, used the story of Abraham and Isaac to build an argument for Christians to offer their "skills as living sacrifices" (p. 280). Early Christian artists used Isaac as a symbolic representation of Christ (Jensen, 1993). For some, recounting of the ram caught in the thicket is a symbolic representation of Jesus wearing a crown of thorns. Others see it as an early example of Christian redemption.

McGee (1991) perhaps represents the extreme form of this interpretation: "We assume that Abraham, Isaac, Jacob and all the Old Testament worthies were great men but that they were not as smart as we are, that they did not know as much as we know" (p. 79), he wrote. "However," he added,

> I am of the opinion that Abraham knew a great deal more about the coming of Christ and the gospel than you and I give him credit for. In fact, the Lord Jesus said, 'Your father Abraham rejoiced to see my day; and he saw it, and was glad' (John 8:56). So he must have known a great deal more than we realize. (p. 75)

Proponents of this view see several aspects of the story that are symbolically and rhetorically interpreted in light of the crucifixion and resurrection of Jesus. Baldwin (1986, p. 92), for example, argued that the ram was a symbolic representation of Jesus—an innocent sacrificed in the place of Isaac. The thicket in which it was caught could represent the crown of thorns worn be Jesus at the Crucifixion. MacArtney (1997) sees a parallel between the behavior of Isaac and Jesus:

> how beautiful an instance it was of supreme faith and unquestioning submission on the part of Isaac. Had he so minded, with his strong robust arm

he might have seized the knife out of Abraham's hand and smitten him there at the altar. But Isaac, whose meekness and submission are always a type of Christ, permitted himself to be bound on the altar. Like Christ, as the prophet described him, "He opened not his mouth." (p. 61)

McGee (1991) also saw parallels between Isaac and Jesus. Based on a comparison of Sarah's age when Isaac was born (90) and when she died (127) soon after the sacrifice, McGee argued that Isaac was not a young child but probably around 30 years old when the incident occurred. If so, that would make Isaac about the same age as Jesus was when he was crucified. McGee found another symbol in the type of sacrifice commanded of Abraham, the burnt offering. "The burnt offering was the offering up until the time of Mosaic law; then a sin offering and a trespass offering were given," McGee wrote. "Here the burnt offering speaks of the person of Christ" (p. 68). "What can we do but submit to God's will, obey His commands, and trust where we cannot see?" McGee asks elsewhere. "We have far better assurance than Abraham had, for we have the assurance of God's love given to us in Christ" (p. 62).

Doctrine Anticipation. A second Christian argument for the sacrifice is that it demonstrated the theological need for Jesus' sacrifice to cleanse the sins of the world. The basic thesis of this rhetorical stance is that the types of sacrifices provided by early worshipers were unsatisfactory as a method of handling redemption. Thus, McGee (1991, pp. 66, 74) concluded that the incident revealed that God required that a life be given before He could save the world from sin. "Through this incident, God is making it clear that there will have to be a Man to stand in the gap, there will have to be a Man capable of becoming the Savior of the race if anyone is to be saved" (McGee, 1991, p. 74). Baldwin (1986) agreed: Jesus, he wrote, "was also the 'only' or unique Son, for whom there could never be a substitute" (p. 92).

Prophetic Symbolism. A third alternative Christian explanation is that the sacrifice was really a scriptural prophecy, one that anticipated the sacrifice of Jesus. Like the "foreshadowing" approach, proponents of this view see a great deal of symbolism in the event, with each symbol serving as a prophetic and rhetorical element. Hence Baldwin (1986) noted, "The words of Abraham, '*God will provide himself a lamb,*' are prophetic, and John the Baptist had evidently meditated on them when he said, 'Behold, the Lamb of God!' (Jn. 1:29, 36)" (p. 92). And, Baldwin added that, "He may also have had in mind the Passover lamb, and the lamb led to the slaughter (Is. 53:7), for these are the outstanding occasions in the Old Testament when the word 'lamb' is used'" (p. 92).

McGee (1991) saw a prophetic symbolism in the relationship between the father and the son.

The transaction that is going to take place is between the father and the son, between Abraham and Isaac. And, actually, God shut man out at the cross. At the time of the darkness at high noon, man was shut out. The night had come when no man could work, and during those last three hours, that cross became an altar on which the Lamb of God who taketh away the sin of the world was offered. The transaction was between the Father and the Son on that cross. Man was outside and was not participating at all. The picture is the same here: it is Abraham and Isaac alone. (p. 70)

Dumont (1971) saw a series of similarities between the sacrifice of Isaac and that of Jesus:

> An interplay of Jewish and pagan themes in the Isaac and Iphigenia stories cast their shadows over Christianity. As Isaac carried the wood for his sacrificial altar on his shoulders to Mount Moriah, so Jesus carried the cross for his crucifixion on his shoulders to Mount Golgotha. Jesus expected a Jewish ending but got a pagan one. Just as Abraham looked to heaven for God's grace to stay his hand, so Jesus looked to heaven for God's grace to stay the hand of fate. But as Jews did not write this script, there was no grace for Jesus. He died with a prayer from the Psalms (22:2) on his lips: "Eli, Eli lama sabachtani"— My God, My God, why hast Thou forsaken me? (p. 207)

Emotional Empathy. A fourth rhetorical perspective, from the Christian view, is that by asking Abraham to sacrifice his son, God could better appreciate the emotional pain that He would face in sacrificing Jesus. Thus, McGee (1991) noted, "God spared Abraham's son, but God did not spare His own Son but gave Him up freely for us all" (p. 74). This approach provides rhetorical justification for some Sunday morning sermons, but suffers from several theological problems.

* It questions God's omnipotence. An omnipotent God should already know what that feeling is like.

* God had already lost a son and a daughter. Adam and Eve were both the children of God (literally, according to the second chapter of Genesis), and he had already experienced their loss (albeit through natural deaths rather than sacrifice).

* At no point in the story does it mention, or even imply, anything that points to this conclusion. Genesis pointedly treats the story as it relates to Abraham's faith. The only reference that it makes to increased knowledge for God is that God now has a clear assessment of the depth of Abraham's faith.

Summary
The story of Abraham and Isaac engenders three distinct perspectives from the three major religions. Each offers a neat theological answer that fits well within the thoughts and beliefs of the individual religion. Ultimately, though, none of these approaches addresses some key elements of the story. Cahill (1983) succinctly summarized the problems when he described such interpretations as rationalizations that avoid key elements of the story. "Without meaning to imply that these interpretations have no basis," he wrote, "I hasten to point out that both serve as frames, giving us categories to stuff this episode into: they are excuses to distance ourselves from the central brutality, so that we may eventually tuck it away out of sight" (p. 83).

That brutality is the subject of our next examination.

Chapter 6
The Legacy of Location

From 1948 until 1967, Mount Moriah and the ruins of Solomon's Temple were part of the no-man's land in the fighting between Israel and its Arab neighbors. In June 1967, General Moshe Dayan led the first Israeli troops into the Old City section of Jerusalem and claimed Mount Moriah as part of Israel. That military success has barely toned down the conflict in the area, though. Fighting remains frequent and deadly, suicide bombers sneak into nearby neighborhoods to kill themselves and others, and a climate of fear continues. Mount Moriah has not been immune to the brutal situation. Because of concern over the behavior of religious fanatics, it is illegal to bring Bibles to the Temple Mount (Feiler, 2001, p. 87).

Yet, in the story, God's instructions to Abraham were specific in pointing out this site as the place to sacrifice his son. Abraham was at Beersheba when God spoke; Mount Moriah was about 45 miles away and no quick trip by any means. As Baldwin (1986) noted, "Even with an early start it would indeed be the third day before their destination came in sight" (p. 90). That is consistent with the book of Genesis that noted "on the third day Abraham lifted up his eyes, and saw the place afar off" (Gen. 22:4).

The context of the instructions indicates that the location was not chosen at random. Quite the contrary, Mount Moriah is arguably the single most sacred place in Jewish and Christian history, while also ranking high among Islamic religious sites. Borg (1987) noted, "Many cultures speak of a particular place as . . . the umbilical cord connecting . . . two worlds" (p. 27). As such, this location qualifies as one of those sites that Eliade (1957) described as the "navel of the world" (pp. 32-47), or the *axis mundi* which connects the real world and the spiritual world. For the three great religions of the world, Mount Moriah seems to be considered such a location, for it was a focal point of several key events in the Old and New Testaments.

The problem is that much of the spiritual significance attached to Moriah is largely the result of speculation. Spiegel (1993) argued that we cannot be sure that the Moriah location was even part of the original story, noting that those details could have been "added at a later date, in order to exalt and proclaim the lineage of the Temple in Jerusalem" (pp. 66-67). If so, though, one would expect that the additions would have been more precise, because the information in the story is too vague to know exactly which location serves as the final scene of the story. Realistically, then, the exact site of Moriah cannot be known for sure. Marks (1983), for example, noted that the language of verse 14 is explanatory in nature, not a place name. The Hebrew words were later reconstructed (2 Chronicles 20:16) to reflect the phrase, "Today, in this mountain, God provides." As Marks (1983) admitted, "This suggestion is the best we have, but the name of the cultic center cannot be satisfactorily determined" (p. 50).

So, given the vagueness of the reference, how has one specific place become so sacred that it is the site of multiple sacred events? Eliade (1957) argued "The sacred always manifests itself as a reality of a wholly different order from 'natural' realities" (p. 10). Further, "Man becomes aware of the sacred because it manifests itself, shows itself, as something wholly different from the profane" (p. 6). Eliade defined this manifestation of sacredness as a "hierophany," or a sign that indicates the sacredness of the place through "an irruption of the sacred that results in detaching a territory from the surrounding cosmic milieu and making it qualitatively different" (p. 26). Mount Moriah seems to have had several such signs. When Abraham and Isaac climbed up Mount Moriah that day, they could scarcely imagine the number of hierophanies that would occur at that location. Centuries later, this same mountain would be considered the place where:

* David would establish his capital city in Jerusalem
* Solomon would build the Temple,
* Mohammed would step to Heaven,
* Jesus was crucified and buried, and where his resurrection was first reported.

(Fritsch, 1983, p. 259) also identified it as the place where God appeared to David (I Chronicles 21). Others aren't as sure. Marks (1983) argued that Moriah's dual designation as the site of the *akedah* and the Temple comes from II Chronicles 3:1 which identifies it as the hill in Jerusalem on which the Temple would later be built. The problem, though, is that this description is not consistent with the references in Genesis to several mountains ("the mountains of Moriah"). Further, it appears likely that Jerusalem was already settled in Abraham's time, a fact that caused Marks to suggest that the text may have been corrupted from an original reference to the "land of the Amorites" (p. 50). Despite the confusion, though, the designation has remained. Much of the credit for this co-identification of the site must go to David, who arrived in the area almost a 1,000 years after Abraham, purchased the rock atop the highest hill in the city, and identified it as Moriah (Feiler, 2001, p. 88). The fact that David may have had little justification for making such a designation seems irrelevant to modern sentiments and conclusions. It is still considered sacred by the three great religions.

A pragmatic consideration would be whether Abraham had been there before. It is likely that he had. When God instructed him to leave Ur, He gave specific directions for the trip. But no directions are included with the command to go to Moriah. Apparently, wherever Moriah might have been, directions were unnecessary because Abraham was familiar with the area and considered it a holy place. Further, if Abraham had any doubts when he climbed the mountain, he certainly had none by the time he descended. His name for the place, *Jehovah-jireh* ("the Lord will provide") has become a proverbial saying (Miles, 1996) that has etched itself into the heritage of the modern church (Baldwin, 1986, p. 91-92).

Jerusalem. Where would Abraham first get the impression that Mount Moriah was a holy place? Perhaps from a friend who was familiar with the area, and that could have come when he called upon the priest-king Melchizedek. An earlier account in Genesis (14:18-2) records that Melchizedek, the king of Salem, met Abram in the valley of Shaveh (Gen. 14:17). While Shaveh would not have been close to Moriah, the priest-king may have come from that area and perhaps talked to Abraham about it. The clue comes from Melchizedek's title, "king of Salem." Some Jewish commentators have argued that Salem is Jerusalem, noting that the book of Psalms (76:2) also refers to Jerusalem with the shortened form of "Salem" (Smith, 1948, p. 581). Gruen (1997) more directly described Salem as a short form of Jerusalem. Others disagree, instead identifying it with the Salem where John was baptized. Still, it's an intriguing possibility that Melchizedek might have influenced Abraham to view the future site of Jerusalem as a holy place. After all, the priest-king appears to be the only religious leader—other than God—to whom Abraham made an offering to during his lifetime. This occurred when he presented the priest with a tithe of the bounty he won in the victory over Chedorlaomer and his allies (Gen. 14:18-20).

Scholars are not certain whether the area around Mount Moriah bore the name of "Salem" when Abraham and Isaac began their ascent of the mountain. Most, though, believe the name Jerusalem eventually became associated with the area. Armstrong (1996b), for example, noted that while there is no mention of Jerusalem in the text, the land of Moriah would become associated with Jerusalem by at least the fourth century BC (p. 28). That date is based upon the dating of the biblical passage (II Chronicles 3:1) that identifies "the land of Moriah" as one of the mountains in which Jerusalem was situated. Others continue to disagree. Alter (1996) submitted that "Though traditional exegesis . . . identifies this (spot) with Jerusalem, the actual location remains in doubt" because "there is an assonance between 'Moriah' and 'yir'eh, 'he sees,' the thematic key word of the resolution of the story" (p. 104).

David's capital city. The ancients considered Jerusalem to be the center of the earth, "the place where God was chosen." Tom Wright (1996), called Jerusalem "the place where the glory and the folly of the world is concentrated" (p. 14). Psalms referred to it as "the joy of the earth" (Ps. 48:1). The history of the area dates back about 5,000 years. The Canaanites inhabited the city around 2500 B.C. It later became a citadel for the Jebusites and first came under Jewish control around 996 B.C. when King David sought to unite the twelve tribes of Israel into a single nation. He conquered the city and made it his capital (2 Samuel 7:10). Davis (1998) noted that Jerusalem was an excellent choice, for both political and strategic reasons, even though it was a small and relatively insignificant Canaanite town at the time. "Occupying high ground at a crossroads with highways running in four directions, Jerusalem is virtually impregnable from assault on three sides and contains a perennial water supply from the Gihon spring," Davis (1968) wrote. "The choice of Jerusalem is politically astute because it was not affiliated with any of the tribes" (p. 182). David solidified the image of the city for the Israelites when he moved the Ark of the Covenant there, thus making Jerusalem the center of worship for the united nation.

After David built his palace, he wanted to build a temple to God that would house the Ark (1 Chronicles 17:1-4, 7, 10-14, 23-27). God—speaking through the prophet Nathan—politely refused the offer (1 Chronicles 17:15) because David had been "a warrior" and had "shed blood" (28:2-3). Instead, he housed the ark in a tent until a temple could be built. David settled for preparing plans (28:11-12) and gathering materials (29:1-5) so that his son Solomon could complete the project.

Solomon's Temple. After David's death, Solomon completed the task of building Israel's first temple atop a mountain in Jerusalem—a house that "would be associated with God's kingdom forever" (Batson, 2000). Construction began around 970 to 967 BC and was completed around 952 BC with the aid of Phoenician artisans. The structure faced east, and it was primarily built of stone. It had a flat wooden roof made from imported cypresses and cedar. Bronze pillars stood in front of the structure, which had three main rooms. Visitors entered through the anteroom, or Ulam. Beyond the anteroom was the Hekal, or main sanctuary. The Hekal was connected to a flight of stairs that led to the Holy of Holies—the room that housed the Ark of the Covenant. Tradition identifies this site with Mount Moriah.

Sitting squarely in the middle of the Temple Mount is an unusual and large rock known as "Abraham's Rock." The impressive formation is 58-feet long, 51-feet wide, and between four and six feet high. Whether this is the exact rock upon which Abraham had bound Isaac is difficult to determine, but all three of the major religions consider it a sacred site. Tradition also identifies it as the site of the altar in Solomon's Temple and the spot from where Mohammed ascended to heaven (Howard, 1999, p. 339). In essence, Wright (1996) concluded, this was "the place where . . . the living God chose to meet with his people" (p. 57) and the temple stood for "the saving presence of Israel's God at the very centre of the world" (p. 65).

Indeed, strange and historic events seemed to have occurred there. It was there that Isaiah supposedly saw a vision of God upon the divine throne surrounded by strange, six-winged creatures. As Borg (1987) noted, the vision was possible because the temple was "the sacred place connecting the earth to the other realm . . . . He did not simply ⬜see' into the other world; he was, in a sense, *in it*" (p. 30).

After the Israelites took control of Jerusalem, many of the Israelites of the day believed that Jerusalem could not be defeated because it was under God's protection (Borg, 1987, p. 161), despite warnings from Jeremiah (7:4). Their feeling of security turned out to be a false one. Solomon's original Temple was destroyed by Nebuchadnezzar and the Babylonians in 586 B.C... A second Temple, considerably smaller than the original, was erected between 525 and 515. During the first century B.C.E., Herod the Great expanded it, bringing back parts of its former glory (Ben-Dov, 1986; Ritmeyer & Ritmeyer, 1989). It was from this second Temple that Jesus drove out the moneychangers (Luke 19:45) in an action that precipitated his Crucifixion and the beginning of Christianity.

By then, the religious significance of the Temple had become ingrained into Jewish thought. The Temple, in fact dominated the city. As Wright (1996) noted, "The Jewish temple that existed back then wasn't simply a large building in one part of the city. It's more that Jerusalem was a temple with a city around it!" (pp. 57-58). It size reflected its importance in Jewish life; the temple, Wright wrote, "wasn't just at the centre of the city. It was also at the centre of Jewish worship. They believed it was the centre of the cosmos itself" (p. 57-58).

By the time of Jesus, the area around Mount Moriah had grown into an urban area with a population that ranged somewhere between 40,000 and 70,000 people (Borg, 1987, p. 173). Its importance was magnified by the fact that the Israelites of the time were under foreign domination. Jerusalem had been occupied by the Romans for half a century by the time Jesus was born, but the Temple stood as a reminder of days of greater glory. Apparently the Romans understood its importance, although they may have underestimated its role. At one point, the Roman emperor Caligula (Borg, 1987, p. 84)—known throughout history for his depravity—sought to have a statue of himself erected in the Holy of Holies in the temple. That proposal created an outcry from the Jewish people. The temple was so holy in the Jewish religion that Jesus could not have completed his ministry without going there. As Wright noted, "Kings have to go to Jerusalem if they are to be crowned" (p. 60). The temple maintained that lofty standing in the Jewish culture until the structure was destroyed by the Romans in A.D. 70.

In 66 AD, the Jewish people in Jerusalem revolted against the Roman government. Rome put down the revolt violently. In 70 AD, after a six-month siege, the Romans captured and destroyed the city—including the temple. The entire compound was burned to the ground. The destruction of the temple may have destroyed the building, but not the cultural importance of the site. The Western Wall remained as a final remnant, and Jews continue to gather there today for prayer (Laperrousaz, 1987). Even secular Jews get angry over the site, because it serves as such a central symbol in Jewish culture. That role was emphasized by the importance of its capture by the Jews on June 7, 1967 during the Seven-Day War. The capture of the site from Jordanian control was announced with the phrase, "The Temple Mount is in our hands," and started a nationwide celebration (Laperrousaz, 1987).

The Dome of the Rock. The perception that Mount Moriah was a holy site was not limited to the Jewish and Christian religions. Overall, the mount was the site of two Jewish temples, at least one pagan temple, and two Islamic structures. Those Islamic buildings serve to punctuate its important to the

Islamic religion. The Mount is revered by Islamic believers as the Haram as-Sharif ("Noble Sanctuary") and is the third most holy site known to Muslims—housing both the Dome of the Rock and the el-Asqa Mosque. Muslim reverence for the site dates back to the seventh century. The Temple Mount had remained in ruins for more than 500 years after its destruction by the Romans. Its re-emergence as a religious site came in 638 when Arab caliph Omar Ibn-Kharib conquered Jerusalem and looked for a place to build a shrine to Mohammed. One of his aides, a converted Jew, recommended a spot on the northern side of the mount, so that Muslims praying south toward Mecca would always overlook the site of the Temple (Feiler, 2001, p. 88). Later, in 715, the Muslims built the silver-domed El Aqsa Mosque at the south end of the Temple Mount. In addition to serving the Islamic religion, it was used by many waves of the Crusaders as the headquarters for the Templars.

But the most awe-inspiring structure on the mount is the Dome of the Rock. Feiler (2001) described it as "the jewel of Islamic architecture" (p. 89). Its reverence to the Muslim religion can be traced back to the prophet Mohammed, who was born in the year 570 in Mecca and was 40 years old when he had his divine revelation. According to Islamic tradition, Mohammed was asleep near the Holy Shrine in Mecca when he was taken by God to Jerusalem, and then ascended to Heaven. The Dome of the Rock marks the site where Muslim's believe Mohammed made that ascension. The stone from which Mohammed is said to have ascended—Abraham's Rock—is in the center of the Dome. Historically, there is trouble with this interpretation. According to Feiler (2001, p. 88), this tradition came after the construction of the Dome, and was not the reason for its original erection.

Still, the Dome is arguably the most beautiful building in Jerusalem, and its 24-karat gold-plated dome dominates the skyline. Its eight-sided base is covered in blue Persian tiles the color of sapphires. Inside, carpets line the floor so that worshipers can kneel in prayer before the peak of the mountain, Abraham's Rock. Directly below the peak is an underground cave. Muslim tradition holds that when Muhammad ascended to Heaven from the top of the rock, the rock tried to follow—creating the cave beneath the rock (Feiler, 2001, p. 89).

The first Muslim dome was built in the seventh century (691-692 A.D.) by Abdal-Malik, shortly after the Arab capture of Jerusalem in A.D. 638 (Howard, 1999, p. 339). Even though the site is under Jewish control, it is under the day-to-day control of Islamic religious leaders. After the Jewish military captured the site in 1967, Jewish rabbis ruled that Jews should not enter the Temple Mount for fear of walking on the holy soil that once marked the spot of the Holy of Holies. The "Holy of Holies" was so holy that only a few select members of the religious elite were allowed to enter it. Entry by anyone who was considered "un-pure" could result in death. Thus, the safe thing to do was to avoid it. While the exact location of the Holy of Holies is not known, at least one archaeologist has argued that it was on the current site of the Dome of the Rock (Ritmeyer, 1992, 1996; 2000). A sign near the original area tells visitors not to proceed any further, because nobody should enter further and take a chance on entering the

Holy of Holies. Jewish respect for the site is so strong that the entire nation surrendered control of the area. Rather than risk accidentally walking over the spot, the Jewish religious leaders recommended avoiding the Mount entirely. The result was the paradoxical situation in which Jews own the land but do not walk over it. The Muslims lost the land in the war, but continue to control its day-to-day activities and continue to view it as a sacred site—so much so that a round of violence between the Jews and Palestinians erupted in 2000 when a Jewish politician visited the mount. The Muslims viewed the act as a desecration of a holy site and responded with violence (Perry, 2000).

The Crucifixion. Christians revere Mount Moriah because it was the site of the crucifixion of Jesus (Gibson, 1999, p. 179). His cross was raised on an outcropping of rocks on the mountain that resemble a skull and is known as Golgotha. Both the location and the nature of the human sacrifice reinforce the parallels between the crucifixion and the sacrifice of Isaac. J. V. McGee (1999) recalled his visit to the Holy City and his reaction to being in an area that was sacred to both Jews and Christians:

> When I was in Jerusalem, I had the feeling that Golgotha and the temple area were not very far apart. They belong to the same ridge. A street has been cut through there, and the ridge has been breached, but it is the same ridge, and it is called Moriah. Let's not say that the Lord Jesus died in the exact spot—we don't know—but certainly He died on the same ridge, the same mountain, on which Abraham offered Isaac. (p. 68)

Despite McGee's writings, we can't be sure. After God offered a ram as a substitute sacrifice, Abraham abandoned the rock where he had planned to kill Isaac. Instead, he built an altar on the site—one that would mark the location as a holy site. Unfortunately, that altar was later destroyed and the site has never specifically located.

So, was Moriah a holy site? Undoubtedly, most Jews believe so. Even before David, Solomon, or Jesus appeared in the annals of history, Abraham had been directed by God to go to this holy site for his biggest test. Mount Moriah was, as Cahill (1998) noted, the site of Abraham's "mountain experience" (p. 83)—one that could inspire future generations. Arab nations continue to revere the Dome of the Rock and its surroundings. And Clarence MacArtney (1997) saw a parallel for Christians seeking God. "Let us climb the slopes of Mount Moriah," he wrote, "and see Abraham in this supreme hour" (p. 57).

The location, it seems, is important to three different religions. As a Muslim once said, "This is a spot where people come to meet God" (quoted by Feiler, 2001, p. 88).

The Rhetorical Implications of Location

Why does it matter? What difference does it make where the event occurred? Isn't the impact of the story the same regardless of where it occurred? Maybe. However, rhetorically, the location can play a vital role—one that is so vital that people will fight and die for it. As Kimball (2000) noted, many fights are "sparked by a controversy over sacred space" (p. 127). What happens is "When a key feature of religion is elevated and in effect becomes an end, some people within the religion become consumed with protecting or achieving that end" (p. 129).

Social psychologists call the concept territoriality, i.e., the tendency to claim and defend a geographic territory as one's own (Burgoon & Saine, 1978, p. 90). Its role in conflict is important but often overlooked (Lyman & Scott, 1967). Territories often play a crucial role in individual, group and national identities. A person's apartment, their house, or their room is representative of their self, and they have a right to defend it against intruders. Apply that same principle to a religion, and the potential for conflict is vast but understandable. When Abraham departed from Ur and began his years of nomadic wandering, he may not have had a specific location that represented his God and his religion. After this story, though, all three great religions had a location that they could call sacred.

Chapter 7
Sacrifice

My grandmother was a frugal lady. She arose early to prepare breakfast, worked in the fields until noon, took a break to cook lunch, and then returned to the fields again. The idea of hiring someone to help her was an inconceivable alternative, as would have been the notion of bringing in fast food for meals. These and similar types of corner-cutting options were frivolities to her. She would say, they were "a waste of money."

Youngsters of today's generation have trouble understanding her attitude. Examples of her frugality strike them as extreme. Perhaps it is, by contemporary generations' standards. But it makes perfect sense for someone who grew up in the 1930s and toiled through the scarcity and hardships of the Great Depression. People who lived through that time typically demonstrate the principle of "waste not, want not." To understand them, we must comprehend the circumstances that they experienced.

Similarly, some scholars argue that the story of Abraham and Isaac cannot be understood unless it is placed in the context of their times. Of particular importance is the construct of sacrifice, as practiced by the other cultures with which Abraham interacted, and how that theological construct was subsequently developed in other passages within the Bible. Despite all of its other theological implications, the over-riding construct that dominates the story is that of sacrifice—particularly human sacrifice. Spiegel (1993) noted that "Echoes of an archaic rite" emerge from the story (p. 62). Spiegel's point is important, as it indicates that Abraham and his religion's predecessors and descendants were not the only religions to perform sacrifices.

Returning to Abraham's sacrifice, McGee (1991) found that, "this is the first time human sacrifice is even suggested" in the Bible (p. 66). Abraham would have known that other cultures in the area practiced human sacrifice. Animal sacrifice had previously occurred in the book of Genesis, beginning with Abel's sacrifice of an animal from his herd. One common interpretation of the story, in fact, is that it is intended to teach mankind that human sacrifice is wrong. Another, taken from the Christian perspective, is that a substitute sacrifice is both acceptable and necessary. Sacrifice was, after all, a major part of the indigenous religions of the area.

Types of Sacrifices

By the time the sacrificial system of the Temple and Tabernacle had been established in Israel, the system had grown into a complex set of alternatives. At least five different types of sacrifice were recognized by the early Hebrews—Propitiatory Sacrifices, Sacrifices for Sin, Thanksgiving Sacrifices, Peace Offerings, and Burnt Offerings (Urban, 1995).

Propitiatory sacrifices were aimed at appeasing the gods. Such sacrifices were common among many other ancient cultures. Homer makes a reference to such a sacrifice in *The Iliad*, when Odysseus explains that he made a sacrifice to Apollo in order to "appease the (god)" (Homer, *The Iliad*, book 1, line 444). As Hammer (1994) noted:

> pagan worship was more than an attempt to influence the gods; it was a method of controlling them. Worship was accompanied by gifts which pleased the gods because they needed those gifts. Sacrifices were not symbolic offerings but actual nourishment to be consumed. They were often part of a ritual of magic which, when accompanied by the appropriate spells, could affect the gods and their actions. (p. 43)

Although this concept of appeasement is often associated with pagan or ancient religions, an element was retained within the Hebrew culture. Some of the Hebrews seemed to view sacrifices as a means of appeasing God's wrath, a function that God seemed to reject (Jer. 3:12-14; Hos. 6:1-6) when God denounced Israel for its sins (Urban, 1995, p. 258). Further, Urban noted, the idea of appeasing God's wrath sometimes creeps into modern rituals; among Catholics, for example, appeasement is sometimes used in describing the sacrifice associated with Mass (p. 259).

Sacrifices for Sins were dictated as necessary by the Jewish Law. Among Christians, this concept of atonement was for the sinful nature of man. For early Hebrews, though, sacrifices were made to atone for specific sins, an instruction dictated by the Law as described in Leviticus 4 and Numbers 15:22-31. The entire litany of rituals for the Day of Atonement (Lev. 16:1-34) illustrates the function of sin-based sacrifices. Their purpose was to show "proper repentance and [were] not commanded as acts of appeasement" (Urban, 1995, p. 260). This idea is expressed by the psalmist who wrote, "The sacrifice acceptable to God is a broken spirit: a broken and contrite heart, O God, thou wilt not despise" (Psalm 51:17).

Thanksgiving Sacrifices were those presented as either public or private acts of saying thanks to God. One example of modern thanksgiving offerings might be donations made to churches by someone who receives a financial windfall. Urban (1995) noted that thanksgiving offerings were more common in the Hebrew Bible than were sin offerings:

> Public sacrifices were offered as acts of thanksgiving at the end of battle (Jos. 8:31: 1 Sam. 13:9) and by David to celebrate the safe arrival of the Ark in Jerusalem (2 Sam. 6:17-18). The sacrifices marking the sealing of the Covenant

between God and Israel (Exod. 24:5) and at the dedication of the Temple (1 Kings 8:64) were acts of public thanksgiving as well as acts of consecration. In addition, the daily sacrifices, the sacrifices required on the Sabbath and the new moon, and the sacrifices on the days of the great festivals—Unleavened Bread, First Fruits, Trumpets, and Booths (Tabernacles)—had thanksgiving as an essential ingredient. Private sacrifices often had this character (Lev. 7:12-15; Ps. 56:12-13, 107:22, 116:17), as did the offering of the first fruits at the time of harvest (Exod. 23:19; 34:26; Lev. 2:14; 23:30) or at the birth of a first child (Exod. 13:1-16). Thanksgiving sacrifices must have been very frequent (p. 260).

Peace offerings were an early form of communion offerings (*zevach*) which symbolized "the unity of God and human beings in the living community founded by the covenant . . . ." (Urban, 1995, p. 261). The ritual of the early Hebrew peace offering had an obvious similarity to the modern Christian rituals in which bread and wine are offered to God and later consumed by the congregation. In the Hebrew peace offering, which is described in detail in the first three chapters of Leviticus, the sacrificial animal was burned and part of it removed from the fire. The worshipers then ate that portion in a communion meal. Urban (1995) noted that the ritual was not confined to Israel but was widely practiced in the rest of the ancient world.

Burnt Offerings (*olah*), which were also common among other cultures, represented the ultimate form of religious sacrifice in that the sacrificial object—animal or cereal—was totally consumed by the sacrificial fire. The burnt offering represented the complete surrender of the worshiper to God. As Urban (1995) noted, "Although an animal or cereal was placed on the fire, it was ultimately the worshiper himself who was being offered" (p. 261). This symbolic element was represented by the requirement, in the Hebrew ritual, that the worshipers lay their hands on the sacrificial animal before it was killed (Lev. 1:4). This "substitute" sacrifice also appears in other Jewish traditions. Girard (1977) noted that according to Islamic tradition, the ram that God provided to Abraham as a substitute for the son was the same ram offered by Abel in the Bible's first recorded sacrifice (p. 4).

In a particularly important ceremony, the burnt offering and a peace offering could be combined into a single religious ceremony. Such an occurrence is recorded in the Book of Exodus when the Covenant was consummated at Sinai. As part of the ceremony, Moses caught the blood of the sacrificial animals and poured out some of it on the steps of the altar and on the people who had gathered (Exod. 24:4-8). Urban (1995) noted that the pouring of the blood was a symbolic expression of purification and binding of a Covenant that was echoed in later accounts of the Last Supper in the New Testament (Matt. 26:28; Mark 14:24; Luke 22:20).

Sacrifice in Various Cultures

In his book, *The Broken World of Sacrifice*, J. C. Heesterman (1993, pp. 7-12) utilized a surprisingly massive body of evidence that enlightens readers regarding the ancient Veda of the continent of India and their perceptions of, and possible uses of sacrifice. His sources (i.e., collections of Veda writings and artifacts, were well over 2,000 years old, and included sacrifice ritual manuals, guidelines for the carrying out of sacrifice, and masses of other literary and historical treasures regarding the ancient civilization's interaction with the construct of sacrifice. He discovered that the Veda people of India apparently understood the moral and practical problems with human sacrifice, as we think of it. However, the manuals are clear—the rituals for human sacrifice existed.

There is evidence in Heesterman's research that indicates the animals and humans who were the sacrificial objects may not have been harmed. One way the Vedas apparently achieved this was by clipping some of the hair of the sacrificial object and destroying it during the sacrifice ritual. The consecrated animal or person was evidently set free at the end of the ceremony. There are questions that accompany such interpretations. Were hairs clipped from non-sacrificed humans kept? If not, would each haircut not be a sacrifice? Further, could the same person be sacrificed multiple times by this harmless manner? Perhaps in this culture, the cutting of hair was not allowed, except in sacrifice situations. The evidence is unclear on many subtle points, regardless, the Veda did recognize that sacrificing humans by killing them was wrong.

Sacrifice in the Old Testament

The ritual of sacrifice would have been an accepted practice by Abraham and his neighbors, even those of pagan religions. They would have seen nothing abnormal about most of his actions on that fateful day. He built an altar and placed the wood in position. The only thing unusual was that normally Abraham would have brought a ram from one of his flocks, which he would have bound and lain on the altar. His behavior, then, followed the standard procedure for sacrificial animals with one exception—the sacrificial offering was his own son. In this interpretation, the sacrifice of Isaac would have merely been "the vestige of a primitive initiation rite, a kind of 'blood baptism'" which represented unconditional submission to God (Keller, 1980, p. 438).

The binding of Isaac was neither the first nor the last reference to sacrifice in the Hebrew Bible. Hammer (1994) noted that the first comment God made about sacrifice was to explain to Cain why his offering was unacceptable, i.e., his motives for the sacrifice were flawed. The use of a blood sacrifice was not unusual. Abel sacrificed an animal to God (Genesis 4:4), and Noah sacrificed several birds and animals upon leaving the Ark (Genesis 8:20). By the time of the prophets, sacrifice was such a common religious act that the prophets protested against those who did it without the right motives (Heschel, 1969, pp. 195-198). For ancient Israel, Telushkin (1997) noted, "animal sacrifices were what prayer services are to their modern descendants, the most popular expression of divine worship" (p. 451).

Still, sacrifice seems to have played a minor role in the lives of Abraham and the other Patriarchs. Neither Isaac nor Jacob is depicted as offering any sacrifices to God. Other than the binding of Isaac, there is only one other reference to God commanding a sacrifice from Abraham (Gen. 15:9-21), and that had to do with his covenant ceremony. While the Bible recounts a number of instances in which Abraham erected altars to God, there is no mention of him bringing offerings to those altars. As Hammer (1994) observed:

Considering the later emphasis on the sacrificial system of the Tabernacle and the Temple, this seems strange. Perhaps it can best be understood as an attempt to underscore the idea that sacrifice plays a totally different role in the religion of Israel than in pagan rituals. Long before sacrifice became impossible because of the destruction of the Temple, it had been so totally reinterpreted that it was not an indispensable element of worship, as it was in all of pagan religion. (p. 42)

Child Sacrifice

Perhaps the most common and theologically easiest explanation is that the story is a simple repudiation of child sacrifice. Keller (1980) noted that one explanation is to interpret the story as an allegorical renunciation of human sacrifice, particularly a widespread ancient East custom of sacrificing boys. Similarly, Hertz (1981) noted that "The story opens the age-long warfare of Israel against the abominations of child sacrifice" (p. 201). Telushkin (1997) agreed, adding, "Only when God makes it clear that He doesn't want human sacrifice does Abraham learn how evil and immoral such behavior is" (p. 39).

Armstrong (1993) contended that human sacrifice in the pagan world

was cruel but had a logic and rationale. The first child was often believed to be the offspring of a god, who had impregnated the mother in an act of *droit de seigneur*. In begetting the child, the god's energy had been depleted, so to replenish this and to ensure the circulation of all the available *mana*, the firstborn was returned to its divine parent. (p. 18)

Human sacrifice was a common practice in ancient times. In North America, as recent as the 15th century, the Incas of South America were still sacrificing their children to their gods. Some Canaanites practiced human sacrifice, and Abraham apparently knew of the practice (Gibson, 1999). As Gibson noted, "Sacrificing children as an offering to pagan gods was practiced at the time, but never by a godly person. The command must have been abhorrent to Abraham for two reasons. First it would have been unbearable to any loving parent. Second, God's covenant promises were bound in Isaac and his offspring" (p. 176).

Nor did the practice end with the story of the *akedah*. Indeed, Bodoff (1993) argued that the story had an adverse impact on Jewish tradition by encouraging Jews to "sacrifice" their children in other situations, such as the mass suicide at Masada. According to Bodoff, the traditional view of the story influenced the willingness of Jews "to turn the Biblical prohibition against murder into an act that became recognized as a legitimate form of *Kiddush Ha-shem* (honoring of God)" (p. 86). Dershowitz (2000) agreed when he wrote that during the

Crusades, the Inquisition, and the Holocaust, "many 'Abrahams' made the decision to kill their own 'Isaacs,' sometimes to prevent their forced conversion, other times to prevent their torture, rape and eventual murder" (p. 127).

Riskin (1997) took a different view, arguing that God used the incident to warn Abraham that the covenant offered included no assurances that such sacrifices would not be required (p. 17). Sometimes God might intervene when those sacrifices might be warranted, but sometimes He would not. Thus Dershowitz (2000) provided cultural context when he wrote, "Every parent in Israel who sees his son off to the army hears the divine command: 'Take your son, you only son, whom you love'" (p. 128). Dershowitz aptly clarified the worldly operation of the covenant. Through obedience by Abraham in this instance, God was warning Abraham and his progeny that accepting the covenant, was not coupled with any assurances that the future would be ideal in every respect. Jewish historians can cite case after case that verifies the covenant is distinct from subsequent earthly bliss. In fact, the seed of Isaac have suffered as much as or more than other tribes and races, since the consummation of the covenant than

One possibility is that the story tried to stop this practice by instituting animal sacrifice as a substitute for human sacrifice. Telushkin (1997) submitted that medieval Jewish philosopher Moses Maimonides believed that animal sacrifices were instituted as a transitional device to wean people from the practice of human sacrifice (p. 451). In the story of the binding of Isaac, this theme is arguably represented by God providing a ram as a substitute for the son. One problem with this interpretation, though, is that animal sacrifice was already established in the Bible with Abel's sacrifice of a ram to God. Dumont (1971) goes further, viewing it as a transitional stage in the Jewish view on sacrifice. "Through this story the Jews learned that God does not want human sacrifice, not even as an act of faith," Dumont wrote, "just as fifteen centuries later the Jews were to learn through their prophets that God does not even want animal sacrifice, but that he can be approached through prayer, humility, and good deeds" (p. 206). Guinness (1988) disagreed with this interpretation, noting that "nowhere in the account is child sacrifice discussed. And later stories in the Bible recount instances of it, which casts doubt on this interpretation" (p. 55).

Indeed, there are several other references to human sacrifice in the Hebrew Bible. Some of those are related to pagan cultures and some to the Israelites themselves. As Marks (1983) noted

> References to human sacrifice in the Old Testament indicate that the Hebrews knew and practiced it . ... Mesha of Moab caused the Israelite armies to withdraw by sacrificing his son in their presence (II Kings 3:27). Ahaz sacrificed his son (II Kings 16:3). And all Israel is accused of practicing barbarity in II Kings 17:17. The sacrifice of Jephthah's daughter (Judges 11:29-40) and Hiel's son (1 Kings 16:34) are additional instances. (p. 50)

Gottwald (1983) paid particular attention to what might be references to human sacrifice in Deuteronomy 18:9-14. In that chapter, which is primarily devoted to a sequence of laws related to offices, these verses interrupt the laws with prohibitions against some pagan religious practices. Two different types of pagan rites are prohibited, but one may have referred to child sacrifice, Gottwald noted.

> The first sort (verse 10a) is denoted by a phrase literally meaning "makes . . . pass through fire" (p. 314) This was apparently understood by the Chronicler as referring to child sacrifice (II Chronicles 28:3; cf. II Kings 16:3) and has generally been so interpreted . . . . Some scholars claim, however, that it refers rather to an ordeal by fire and that occasional failures to survive the test explain such references to it as 12:31, Jeremiah 7:31, 19:5, and Ezekiel 16:20-21; 23:37-29. (Gottwald, 1983, pp. 314-315)

Levenson (1998) noted that in the days of the Patriarch, child murder was distinguished from child sacrifice. The former was almost universally condemned, while the latter was widely accepted as a show of gratitude toward the gods. Dershowitz (2000) later wrote that the distinction applied to this story:

> God did not order Abraham to "murder" his son; such a command would have violated the Noachide laws against shedding innocent blood. God ordered Abraham to "sacrifice" his son . . . . You murder those you hate; you sacrifice what you love most. (Pp.110-111)

Nahum Sarna (1970) identified a troubling aspect of the story: "We cannot evade the fact that the core of the narrative actually seems to assume the possibility that God would demand human sacrifice . . . . God does not denounce human sacrifice as such" (pp. 157, 159). Quite the contrary, in later passages, God seems to accept human sacrifice. As Kirsch (1998) noted, "God's troubling indifference toward child sacrifice . . . sheds an ominous light on the events of Exodus," specifically God's plan to kill the first born sons of the Egyptians as recorded in Exodus (p. 177). According to the Bible, at midnight, God himself "rampages through Egypt and slays every firstborn child," Kirsch wrote. "Yet God seems to know himself well enough to realize that he is not likely to distinguish between the Egyptians and the Chosen People once he has begun to kill" (p. 178) Thus God decreed that a lamb must be sacrificed its blood must be smeared on the doorposts so that he would know which children to spare.

A few other passages in the Hebrew Bible have also been viewed as potential indirect references to human sacrifice. In the story of King Ahab and his marriage to Jezebel, a reference is made to her efforts to substitute the worship of Baal for that of Israel's God. An incidental note mentioned in the introduction of this story (1 Kings 16:34) refers to the official refortification of Jericho by Hiel, with Hiel suffering the loss of two children. The traditional interpretation of this passage is that the loss of the children was the fulfillment of an ancient curse, a reference made in Joshua 6:26. However, archaeological excavations at Gezer have revealed skeletons of persons apparently sacrificed to secure divine approval for the construction. Such findings lead to the conjecture that the verse may refer to such a foundation sacrifice instead of an "unwary builder's double misfortune" (Wevers, 1983a, p. 199).

A more overt description of child sacrifice is found in the second book of Kings (3:26-27). In this story, Mesha, King of Moab realizes that his troops are on the verge on losing a battle to the Israelites. Desperate to save his kingdom, Mesha sacrifices his oldest son to his deity. The story is not intended to condone the action, even though it achieves the purpose sought by Mesha. After viewing the act, the Israelite soldiers abandon the siege—perhaps due to either repulsion from what they viewed or panic over the thought of facing such a bloodthirsty foe (Wevers, 1983b, p. 211). Some critics point to this story as an indication that the Israelites found child sacrifice to be abhorrent. If so, then perhaps the narrative of Abraham and Isaac had served its goal and had become ingrained within the Israelites by the time of the Kings.

Dershowitz (2000) noted that some commentators have interpreted Isaac's silence and passive acceptance of his father's action as an indication that Isaac may have been retarded. Medical knowledge has progressed to the point that many laymen now know that children born to aged parents often suffer from some mental, emotional, and/or physical maladies. And Isaac's behavior throughout most of the Bible is limited. Later, on his death bed, he lacks the mental capacity to distinguish one of his sons from another. However, there are certainly alternative possibilities for an aged and dying man to exhibit such behavior. Such speculation has led some to suggest that such an interpretation would explain both Isaac's silence and Abraham's willingness to sacrifice his son. Dershowitz's (2000), reminder that until relatively recent times, parents have killed—sacrificed—children who were born with physical or mental handicaps. This could have been a factor in Abraham's decision to sacrifice Abraham. However, such sacrifices were usually carried out very early in the child's life—usually within days of birth. After considering all of the problems that could accompany this possibility, it is unlikely that it, as an explanation, could contribute toward settling the moral qualms of modern readers. In fact, if God encouraged such sacrifices, it could raise more questions than it resolves. At the end of the day, human attempts to exhaustively explain the rationales for God's need for Abraham's obedience, leave detached and neutral scholars with questions. For those scholars and lay believers in locales where human life carries special dignities and intangible worth, the story retains a repulsive element.

The Christian View of Sacrifice

The typical Christian view of sacrifice combines elements of two forms of Jewish sacrifice—sacrifices for sins and blood sacrifices. From this perspective, the crucifixion of Jesus was a blood sacrifice done as redemption for the sins of humanity. Some Christians see the sacrifice of Isaac as the Old Testament's preview version of the Christian concept. Abraham was asked to sacrifice his son in the same manner that God would later sacrifice his own Son, Jesus.

Another interpretation, from the Christian perspective, is that the sacrifice of Isaac was a dress rehearsal for God. By asking Abraham to sacrifice his son, God would be able to appreciate the amount of emotional pain that he would have to suffer when he sacrificed his son Jesus. The idea makes for an interesting perspective and provides the Christian community with a psychologically comfortable way of interpreting Abraham's action. Still, several problems remain with this approach.

First, it questions God's omnipotence. Theoretically, an omnipotent God should already know what that feeling is like. Otherwise, the God of Abraham was an incomplete God, still searching to find his own identity. Such an idea is consistent with some theologians. For example, the critically acclaimed "biography" of God by Jack Miles (1995) explores the concept of God from a developmental perspective. Regardless, it conflicts with traditional views of God as an all-knowing entity.

Second, God had already experienced the loss of a child—two of them, in fact. According to earlier chapters of Genesis, Adam and Eve were both the literal children of God. He had thus already experienced the loss of both a son and a daughter. Granted, their deaths were due to natural causes—not by sacrifice. But as mentioned before, it could also be argued that, in a way, God essentially sacrificed Adam and Eve too. Their deaths were slow, but they knew their lives on Earth would end. Either way, God had already experienced losses of children.

Third, despite the appeal of the interpretation, there is nothing in the story that firmly supports that conclusion. At no point does the story mention, imply, or even hint that such an interpretation is warranted. Quite to the contrary, the story directly treats the episode as a test of Abraham and his faith. There is only one reference to God learning or experiencing anything from the events, and this is an increased understanding regarding the strength of Abraham's faith. There is no reference in the story to God learning about the meaning of sacrifice.

So why has this interpretation persisted? Partly because of the metaphorical similarity between the incident and the sacrifice of Jesus and partly because of semi-submerged strains of Jewish theology. The similarity between the binding of Isaac and the crucifixion of Jesus are numerous: (1) the willingness of the Father to sacrifice the Son, (2) the symbolism of the Lamb of God as a substitute for the lives and souls of others, and (3) the three-day journey to Moriah compared to the Resurrection occurring on the third day after the Crucifixion. No wonder, then, that some Christian writers might argue that the binding and sacrifice of Isaac has become a symbol of redemption (Lerch, 1950). As Pelikan (1985) noted

> In using the Hebrew Bible and the Jewish tradition to explain the meaning of Jesus, Christians had applied . . . foreshadowings of the cross, anticipations of doctrine, and prophecies of the coming of Christ to their interpretation . . . .

[The] description of the binding and sacrifice of Isaac became one of the most
pervasive figures of redemption: God, like Abraham, had willingly offered his
own first-born Son as a sacrifice. (p. 43)

Such interpretations come easily to modern-day Christians. Somewhat
surprisingly, though, similar interpretations can be found among Jewish
theologians. Hammer (1994, p. 173) noted that, according to two 13th century
Jewish works (*Sefer Ha-Eshkol* and *Shibolei Ha-Leket*), Isaac was the first
instance in which God demonstrated his power to restore life. Spiegel's (1993)
study of these same texts also noted that the legends claimed that the sacrifice
was no sham. To the contrary, according to these legends, Isaac was actually
killed and then resurrected from the dead. In this view, Isaac was the first person
to experience in the flesh the meaning of death and resurrection. In other words,
the identification of resurrection with the binding of Isaac is not a uniquely
Christian concept. No wonder, then, that the interpretation has persisted.

The Silence of Abraham

Ellen Gunderson Traylor's (1988) *Song of Abraham*, a novel designed as a
biography of the Patriarch, depicted Abraham as first sensing God's presence in
the wind before he heard God's voice. She has God asking Abraham, "How
much do you love me, Friend Abraham?" before proceeding to the instructions.
When God gives Abraham his instructions to sacrifice Isaac, Traylor depicted
the Patriarch as thinking to himself, "Merciless, Cruel One! What monstrous
thing is this You ask of me? What deviltry is this You set my hand to do?" (p.
422).

Abraham may have thought it, but he never said it. According to Genesis,
Abraham voiced no outrage, counter-arguments, or doubts at any point in the
story. As Guinness (1988) pointed out, "the Bible does not portray Abraham as
outraged against such a horror, but rather as an obedient and silent servant of the
Lord" (p. 54). Such a response is puzzling, given Abraham's willingness to
argue with God over other moral issues such as the destruction of Sodom and
Gomorrah (Laytner, 1900). Dershowitz (2000) questioned why Abraham did not
resist by using God's existing directions for mankind. For example, Abraham
could have asked the following: "God I understood your covenant with Noah as
prohibiting killing human beings, when You said, 'Whoso sheddeth man's
blood, by man shall his blood be shed: for in the image of God made he man.' I
thought Cain killing Able was seen as punishable by you, because you told him,
"Therefore whosoever slayeth Cain, vengeance shall be taken on him seven-
fold." And then You placed a mark on Cain indicating that anyone finding him
should kill him. So, God, am I exempted by you from your previous injunctions
upon killing another human? Will my sacrifice of Isaac mark me, like Cain?

The Moral Dilemma

Levenson (1998) argued that modern critics should go easy on Abraham.
After all, his actions took place before the Commandments were given to Moses

at Sinai. Unlike later Hebrews, the Patriarch had no written guidelines for making judgments about right and wrong. This may be true, but he seemed to have no trouble in making other ethical judgments, such as defending the innocents at Sodom and Gomorrah. In sacrificing his son, though, he faced a tougher moral challenge.

Armstrong (1993) noted that the moral dilemma presented by pagan sacrifices was not present for Abraham. Pagan parents sacrificed their eldest sons because they thought the child was a son of a god; by sacrificing their child, they were merely returning the child to its rightful owner. Abraham knew that wasn't the case.

> Isaac had been a gift of God but not his natural son. There was no reason for the sacrifice, no need to replenish the divine energy. Indeed, the sacrifice would make nonsense of Abraham's entire life, which had been based on the promise that he would be the father of a great nation. (p. 18)

Fromm (1966) interpreted the moral dilemma as Abraham's willingness to separate himself from his family. The first such test, Fromm noted, came when God ordered Abraham to leave his father's house. The command to sacrifice Isaac, Fromm argued, was the second such test. "This command is interpreted as implying a test of Abraham's obedience, or an attempt to show, though indirectly, that God does not approve of the heathen ritual of child sacrifice," Fromm wrote. "While these interpretations are probably correct, the text suggests still another: namely, the command to cut the ties of blood to the son" (p. 72). In essence, Fromm argued, God was insisting that Abraham be free all ties—not only with his parents, but also with his own son.

Some argue that God's intentions are not an issue, because the entire incident was merely a test. Gibson (1999), for example, argued that "God never intended that Abraham would actually sacrifice Isaac. He let Abraham make the preparation, and then he intervened" (p. 179). The problem with such an explanation is that it implies that God is capable of duplicity or outright lying. If God never intended for Abraham to truly sacrifice his son, then was his instruction to the Patriarch an outright lie or merely a little white lie? Or was it simply a misrepresentation that was necessary given the situation? If so, it could be argued that this was essentially the first recorded example of "ethical deliberation" in that it might be considered ethical even if immoral. Regardless of the answer, what are the moral implications for God's own behavior?

These questions, even without infallible answers provide implications regarding Abraham's values. Some critics argue that if it was a moral test, then Abraham failed it. As Dershowitz (2000) wrote, "The message of this story is not in what Abraham did in setting out to sacrifice his son. It is in what God did in refusing Abraham's sacrifice. Abraham passed the test of obedience but failed the test of moral self-determination" (p. 125).

Dershowitz (2000) also took issue with positive comparisons between Abraham and his neighbors. Indeed, moral repulsion at the act does not seem to be an issue for Abraham. As Dershowitz wrote:

> I do not understand the distinction . . . between Abraham's actions and those of his Molech-worshiping contemporaries. . . . Abraham's *own* conduct cannot be contrasted favorably with that of Canaanite parents who willingly sacrificed their children to Molech, unless Abraham never really intended to carry out God's commands, in which case he loses points on the faith scale. (p. 116)

"Even a heavenly voice cannot make the killing of an innocent child right," Dershowitz added. "The Talmud . . . makes the point that once God gives humans his law, He may not interfere with the human process for interpreting and applying it" (p. 117).

There appears to be a sadistic element in God's orders to Abraham. Guinness (1988) noted that the instructions came after Abraham had already sent Ishmael away, leaving Isaac as his sole heir (pp. 54-55). That would have made the request hard enough for Abraham to bear, but God seems to ensure that Abraham knows the extent of his dilemma. As Telushkin (1997) noted, "The language with which God instructs Abraham to sacrifice Isaac is deliberately intended to magnify the pain the command raises" (p. 38). Yet, Telushkin disagreed that Abraham's actions represented a lack of moral fiber. Instead, he argued that Abraham was still learning the moral standards of his God. Thus he noted:

> Abraham's readiness to obey God's command shows him to be ethically deficient by later standards, but not by those of his age. True, God had revealed Himself to Abraham, but He had not made known to him the full ethical implications of monotheism. Since other contemporary religious believers sacrificed sons to their gods, God, in essence, was asking Abraham if he was as devoted to his God as the pagan idolaters were to theirs. (pp. 38-39)

Given the trauma that Isaac likely suffered during the incident, it is perhaps not surprising that the Bible records no instance of Isaac offering a sacrifice. Similarly, neither did his son Jacob. Hammer (1994) contended that these omissions were deliberate and contributes to the meaning of the story: "Perhaps it can best be understood as an attempt to underscore the idea that sacrifice plays a totally different role in the religion of Israel than in pagan rituals," he wrote. "Long before sacrifice became impossible because of the destruction of the Temple, it had been so totally reinterpreted that it was not an indispensable element of worship, as it was in all of pagan religion" (p. 42).

In conclusion, what is the biblical attitude toward sacrifice? Abraham Heschel (1955) may have summarized it best. "The value of sacrifice is determined," he wrote, "not only by what one gives away, but also by the goal to which it is given" (p. 399). Indeed, the Hebrew verb for "to sacrifice" literally means "to come near, to approach." The *akedah* plays a key role in defining that concept. As Spiegel (1993) concluded, the *akedah* "came to enforce and validate a new way of worship," (p. 73) which abolished human sacrifice and still brought people close to God.

Chapter 8
The Story of Jephthah's Daughter

If you think the *akedah* is a terrifying story then perhaps you haven't read Chapter 11 in the book of Judges. This collection of verses recounts the story in which an Israelite judge named Jephthah sacrifices his only child—his daughter—in exchange for a victory in battle. The *akedah* is scary and uncomfortable. The story of Jephthah's daughter is that and more, inspiring literary works that are just as gruesome (Hanusa, 1999). As Murphy (1998) said, this story is "one of the most disturbing in the Bible" (p. 122). Davis (1999) notes that the story is particularly disturbing to all those who "thought old Abraham had wiped out the practice of human sacrifice" (p. 164).

Jephthah ("He opens"), an 11th century B.C. warrior, was the son Gilead, an Israelite leader. His mother, though, was a prostitute. That background made him a social outcast who was even rejected by his own family (Mendelsohn, 1953). Willis (1997) wrote that he was "a man with exceptional military prowess who had lost his right of inheritance in his tribal segment of Gilead by being disinherited by his 'brothers'" (p. 41). He started out as an outlaw, an ancient Hebrew version of "Robin Hood." His reputation for fighting the enemy eventually led the Israelites to offer him the leadership of the kingdom—if he defeated the invading Ammonite army (Marcus, 1989).

Jephthah accepted the challenge. Before going into a critical battle, though, he made a promise to God, hoping to improve his chances. If he won the battle, he vowed, he would make a burnt sacrifice of the first to greet him upon his return home (Judges 11:31).

Naturally, he won. When he returned home, however, the elation of victory quickly dissipated when the first person to meet him was his only child—his daughter, wearing timbrels—who comes to greet him with a dance. The despondent Jephthah then told his daughter of his vow. She understood, acknowledged her duty, and agreed to go to her death. Her only request was that she be given two months to "bewail her virginity" with her friends before submitting to the knife at the altar.

Jephthah agreed. She and her friends retired to a forested hilltop nearby in a final round of celebration. Afterward, she courageously returned to the town and apparently faced her death as a burnt sacrifice. Jephthah went on to lead Israel for six more years.

The *akedah* was a horror story, but at least it had something of a peaceful ending. This one is gruesome from start to finish. It poses serious questions about the nature of God and of the Jewish religion. Explanations and rationalizations are always possible, but—like the *akedah*—most still leave the reader feeling uncomfortable.

Most explanations for this story start with the cultural context in which it occurred. It was, the apologists would argue, a different time with different expectations for God's people. The biggest difference between then and now is the cultural view of women. Jephthah and his daughter lived in a culture that was not friendly to women, at least by modern standards.

Women in the Middle East have traditionally lived a second-class existence, particularly among non-Jewish religions in the area. In some pagan societies of the Middle East, it was the custom to bury unwanted female babies alive. Their rights to inherit were limited, and penalties for killing a woman were lighter than if a man were the victim. Husbands or male relatives were allowed to kill women—so-called Arab "honor killings"—if they were suspected of a sexual indiscretions; and, as recently as the 1990s, women in Saudi Arabia were not allowed to have their own identification cards (Beyer, 2001). One view pointed out that a typical Bible-era house was built around a courtyard where livestock was kept. Based on this idea, some scholars have argued that perhaps Jephthah anticipated that a goat or chicken would be the first one to encounter him (Boling, 1975, p. 208). But, by most accounts, it would also have been reasonable to expect his daughter to be among the first to greet him. The men were the fighters who went to war; the women were the servants who waited and greeted them on their return.

There may also be other cultural influences on the story, particularly from Greek legends. Dumont (1971) noted that there are similarities in the story with a portion of Homer's *Iliad* in which Agamemnon sacrificed his daughter Iphigenia. Thus, Dumont wrote:

> In the Iliad story, an oracle advises Agamemnon, commander of the Greek forces, that only by sacrificing his daughter Iphigenia as atonement for a trifling crime he has committed will the gods give him the wind he needs to set sail for Troy. Agamemnon cuts her throat but she is whisked away, still alive, by the goddess Artemis, not as a moral lesson for man, but to consecrate Iphigenia as a priestess in the temple of Artemis, where she is taught to prepare victims for sacrifice. (p. 38)

Smith (1983) wrote that the reference to the "only child" is also analogous to the Iliad story (p. 69).

Comparisons to Abraham and Isaac

The story of Jephthah's daughter is included in this study because of his obvious comparisons with the *akedah*. The key word here is "comparison," not "similarity." While there are many parallels between the two sagas, the differences are also apparent and important. This combination of parallels and key difference is the reason that Webb (1986) described the story of Jephthah's daughter as "a grim inversion of the Abraham-Isaac narrative" (p. 40).

First, let's consider the similarities. Both stories involve a situation in which a father believed he must sacrifice a child. Further, it's not just any child but their "only child." Smith (1983) noted that, "The storyteller heightens the pathos by presenting the girl as his only child" (p. 69)—the same language used in the *akedah*. Similarly, Tapp (1989) noted, "the Hebrew word used by the biblical author to describe Jephthah's daughter as his 'only' (or 'beloved') child is the same one that God uses to describe Isaac when calling on Abraham to offer him as a sacrifice" (p. 174).

Further, both children seemed to be willing participants in their unfortunate and unfair situations. Jephthah's daughter is overtly willing to participate, asking only that the sacrifice be delayed. Isaac seems to be a willing participant by omission; he makes no apparent objection to the sacrifice, even when he is bound and prepared. Such lack of objections have led some to characterize Isaac's role in the story as that of willing compliance (Ginzberg, 1938, p. 44). Others still point out that there "is no indication in the biblical narrative that Isaac willingly consented to anything—he seems rather to be an unknowing victim, virtually a prop" (Kugel, 1997, p. 173).

Still, the differences are even more dramatic. The most obvious difference is the final result. In the Isaac story, the sacrifice is not completed and ram is substituted for the child. Jephthah's daughter, conversely, has to die. Exum (1989) noted that Jephthah's daughter even refers to Isaac, possibility hoping for a similar fate. Kirsch (1997) described the reference as "darkly ironic" in that God stops Abraham from killing his son, "but no such *deus ex machina* appears in the story of Jephthah and his daughter" (p. 206). Further, Jephthah's loss is probably more than Abraham would have suffered. After all, Abraham subsequently had several wives and a number of children (Gen. 25:1-5), but Jephthah had already lost his wife and this was his only daughter (Exum, 1989, p. 71).

The second major difference lies in the motivation of the parents. Jephthah is looking for a personal gain, while Abraham has nothing to gain. As Dumont (1971) noted:

> In the Genesis story, Abraham stands to gain nothing by sacrificing his son Isaac. God promises him no favors. Faith carries Abraham to Mount Moriah; hope sustains him. Faith makes him heroic; hope makes him human. The sacrifice is never consummated; an angel stays his hand, and a sacrificial lamb is substituted for Isaac. (p. 38)

It should also be noted that in one important aspect Jephthah's story is the obverse of Abraham and Isaac. It was Jephthah's idea to make the vow. God had previously forbidden human sacrifices (Leviticus 18:21, 20:1-5). It could be argued that Jephthah tested God rather than God tested Jephthah, as he did with Abraham. After all, Jephthah could have possibly won without the vow.

Theological Implications

The Silence of God. Kirsch (1997) noted that one theological question raised by story is the apparent silence of God during the entire episode. The Bible records that the spirit of God came over Jephthah before he made the vow. Afterward God falls "uncharacteristically silent" even though the lengthy preparation leading to the ritual provided plenty of time for God to consider commuting "her death sentence" (pp. 206-207). Exum (1989) agreed, noting that the source of the tragedy in the story "is not divine enmity, but divine silence" (p. 79). Amos Oz (1981) depicted Jephthah as begging in vain for a sign that God wants him to disregard his vow and spare his daughter (p. 217).

Is there a lesson here? Kirsch (1997) believed so, noting that "sometimes the Almighty expresses His will, however indistinctly or indirectly, by simply clamming up" (p. 206). Did Jephthah plead for a reprieve for his daughter? That wouldn't have helped, Kirsch added, because the Israelites had made such requests too often. "God has already complied with countless such pleas and demands from his people ever since he first befriended Abraham," Kirsch wrote (p. 207). Kirsch also considered the possibility that the silence of God resulted from a divine trial in which God tested Jephthah by allowing him to win the battle "and then waiting to see if the father is really willing to slay his only child" (p. 207).

Bribing God. Webb (1986) described Jephthah's vow, made on the eve of a crucial battle, as a "bribe under the table." Such a vow was not an impulsive response to the situation, but a shrewd and calculating decision on the part of Jephthah. As such, the vow would be a promise of a "Thanksgiving sacrifice." Urban (Urban, p. 260) noted that such rituals were a common means of celebrating the end of a battle for the Israelites, as recorded in the books of Joshua (8:31) and 1 Samuel (13:9). Murphy (1998), though, characterized it as a "transfer of ownership" in which Jephthah trades his daughter for the victory in battle (p. 122).

Smith (1983) saw duplicity in Jephthah's strategy. If he believed that such a sacrifice could help him win the battle, he could have done it as a pre-battle ritual. While this is "the most extreme of all prebattle rites" (p. 69), it would not have been an isolated incident in the Bible. Mesha of Moab did precisely that, presenting his own son as a burnt offering while the Israelites lay in siege of his stronghold. The action caused the Israelite armies to withdraw (II Kings 3:27). Jephthah could have done the same, but Smith argued he was a shrewd man who did not "wish to make his sacrifice in vain" (p. 69). Instead, he promised Yahweh a human offering only if he won the battle.

In this view, Jephthah's action was the promise of a *propitiatory sacrifice* aimed at appeasing the God. As Hammer (1994) noted, such an action "was more than an attempt to influence the gods; it was a method of controlling them" (p. 43.). From this perspective, Jephthah's actions were not those of faith and obedience, but an attempt to manipulate God. Smith added that Jephthah's promise to sacrifice the first person whom meets him was not an act of faith, but a manipulative safeguard that kept him from having to choose his victim in advance (p. 69).

God's Disapproval. Most theologians argue that God's silence reflected his disapproval of Jephthah's actions. Kirsch (1997), for example, argued that one explanation is that God allowed the sacrifice to continue as a way to punish Jephthah (p. 207). Kirsch (1997) added that God would have rejected the sacrifice because the Hebrew religion at the time had a strong position that "God does not require or even permit human sacrifice of any kind" (p. 212). Frye (1982) agreed, noting an anti-feminist trend in Jewish sacrifice, i.e., the ritual of sacrifice described in the book of Exodus doesn't condone the sacrifice of any female—human or animal (p. 185).

The Feminist Angle. One interpretation is that, when compared to the sacrifice of Isaac, the story represents the lower esteem and bias faced by women in ancient Israel (Fuchs, 1989). Penchansky (1992) described the story as part of the "literature of the feminist intelligentsia in ancient Israel," a collection of narratives that "gave them courage to live marginally" (p. 84). Kirsch (1997) considered it significant that the Bible does not deem her important enough to provide her name, "a fact that takes on special significance in a book whose authors regard name and naming as something sacred" (p. 203). Exum (1989) argued that Jephthah thoroughly expected to be greeted by his daughter, "who in the Patriarchal society would have been more expendable than a man." Kirsch (1997) noted the possibility that "Jephthah might have expected and even hoped for such a greeting" (p. 204). As Murphy (1998) contended, "Feminist critics have long contrasted the story angrily with that of Abraham and Isaac, noting that God stayed the hand of Isaac, a son" (p. 122). Davis (1999) agreed: "So why doesn't God stay Jephthah's hand? The Bible doesn't tell us so. The only conclusion to be reached: Jephthah's daughter was not as precious as Abraham's son" (p. 164).

Feminists also argue that, even if Jephthah did not expect his daughter to greet him, he probably expected some woman to be the first person he saw. Kirsch (1997) noted that the Bible explicitly describes the women of Israel celebrating a battle victory "with timbels and with dances"—precisely the same phrase used in the story of Jephthah (p. 204). At least two other instances of women leading such post-war celebrations are recorded. The Israelite women greet King Saul in such a manner after David defeated Goliath (1 Sam. 18:6), and Miriam led such a celebration after the defeat of Pharaoh's army at the Red Sea (Exod. 16:30). If such celebrations were traditional, then Jephthah would have expected some woman to be the first to greet him—but not necessarily his own daughter. Again, this line of reasoning serves to lower the value of women in the Hebrew Bible.

The Women with No Name. The Bible doesn't mention the name of Jephthah's daughter or of her mother. Kirsch (1997) noted that Jewish tradition, going back to an ancient storyteller, called her "Seila" (p. 203). Kirsch credited Pseudo-Philo with naming the child, by selecting a name "that reflects her destiny: 'Seila' means 'she who is demanded'" (p. 213). Despite the lack of information on "Seila," we still know more about her than of her mother. The story gives no information on her.

The Sex Cult Theory. One theory is that Jephthah's daughter and her friends were members of a pagan sex cult that was dedicated to a pagan deity, perhaps a local cult whose origins are forgotten. As Kirsch (1997) speculated:

> If so, we can begin to imagine that her death was not the result of a rash vow to Yahweh, but rather of a death sentence pronounced on an apostate in the name of Yahweh. Either one of these imagined endings might have prompted the biblical authors to turn Jephthah's daughter from a goddess-worshiper into a pious martyr. And either one is reason enough to explain why they dared not write her name into the pages of the Bible. (pp. 228-229)

Kirsch (1997) added that there are traces of a "forgotten ritual" in the story (p. 214), a position supported by other scholars (Willis, 1997). Later Kirsch also wrote of another aspect of the event that might be related to the pagan gods of the area, noting that, "we might imagine that she is being punished for doing something that the pious authors of the Bible simply refuse to speak aloud" (p. 223).

Persephone, a Greek goddess, would fit such a description (Ramras-Rauch, 1990, p. 167), and any number of local pagan religions could have had a comparable deity. Kirsch (1998) noted that, according to the Bible, the Israelites often demonstrated a fatal attraction to the pagan Gods of the Canaanites and other groups in the region. Davis (1999) believed that the story occurred during a time when the Israelites were turning to the idols of pagan religions. Further, the shrines and altars of these pagan deities were often in "high places" such as hill tops and mountains, with the rituals were "conducted under the boughs of sacred oaks and around stone columns placed upright in the ground" (p. 217). Jephthah's daughter chooses such a location for her own final ceremony. Thus, in this theory, the romp in the forest by the young people was simply a ritualistic representation of her loss of virginity (Day, 1989, p. 14). Boling (1975) identified it as a pagan fertility cult 'based on the ancient and primitive custom of annually bewailing the dead or ousted spirit of fertility during the dry or winter season" (p. 209).

Frye (1982) suggested that Jephthah's daughter herself subsequently became the center of such a cult, one in which a virgin goddess is depicted as the protector of childbirth (p. 185). In this theory, the story was invented to account for the existence of the cult and to justify its existence (Kirsch, 1997, p. 204). Regardless, an annual Jewish festival has also developed, even though the ritual is not mentioned anywhere else in the Bible (Exum, 1993, p. 140). The ritual calls for four days to be set aside each year for the daughters of Israel to lament her death (Ostriker, 2001). Kirsch (1997) argued that the rituals on the mountain were probably a coming of age rite of passage for the young girl, adding that the rite becomes ominous only because the celebration is held while she is facing a death sentence (p. 215).

Smith (1983) argued that the story also seemed to provided the Jewish nation with an "explanation for the existence of ceremonial mourning— probably over the death of growing things which occurred each winter, here symbolized by the descent of a virgin to the realm of the dead (cf. the Greek myth of Persephone)" (pp. 69-70). At the very least, it represents a mourning-based story (Trible, 1981). Traces of a cult with this type of ceremonial mourning were known to exist throughout the Near Eastern and Mediterranean world. However, the story of Jephthah's daughter does not have the restoration of life that is central to those other fertility myths (Smith, 1983, p. 70).

Jewish and Christian analogies. Some scholars see the story and the ritual as "a paradigm for later Jewish and Christian martyrology" (Brown, 1992, p. 94). Tapp (1989) saw her as an early Christ figure, pointing out that "The only other biblical character who was sacrificed by a Patriarch for the good of his people is Jesus" (p. 172). It is thus understandable that the story has remained part of Jewish tradition. In this tradition, the young women of Israel make an annual, four-day pilgrimage to the mountains in her memory "recalling her life and lamenting her death in a manner that befitted the daughter of a chieftain" (Kirsch, 1997, p. 201).

The Unwilling Martyr. None of the Israelite public would have witnessed the actual sacrifice, but word soon spread that Seila had gone to her death bravely and eager to offer herself to God. "Indeed," Kirsch noted, "her only anxiety is that she will not be acceptable as a sacrificial offering and that her father's vow would be in vain" (p. 210). Once Jephthah assures her that she will be worthy of such a sacrifice, even though she is a female, the young girl turns to comforting her father rather than bemoaning her own fate. However, other rumors were also circulating. One such rumor related to her request for a two-month reprieve. Perhaps she made the request, hoping that her father or God would intervene. More directly, maybe it was not a request at all. Perhaps she merely fled, hoping to escape from her fate before she was located two months later and returned to the altar. Kirsch (1997), for example, argued that the "taking to the hills" phrase in the story may have indicated that she was an unwilling victim (p. 203).

Theories of Escaping Death. As Kirsch (1997) noted, few people were actually witnesses to the sacrifice of Seila or were in a position that would have allowed them to hear her father's final comments. Those who were present (probably fellow soldiers of the battle and Seila's friends) likely "never spoke of it to anyone except themselves" (p. 200). But plenty of talk was triggered among others. Kirsch argued that it was the secondary talk that led to the perception that the young girl died bravely. The locals, she argued, would have found it reassuring to tell themselves that the child was brave, did not beg for her life, and "did not groan in misery as her blood spilled over the stones of the altar and the flames turned her beautiful young body into charred meat" (p. 200).

Another interpretation that has developed from that tradition is that "Seila" was never sacrificed at all (Landers, 1991). In this version, "Seila's" sacrifice was that she had to serve in the synagogue as an isolated virgin, away from all men, much like cloistered nuns do in the modern Catholic Church. This interpretation has the moralistic appeal of rationalizing away the death of the girl and elevating the status of God by assuming that He would have stopped the sacrifice if the child actually had to die.

The Legal Interpretation. The story of Jephthah is not only a moral issue, but also a legal one (Marcus, 1990). The story has triggered legal debates among Jewish rabbis over whether—according to Jewish law—Seila should have been sacrificed. Davis (1989) doubts that Jephthah would have won, had the case been taken to a rabbinical court because the law would have required that a sacrifice be selected from the flock, not from one's own family (Lev. 1:2). Further, the law permitted Jephthah to make a cash payment equivalent to the value of the sacrificial victim (Lev. 27:2-8), a tithing vow specifically excluded the sacrifice of one's own children (1 Sam. 1:11). The bottom line, according to Kirsch (1997) is that there is a legitimate rabbinical argument that concludes that Jephthah had no legal requirement to fulfill his vow. If so, then why did the sacrifice continue with no objections?

The Sanctity of the Vow. The answer to the above question appears to lie in the sanctity of the Jephthah's vow (Marcus, 1986). Kirsch (1997) noted that the nexus of the story is that assumption that his daughter "must do exactly what he has vowed to do" (p. 208). There is no indication in the story that Jephthah ever considered renouncing his vow or that his daughter might refuse to accept her role in the ceremony. Part of the sanctity of the vow comes from the high regard that the Israelites placed on words and letters. Remember, these are the people who were in awe of even mentioning the name of God. The Hebrew Bible specifically speaks to the sanctity of such vowels, with Moses pointedly saying, "When a man voweth a vow unto the Lord, he shall not break his word; he shall do according to all that proceedeth out of his mouth" (Num. 30:3). How widespread was the perception that such a vow could not be broken? Apparently extensive, judging by the tone of the story. As Kirsch added, the author of the narrative assumed that the readers would "understand and accept the fact that Jephthah's rash words cannot be ignored or defied even though they amount to a death sentence by a father on his own child" (p. 209).

The Virgin Factor. The Bible states that Jephthah's daughter goes to the mountain not to mourn over her fate but "bewailing her virginity." Kirsch (1997) noted that the word *betulum*, which is usually translated "virginity," is more accurately translated as a reference to "the stage of a young woman's life when she is capable of having children" (p. 214). From this perspective, Jephthah's daughter is "bewailing" the fact that she will never become a mother.

An Argument for Child Sacrifice. If the fate of Isaac and Seila were different, then perhaps so were the themes of the two narratives. Reis (1997) raised doubts about the moral purity of Jephthah's daughter. Kirsch (1997) argued that the story of Jephthah indicated that the narrators of the story "were neither surprised nor shocked by the notion that God would countenance the sacrifice of a child by her own father" (p. 212). Smith (1983) seemed to agree, at least in terms of how God was known to the Israelites of the time. The tale "presupposes a primitive concept of what God demands of humans," he wrote. "One should not try to soften its hardness by emphasizing the fidelity with which Jephthah and his daughter carry out the grisly deed" (p. 69).

The Impulsive Vow vs. Deliberate Barter. Generally, the Bible and most theologians place the blame for the death of Jephthah's daughter on Jephthah himself. The most common interpretation is that his vow to sacrifice the first to greet him (Judges 11:31) an "impulsive, shortsighted, even vain and downright stupid—but essentially innocent" (Kirsch, 1997, p. 204). This interpretation assumes that Jephthah simply does not take the time to consider the problems that his vow might cause.

Was that really the case? As Kirsch (1997) noted that Jephthah likely knew that his daughter could be one of the first to greet him when he returned. Perhaps he realized the possibility but was willing to risk the loss of his daughter in exchange for a victory (Landers, 1991). Such bartering would have been nothing new to this mercenary. After all, he had already worked out a deal that had put him into higher office. Perhaps, as Kirsch mused, he was willing to sacrifice his daughter as an inducement for God to assist him in winning "the battle that will determine if he will live in glory in Gilead or die in shame in Mispah" (pp. 204-205).

Jephthah's Authority. Several studies have focused on Jephthah as a pivotal character in understanding the portrayal of judges as leaders of the Israelites. Willis (1997), in particular, noted that the author of the book did not use any term of leadership to describe Jephthah after Judges 11:11 until the concluding phrase "Jephthah judged Israel" in Judges 12:7. Assuming that the final statement was placed there simply as a conclusion to the story, Willis re-examined those verses that attributed a leadership position to him and concluded that after Jephthah negotiated his way back into a position of leadership, he used that position as a springboard for claiming broader charismatic authority. If so, his broader charismatic authority would have required support from God. This seems to be provided by Judges 11:29, which reads that, "the Spirit of the Lord came upon Jephthah." However, to convince the Israelite public of such an association, an event or sign was needed. Nothing could accomplish that better than a vow and a sacrifice that ensured victory for Jephthah and the Israelites.

God's Rejection of the Vow. Pseudo-Philo, an anonymous first-century B.C. author, took familiar stories in the Bible and beefed them up with more details in a work called *Biblical Antiquities.* In his version of the story, God is upset with the vow. The problem, in this version, is not that the daughter will be sacrificed, but that something unworthy of his glory may be selected for the sacrifice. In the Pseudo-Philo story, God asks, "If a dog should meet Jephthah first, would a dog be sacrificed to me?" (Biblical Antiquities 39.11). To punish Jephthah, God in essence decreed that the Jephthah's vow would "be visited on his first-born, his own offspring" (Kirsch, 1997, 212). Perhaps Jephthah was hoping that a dog or other animal would be the sacrificial object. But, as Smith (1983) pointed out, "Jephthah cannot cheat Yahweh" (p. 69). Thus, Smith concluded, "the story is less a historical recollection than a moral tale teaching the futility of scheming against God" (p. 69).

Jephthah's Guilt. How badly did Jephthah feel about losing his daughter? That question is difficult to evaluate in retrospect, but his actions indicate he did little to try to save her. After all, he could have put the question to a rabbinical court and at least had a chance of saving her life. That is why Kirsch (1997) suggested that Jephthah appeared to blame his daughter for greeting him first (Judges 11:35). His words might indicate that "the guilt-ridden Jephthah may be desperately trying to comfort himself by shifting some measure of guilt to his wholly innocent child" (p. 205).

The Nature of the Israelites' God. The Israelites' unique contribution to theological theory was the concept of one God. Other pagan religions in the area had religious beliefs related to gods, and the concept of a supreme god was also embodied in some other earlier religions. In Greek mythology, for example, Zeus is often presented as a supreme being with dominion over other gods. Still, none of the competing religions at the time had developed the concept of a single god. One possibility is that it may have taken the Israelites some time to develop this concept. If so, then this passage may represent a transitory period of Jewish history when the theologians of the day were still refining the concept of one God.

Early in Jewish theology, there seems to be an acceptance of multiple Gods. God speaks in the plural when announcing the creation of mankind, using the phrase, "Let us make man in our image, after our likeness" (Gen. 1:26). Kirsch noted that such utterances could cause the reader "to wonder whether even the ancient Israelites regarded Yahweh as merely one god among many" (pp. 220-221). Similarly, when Abraham was visited by God, it was occasionally in the form of multiple (three) visitors—not just one. Even when Abraham embraces God (Gen. 14:19), he does so in the name of El Elyon ("God, Most High, Maker of heaven and earth"). Such a name implies a Supreme Being, but not necessarily the only God. In fact, it could have been the Canaanite god called "El," who was the supreme god of the Canaanites. Kirsch (1997) noted the Israelites likely saw some similarity and relationship between their God and the pagan God of the Canaanites, adding that, "perhaps, at some early moment in their history, the Israelites saw the two gods as one and the same" (p. 63). At the very least, many of the laws, rituals and beliefs of the Jewish religion were borrowed from these other religions (Kirsch, p. 221).

The Desire for a Goddess? One contribution to theology from the feminist perspective has been an understanding of the concept of a dual god—one with male and female characteristics. As Kirsch (1997) noted the pagan religions of the area generally viewed their gods as coming in male-and-female pairs. The Israelites were unique at the time in that they were "told that their God is a bachelor and a loner who lacks father or mother, brothers or sisters, friends or lovers" (p. 224). Perhaps, living in an area where a female goddess was a common concept, some members of the Jewish community were seeking a comparable heroine. If so, then Jephthah's daughter may have been an embodiment of this desire for a goddess.

Chapter 9
The Problem of Evil

During the spring of 2000, NBC tried its hand at an animated series called *God, the Devil and Bob*. The premiere episode included an exchange between God (voice of James Garner) and Bob (French Stewart). Bob complains to God for being unknowable and willing to let "good people suffer and lousy people prosper."

"You call yourself a father?," Bob complains. "You're more like a deadbeat dad!" (Bark, 2000).

That exchange represents one of the most difficult problems in theological debate—the problem of evil. Did God commit an evil act with Abraham? Granted, the act produced long-term benefits for the Jewish people by sealing the covenant between God and Abraham. Theologically, the *akedah* established Abraham as the founder of monotheism—a religious concept that has no equal. But, do the benefits of the act justify the suffering that Abraham, Sarah, and Isaac must have experienced? After all, most religions have basic tenets that question the "ends-justifies-the-means" argument. If such principles apply to humans, should they not also apply to God?

The Bible gives glimpses of the heavy heart that follows Abraham's actions. It may have caused the permanent separation of Abraham and his wife, since the Bible never mentions them living together again. Sarah dies soon afterward, possible hurried to her death by the trauma of knowing that her husband was willing to kill again.

We must also consider Isaac. He was the son who must have felt expendable. One can only imagine the terror he must have felt as he was bound, placed on the altar, and the knife poised to slice into his body. No wonder that the Bible never records another conversation between Isaac and his father. Indeed, Isaac appears to have been so traumatized by the event that he says little for the rest of his life. The event even perplexed Christian writer C. S. Lewis. Lewis (1996) wrote, "If God is omniscient He must have known what Abraham would do, without any experiment; why, then, this needless torture" (p. 100)?

The Philosophical Issue

When approached from this manner, the story of the *akedah* becomes a single incident that is representative of the problem of evil. The question raised by the problem of evil has been used to justify atheism and to glorify the mystery of God. The fundamental issue: How can a God who is supposed to be both all-good and all-powerful permit evil to exist in the universe?

Consider the implications of the question. If He is all-good, He does not wish for evil to exist. If He is all-powerful, He is able to do away with it.

Philosopher David Hume (1779) summarized the argument in three points: (1) God is supposedly omnipotent, omniscient, and omnipresent, (2) God is wholly good, and (3) these propositions cannot be held together. As Pike (1964) noted, a logical inconsistency is developed, because the first two arguments contradict the third. Similarly, Alston (1963) asked, "Given the fact that there is evil in the world, how can we maintain that the world owes its existence to a personal being that is both all-powerful and perfectly good" (p. 221)? Similarly, C. S. Lewis summarized the issue in this manner:

> If God were good, He would wish to make His creatures perfectly happy, and if God were almighty, He would be able to do what He wished. But the creatures are not happy. Therefore God lacks either goodness, or power, or both. (p. 23)

Orr (1977) had a similar impression about the importance of the debate. "The problem of evil is one of the most crucial protests raised by unbelievers against the fact of God," he wrote. "Believers may insist that countless experiences simply make no sense apart from God's existence; likewise unbelievers may protest that specified experiences make no sense if God exists" (p. 79). Theologically, it is an arduous question. As Jones (1975) noted, every religious system ever created has addressed the issue because "All of them in order to exist in the real world thought they had to give some plausible answer" (p. 94).

So, if God exists, then why does evil exist? If God is good, why did he allow six million Jews to die in concentration camps during World War II? Why did he allow 19 Islamic extremists fly airplanes into the World Trade Center and the Pentagon, killing nearly 3,000 people? Why do good people have to suffer? Why would a good God allow such evils and the millions of other evils that happen every day?

These are certainly troubling questions with no easy answers. Therefore, the argument goes, either God does not exist, or—if He does exist—He is not the kind of God we envision. No wonder, then that the problem has been addressed by all three major religions (Ghazali, 1994). It appears reasonable that philosopher William Davis (1969) concluded, "The problem of evil is perhaps the most difficult problem faced by anyone who believes in an all-good, all-powerful God" (p. 33).

Even believers admit the problem of evil is a tough theological problem, judging by the defensive terminology of some of their arguments. Murphy (1995) described his explanation as being only a "plausible" defense. Others answer with theories or explanations that other believers find unacceptable, such as retreats into pantheistic solutions (Levine, 1994). No wonder then, that some people simply give up and conclude that God does not exist or, at least, that His existence is improbable (Beilby, 1996).

Freud (1961), for example, viewed the evil in society as the psychological stimulus for religious beliefs. In his view, whenever a person ran into something that was difficult and unpleasant, the person would regress to simple modes of thinking and latch on to childhood desires. Consequently, the presence of evil in their lives would make some of them more receptive to religious beliefs and practices. Similarly, Cornforth (1954) viewed the story as representative of the sociological impact on cultures, eventually linking religious beliefs to the economic structure of the society.

Doctorow (2000) made the problem of evil the basis of his novel about a writer struggling with the philosophical issue, managing to discuss many of its 20th century manifestations. The book is cast in the form of a novelist's notebook, the record of a writer at work. Doctorow's character examines the ultimate destructive outcome of the expanding universe in the following manner:

> a truth so monumentally horrifying—this ultimate context of our striving, this conclusion of our historical intellects so hideous to contemplate—that even one's turn to God cannot alleviate the misery of such profound, disastrous, hopeless infinitude? That's my question. In fact if God is involved in this matter . . . , He is so fearsome as to be beyond any human entreaty for our solace, or comfort, or the redemption that would come of our being brought into His secret. (p. 4)

The character asks his scientist how to reconcile the idea of God with evils such as the Holocaust. He answers with a reference to the physical laws that hold the solar system together. This leads to the simple answer that Whatever created the universe insisted on conditions that were conducive to human existence. Doctorow's final answer? If God exists, He is a human-created god.

The Search for a Solution

Understandably, given the enormous implications of the problem-of-evil argument, numerous philosophers and theologians have taken stabs at providing answers to the question. From a rhetorical view, these "answers" would be classified as justifications rather than true arguments. Even a conservative Baptist theologian concluded that, "As a matter of fact, there is no simple, airtight answer to the problem of innocent suffering, given faith in an all-powerful and all-loving God" (Johnson, 1971, p. 73). Still, the variety and range of possible answers represent the diversity of religious thought in the theological and philosophical communities. Several different explanations will be examined.

The Augustinian Theodicy. St. Augustine (354-430 A.D.) received credit for first formulating the Christian response to the problem of evil. His principal theory revolves around the idea that the universe is inherently good, but its goodness necessitates a negative component called evil. As Hick (1990) noted, this approach essentially absolves "the creator of any responsibility for the existence of evil by loading that responsibility without remainder upon the creature" (p. 42). That concept has since been expanded along several different lines.

Humans, the Source of Evil. One simple way to eliminate the problem of evil is to identify humans as the source of evil. Keller (1995), for example, talks of the dichotomy created by Divine transcendence and human defectiveness. The concept of original sin identifies an inherent shortcoming in the souls of people. In this view, that capacity for sin is also a capacity to create evil. That evil deed was by men. Thus, it is humans, not God, who are the sources of evil. Examples of human evils abound. Nazi Germany killed more than six million Jews for no other reason than that they were Jewish. Sexual deviants rape and kill innocent women and children. Serial killers randomly select victims to fulfill their own fantasies. Even so-called moral and normal individuals are susceptible to evil deeds although they get less news coverage.

Critics, though, quickly dismiss this argument. Granted, the possibility of pain is inherent in the world in which we live. Still, there seems to be a great deal of suffering that cannot be blamed on man. As Davis (1969) noted, even if this argument is accepted, it only helps to explain moral evils (killing, lying, etc.). It does nothing to explain those physical sufferings that are not caused by moral evil. "Not all physical suffering is caused by moral evil," he wrote, ". . . earthquakes and tidal waves and epidemics of disease destroy good and evil people alike" (p. 33). In August 1992, for example, Hurricane Andrew struck south Florida, causing $26 billion in damages, killing 40 people, and leaving 250,000 homeless (Provenzo & Provenzo, 2002). The tsunami of December 26, 2004 killed more than 120,000 people, left more than 100,000 homeless, and within days resulted in many more deaths from disease and dehydration. This suffering came from a force of nature that should hypothetically be under God's control. Further, even if all evil and suffering were created by humans, doesn't such suffering require God's permission to continue? Couldn't an all-powerful God stop such evil?

The most extreme form of this argument accounts for this counter argument by dividing evil into two distinct categories—natural evil and moral evil. In this version, natural disasters are not really evil because they are spontaneous and impersonal—they are results of laws of nature that God created before shorelines were heavily populated and population centers grew in other high-risk locations. Orr (1977) noted that carrying such an argument to a logical conclusion had staggering implications. However, if everything is natural, then nothing is wrong. Even death is something that nature imposes on every living thing, because every living thing must die.

The extreme theological version of the "all-powerful God would preclude suffering" theory assumes that all suffering is punishment for some sin. While that approach is apparently dismissed today, it was a common idea during the Old Testament eras. When Job was suffering, for example, his friends tried to get him to identify what sin he might have committed to have caused such suffering. Similarly, the New Testament's Gospel of John recounts a story in which Jesus and his disciples come upon a man "which was blind from his birth" (9:1). The encounter prompts the disciples to ask, "Master, who did sin, this man, or his parents, that he was born blind?" Note the assumption that any suffering was caused by sin, either directly or indirectly.

The three major religions handle this dichotomy by making it clear that everyone should be prepared to die at any moment. Mill (1874) understood the irony of the argument by writing, "Death is inevitable. Yet it is a great world in which we live" (pp. 81-82). Most if not all human beings have a strong will to live, yet they know everyone will eventually die. It is often when they are surprised or angered by unexpected and seemingly unjust deaths that God's control or evil characteristics become salient. God is largely irrelevant to many until death unexpectedly enters their worlds—worlds created by them that encircle the fenced taboo territory of unanticipated and stinging death.

The Best of All Possible Worlds. During the 1970s, singer/songwriter Kris Kristofferson wrote and performed a song called "The Best of All Possible Worlds." The song recounted the travails of a man who continuously ran into problems. Kristofferson, who studied in England as a Rhodes Scholar, was undoubtedly familiar with one philosophical response to the problem of evil, i.e., that God created the "best of all possible worlds." While the phrase may not eliminate the problem of evil, it at least changes the nature of the argument. As Alston (1963) noted, the phrase "might suggest that it is up to the theist to show that the world we have is the only sort that a theistic God would create" (p. 221). Thus, rather than arguing about the difference between the possible world and an ideal "impossible" world, the focus should be on the similarity between the possible and the actual. As Johnson (1971) argued, our world "is the kind of world in which the suffering of the innocent is a necessary possibility" (p.73).

In this view, evil is necessary for the existence of a good world. Perfection requires a static world, while the world of God is one of action, progress and change. Creating a perfect world without the possibility of evil would be inherently contradictory, and, as Thomas Aquinas noted, "Nothing which implies contradiction falls under the omnipotence of God" (*Summ. Theol.,* Ia Q XXV, Art. 4). As Davis (1969) argued, "without the possibility of evil and pain it would be impossible to have certain important and valuable goods" (p. 36). It would be possible for a parent to raise a child in an all-but totally safe environment. All they would have to do is to restrict the child's activities to a sterile environment and never expose the child to an outside threat. It is intuitive that, such restriction would not be in the best interests of the child. This child would never develop, never mature to its full potential. To provide only one specific problem for such a hypothetical child, he or she would not be exposed to the germs with which all other children regularly come in contact. Hence, the child's immune system would never have the opportunity to form the antibodies that dirtier and unprotected children develop by their natural tendencies to get dirty. The lack of a runny nose and a cough during early childhood would likely put the child at great risk when he or she becomes emancipated and escapes the sterile environment. The psychological disadvantages of such overprotection could be discussed at great length. Similarly, God could have created a better world, but it would not have been a better world for us. We, as His children, would never have a chance to reach our full potential. Thus Johnson (1971) concluded, "Sometime the parent has to risk the child suffering injury in order to allow him to exercise his [sic] freedom" (p. 73).

Heschel (1955) argued that evil is an essential component of God's world.

> The dreadful confusion, the fact that there is nothing in this world that is not a mixture of good and evil, of holy and unholy, of silver and dross, is, according to Jewish mysticism, the central problem of history and the ultimate issue of redemption" . . . . Evil is not only a threat, it is also a challenge." (p. 377)

Tennant (1930) argued that the best possible world is also an essential element of God. If God had not created the world, God himself would only be an irrelevant abstraction. Further, any god who would have created a different world would not have been the moral God that is worshiped by the Judeo-Christian religion. The world is what it is because God is who He is. It is not just the best of all possible worlds, but the only possible world that can be created by a moral God.

The Free-Will Argument. Another argument, closely related the Best Possible World Argument, is that evil is an unfortunate consequence of God having created creatures who had free will—the ability to choose right from wrong (O'Connor, 1996). "There was no virtue in doing good in the absence of some opportunity of doing wrong," Orr (1977) wrote. "God can create free creatures, but cannot force them to do good, or they would not be free . . . . God can do anything that is within His power. He cannot fake free will for men" (pp.83-84).

The common perception of God that is shared by all three great religions— Judaism, Christianity, and Islam—is that God is a moral God. God's world must have a moral order. There cannot be moral goodness in a creature such as man without the possibility of his sinning. Without freedom to choose evil, a human might be a well-behaved puppet but he or she is not a moral agent. Virtue would be an unknown concept without the availability of temptation for humans to behave in evil manners. The best world, then, must include free agents, people who are truly capable of understanding God's moral order on their own and freely capable of choosing to follow that moral order. Morality cannot exist without the possibility of immorality. Good cannot exist without the possibility of evil. The free will of humans must mean freedom to choose, and that implies that bad things must exist as options that can be chosen. That's why the author of Job can conclude that "man is born unto trouble" (Job 5:7). Trouble is a necessary by-product of free will. Are such conclusions necessarily so? Is it not possible that God could have a good reason for allowing evil in the world? Zagzebski (1996), in her agent-based approach to the problem, questioned the premise that an all-good being is automatically motivated to produce good and to prevent the existence of evil. Lewis (1996) argued that the potential for evil was inherent within the very concept of God and his creation. "We can, perhaps, conceive of a world in which God corrected the results of this abuse of free will by His creatures at every moment . . . ," Lewis wrote. "But such a world would be one in which wrong actions were impossible, and in which, therefore, freedom of the will would be void; nay, if the principle were carried out to its logical conclusion, evil thoughts would be impossible" (p. 30). Some theologians even go so far as to describe evil as a gift from God to secure good ends (Whitney, 1994).

The most current version of the free-will argument is called the openness model, or relational theism, an interpretation that was first articulated in the early 1990s (Pinnock, 1994) and since examined in more detail by other theologians (Boyd, 1997, 2000, 2001; Sanders, 1999). Sanders' (1999) view of the openness model focused on God's relationship with his creation. God is a God of love and thus created beings who could reciprocate that love. His creation initiated a genuine give-and-take relationship, but—because love cannot be forced—God chose to make himself vulnerable to those He loved. He allows evil to enter the world in order to take the risk that we will reciprocate His love. As Lewis (2001) wrote, "Desiring their freedom, He therefore refuses to carry them, by their mere affections and habits, to any of the goals which He sets before them: He leaves them to 'do it on their own' " (p. 7).

Boyd (1997) used open theism to argue against St. Augustine's response to the problem of evil. Augustine attributed pain and suffering to God's mysterious "good" purposes. Boyd argued that evil comes not from God, but from Satan (Boyd, 2001). God is both omnipotent and sovereign and yet vulnerable because he is involved in an age-long battle against Satan (Boyd, 2000). Early Christians, he argued, understood that battle and they tried to join in the fight by seeking to overcome evil. Modern Christians generally don't expect evil and are baffled but resigned when it occurs; New Testament writers expected it and fought against it (Boyd, 1997).

So what are the problems with the free-will argument? First, it implies some limitations upon God's powers, something that many believers have trouble reconciling with their own image of God. Second, for those who have a deterministic theology, it amounts to heresy. Many of the proponents of open theism are members of conservative religious denominations. However, for some of their fellow believers, they are not conservative enough. In 2001, the Evangelical Theological Society voted (with 70 percent approval) to pass a resolution rejecting "open theism." Open theism is the belief that God does not fully know the future because people have been given the freedom to help shape it through their decisions. Open theism, or free-will theism, was introduced to the general public in 1994 with the publication of *The Openness of God* by five evangelical scholars. One of the evangelists voting for the resolution noted that the vote was a "nudge" to warn the open theism supporters to re-think their position or drop out of the organization.

Evil as the Enemy of God. That portion of the openness model that emphasizes Satan as the source of evil is nothing new. In 1955, Heschel wrote that "Life is lived on a spiritual battlefield. Man must constantly struggle with "the evil drive'" (p. 366). Theologians since the beginning of the Bible have depicted evil as the enemy of God. As Heschel continued, "With the exception of the first chapter of the Book of Genesis, the rest of the Bible does not cease to refer to the sorrow, sins, and evil of this world" (pp. 367-368). In Genesis, for example, the Bible records that "The Lord saw the wickedness of man was great in the earth . . . . And the Lord was sorry that He had made man on the earth, and it grieved Him to His heart." (Genesis 6:5-6). Later, in the book of Job, a similar description is given: "The earth is given into the hand of the wicked" (9:24).

Heschel (1955) also opined the following:

> Even more frustrating than the fact that evil is real, mighty and tempting is the fact that it thrives so well in the disguise of the good, that it can draw its nutriment from the life of the holy. In this world, it seems, the holy and the unholy do not exist apart, but are mixed, interrelated, and confounded. (p. 369)

Lewis (1996) argued that the battle between good and evil have caused some to misinterpret God's actions, attributing evil to God where none existed. "When our ancestors referred to pains and sorrows as God's 'vengeance' upon sin they were not necessarily attributing evil passions to God," he wrote; "they may have been recognizing the good element in the idea of retribution" (p. 84).

Evil as the Opposite of Happiness. Some philosophers have approached the problem of evil as a semantic issue, one in which "evil" is incorrectly viewed as the opposite of "happiness" or "pleasure." "Good," this approach argues, should not be interpreted as "happy" but as 'morally right." Proponents of this approach would argue that Abraham may not have been happy about following God's instructions to sacrifice his son, but it was the morally right thing to do.

Similarly, Job may not have been happy to suffer the afflictions that beset him; again, though, it was the morally right thing to do. The key here is the assumption that modern humans associate good with things that bring them pleasure, not with morality. God, though, has a different standard; He wants us to seek that, which is morally right, not what is physically pleasurable. Mere happiness could be the real evil because it could lead to moral and emotional stagnation. A person's character is created by a lifetime a living, not given to people with their birth. Building character in people requires addressing and overcoming obstacles in life.

The Finite God Theory. Alston (1963) noted that "if we conceive of God as limited to some extent in carrying out His intentions, the problem of evil is no longer insoluble" (p. 228). Indeed, not only does the idea of a God with limited powers eliminate the problem of evil, it also explains the presence of evil. Davis (1969), for example, argued that "God is not all-powerful and cannot merely speak evil away . . . rather, God is engaged along with good men in a real struggle with the powers of evil" (p. 34). How can God still be God if He is not all-powerful? Davis explained it in the following manner:

to say that God is all-powerful means only that God can do everything that can be done, not that He can do contradictory things like make square circles. Perhaps the creating of real people is impossible without the existence of evil—"impossible" in the sense that square circles are impossible. (p. 36)

Alston (1963), in fact, argued that the Bible presents God as a finite Supreme Being, noting that, "the supposed revelation of God in the Bible is not carried out as effectively and fairly as would be expected from an omnipotent and perfectly good deity" (p. 222).

Critics, though, cannot always reconcile their images of an omnipotent God with the limited version required by this approach. For example, Hunt (2001) criticized such attempts to minimize God in terms of the specificity of His divine attributes. If God is not all-powerful, is He really God?

God's Goodness. Davis (1969) contended that the answer to the problem of evil lies not in the nature of God's power, but in God's goodness. "Men have never found it easy to trust God's goodness," he wrote. "But this is surely the answer to the problem of evil in all of its forms, namely that God in fact is good, and His goodness is sure to prevail" (p. 37). NBC's short-lived series—*God, the Devil and Bob*—adopted a similar view. God was depicted by James Garner as good, tolerant and had a wry sense of humor.

C. S. Lewis (1996) similarly argued against the problem of evil by pointing to the goodness of God. "If the universe is so bad, . . . how on earth did human beings ever come to attribute it to the activity of a wise and good Creator?" Lewis wrote ". . . The spectacle of the universe . . . can never have been the ground of religion; it must always have been something in spite of which religion . . . was held" (p. 13). Heschel (1955) agreed, noting, "Evil is not man's ultimate problem. Man's ultimate problem is his relation to God . . . . The Biblical answer to evil is not the good but the holy. It is an attempt to raise man to a higher level of existence" (p. 376).

Evil Does Not Exist. Perhaps the easiest way to resolve the problem of evil is to dismiss the existence of evil. Two different philosophical approaches have taken this view—those that view it as (1) a lesser good or (2) only an illusion. The most unusual of the "lesser good" arguments is the approach that dismisses evil through the use of a semantic argument. Tennant (1930) described the argument as having two logical premises and a conclusion: (1) there is nothing that the omnipotent God cannot do, (2) He cannot do evil, and (3) therefore evil is nothing. Hindu tradition views evil as simply another manifestation of God, a manifestation that is just as reflective of God as others. Lewis (1996) described it from the perspective of those who believe in the goodness of God. "It has sometimes been asked whether God commands certain things because they are right or whether certain things are right because God commands them" (p. 89). The apparent problem is that this line of reasoning is not particularly appealing to either the atheist or the believer. As Davis (1969) noted, this line of argument doesn't really solve the problem, but merely "changes the name of the problem" (p. 34).

The second version of this argument is that evil is not real, but is merely an illusion. Again, though, this does not really satisfy many proponents on either side of the debate. Tennant (1930) noted that even if we were to accept that premise, then the illusion would still be real and that would—in and of itself—still represent evil, pain, and suffering.

Universalism. Davis (1969) described the Universalism argument as the belief that "ultimately and somehow all men will be saved, including even the devil and his angels" (p. 35). Universalists look to St. Paul when seeking biblical support for their position, arguing that Christ provided the means for the salvation of everyone. Two verses, in particular, are cited as evidence of their position. In the Book of Romans, Paul is discussing Adam's sin when he writes, "Then as one man's trespass (Adam's) led to condemnation for all men, so one man's act of righteousness leads to acquittal and life for all men" (Romans 5:18). Later in the First Epistle to Timothy, Paul again pens a similar theme: "We have set our hope on the living God, who is the Savior of all men, especially of those who believe" (I Timothy 4:10). The final phrase of that sentence, they argue, indicates that the purpose of Jesus' ministry was not merely to save believers; instead, as stated earlier in the sentence, he came as "the Savior of all men." Taken to its extreme, Universalism implies that salvation is automatic regardless of one's behavior or beliefs

Faith That an Answer Exists. Dodson (1993) argued that Christians have to use their faith to deal with such problems. Davis (1969) agreed:

> The truth is, of course, that in a very real and basic way we all feel that life is worth it. With all of life's dangers, pains, struggles and disappointments, we share what is evidently God's judgment too on the matter—namely, that it is better to be than not to be. (p. 37)

Because we sense the innate value of life, we must have faith in God to cope with this problem. Believers, he stated, "are called upon in this very crucial problem . . . not merely to trust God's wisdom, but also to trust His goodness, to believe that whatever the complete truth is, it will be good for us" (p. 37). Supporters of this approach argue that humans simply cannot understand God's purposes, but we must have faith in His sovereignty (Tinker, 1995). Keller (1995) looked to the answer in God's transcendence over humanity and the hidden nature of God. Abraham apparently believed the God had good motives despite the counter-intuitive nature of his order to kill the son.

Satan as the Source of Evil. One common argument about the existence of evil is that it comes not from God but from the Devil (a.k.a., Satan, Beelzebub, among others). Satan is traditionally characterized as one of God's former angels who now stands in open rebellion to God. As such, he is the origin of sins—such as greed, envy, and lust—pain, and suffering. Thus, evil exists because Satan exists, not because it was created by God or allowed to exist by God. Early theologians attributed the existence of both affliction and natural disasters to the "malevolence of Satan" (Pagels, 1996, p. xvi). The universe was seen as the arena in which God and Satan wage their battles. God does so with the Supreme confidence that—in the end—the Goodness of God will ultimately win out over the Evil of Satan.

Generally, the existence of Satan is primarily a Christian concept, not a Jewish one. Pagels (1996) points out that while angels often appear in the Hebrew Bible, Satan himself makes few appearances. There is, of course, the famous wager between God and the Devil over the faith of Job, but few other references to the Devil are made in the Old Testament. Regardless, Satan emerged as a major figure during the first-century A.D. with both Christians and first-century Jewish groups such as the Essenes. Pagels also argued that what people find fascinating about the concept of Satan is "the way he expresses qualities that go beyond what we ordinarily recognize as human. Satan evokes more than the greed, envy, lust, and anger we identify with our own worst impulses, and more with what we call brutality" (p. xvii).

The character of Satan has inspired a number of popular literary works, often with a plot based upon a combat myth (Forsyth, 1987), such as Dante's *Faust.* Among popular American works, one of the most famous is the classic Broadway play and subsequent movie *Damn Yankees.* In the latter, a middle-aged baseball fan sells his soul to Satan in exchange for a chance to play outfield for the Washington Senators and lead them to the World Series. To do so, he will need Satan's help to defeat baseball's incarnation of evil—The New York Yankees.

Although strongly associated with the Christian tradition, Satan is not a unique concept among world religions. Russell (1970) noted that there are cross-cultural parallels between Satan and an evil Egyptian god ("Set") and the Zoroastrian evil entity called "Ahriman." There is also a Jewish counterpart called "Mastema," which is the Hebrew world for "hatred" (Pagels, 1996, p. xviii). Such widespread use of the concept is perhaps one reason that Jung (1954) studied the psychological implications of beliefs in Satan.

One interesting answer to the problem of evil as it applies to the *akedah* is the possibility that it was Satan who was behind the instruction—not God. This interpretation was presented in a first century B.C. apocryphal Hebrew book known as *Jubilees.* The book, probably written by a Jewish patriot (Pagels, 1996, p. 53) includes a section that recounts the story of Abraham and Isaac. In this version of the story, it is the Hebrew demon Mastema who commands Abraham to sacrifice his son (Pagels, p. 54).

Are there any problems with this interpretation? The most obvious is that it apparently does not apply to the *akedah,* at least not as far as the Bible is concerned. The Book of Genesis makes a definite point to identify God as the source of the command. Second, when the story was first recorded, the concept of an evil force outside of God was not a common concept. To the contrary, the early Hebrews' concept of evil demons was largely limited to their perception of the pagan gods worshiped by other cultures (Pagels, pp. xv-xvi). Finally, even if Satan is the source of evil, why can't an all-powerful God defeat him?

Answering that latter question, the proponents of this theory would say, is to understand the purpose of God and the Universe.

The Answer Is Love. Actor Martin Sheen plays a religiously oriented U. S. president on *The West Wing*, a television current series. In many ways, the faith of Sheen's character mirrors his own religious views. Sheen was raised a Catholic before drifting from the church during his early days as an actor. A personal rededication to his faith came in 1981. Sheen, in a 2001 magazine article, said he found that pain and suffering was an essential part of humanity (Rader, 2001). "To keep your life from becoming self-contained and useless," he said, "You have to feel other people's pain and act to help them. That is what faith and love are all about" (p. 6). Similarly, he noted that pleasure and riches are not the sources of happiness. Recalling his experiences as a childhood caddy to the wealthy, he said, "The rich were my best teachers: I saw their inhumanity, selfishness, dishonesty, but I never saw a satisfied rich man. They were never happy with themselves. They always wanted more" (p. 4).

Sheen may be an amateur theologian, but others share his view that love is the answer to pain, suffering, and evil. Lewis (1996) identified God's goodness as emanating from this love.

> The problem of reconciling human suffering with the existence of a God who loves is only insoluble so long as we attach a trivial meaning to the word "love," and look on things as if man were the centre of them. (p. 43)

Instead, God is the center of creation, and man the creature must "surrender itself to its Creator" (p. 80). Unfortunately, man resists most efforts by God to reach out to man. "We are not merely imperfect creatures who must be improved," Lewis wrote; "we are . . . rebels who must lay down our arms" (p. 81).

In this scenario, it is the rebellion of man that creates pain and suffering. That is why, Lewis argued, that "our cure must be painful" (p. 81). "The human spirit will not even begin to try to surrender self-will as long as all seems to be well with it," Lewis said (p. 82). Pain and suffering, he added, are sometimes necessary because the distress "shatters the creature's false self-sufficiency" (p. 91).

The Biblical Options
The Old Testament View

Jones (1975) noted that the Old Testament actually takes two views about the problem of evil, approaching both from the perspective of why righteous people suffer. One view is that righteous people do not actually suffer. This view was expressed by the psalmist who wrote, "There shall be no evil befall thee" (Ps. 91:10). The problem, as Jones noted, is that the statement "is only a half-truth for the righteous do suffer as other people and are not exempt from the sorrows that come from living" (p. 96). Not surprisingly, Old Testament believers accepted the idea but it continued to be "a point of puzzlement to the prophets" (p. 96). Their general way of resolving the issue was to say joy would be found in the eternal.

The View of Jesus

Jones (1975) observed that the view of suffering espoused by Jesus is distinctly different from other biblical perspectives. He wrote that "one is shocked by the fact that so few Christians have adopted Jesus' attitude toward suffering. He accepted the fact of human suffering. He neither explains it nor explains it away" (pp. 97-98). To explain it, Jones argued, would reduce Jesus' message to that of a mere philosophy. Rather, Jesus sought to use His suffering to change the lives and souls of individuals. "The Gospel may not explain [suffering], but it does utterly change it," Jones wrote. "Jesus transforms suffering by using it . . . . A test is turned into a testimony" (p. 98).

Paul's Eternal View

In the New Testament, Paul also addressed the problem, but gave no answers. He never specifically said why anybody has to suffer. He merely accepted it as part of the human condition. Everyone suffers, he said, but Christians have hope for the future. Thus, in the book of Romans he wrote, "the sufferings of this present time are not worthy to be compared with the glory which shall be revealed in us" (8:18). His advice is for us not to focus on our suffering. We should look forward to what God has in store for us.

Later, in the same chapter, Paul recognized suffering as something that creates religious doubt. "Who shall separate us from the love of Christ?" he asked. "Shall tribulation, or distress, or persecution, or famine, or nakedness, or peril, or sword? As it is written, 'For thy sake we are killed all the day long; we are accounted as sheep for the slaughter'" (Romans 8: 35-36).

However, he rejected the argument, adding,

> Nay, in all these things we are more than conquerors through him that loved us. For I am persuaded that neither death, nor life, nor powers, not things present, nor things to come, nor height, nor depth, nor any other creature, shall be able to separate us from the love of God. (Romans 8:37-39)

In Paul's second letter to the Thessalonians, he opened the letter with a greeting that praises them for enduring persecution and trials and describes them as a positive example to other believers (II Thess. 1:1-4). Some of those persecuted Christians may have been addressing the problem of evil, questioning the justice of God (Younce, 2001). Paul dismissed those doubts as being temporal in nature. Instead, he recommended that those enduring pain and suffering take an eternal perspective. By enduring such persecution, they were examples of spiritual faith facing an extreme test. Their faithfulness in the face of such persecution proved that they were truly God's people.

For Paul, then, their suffering was neither senseless nor unexpected. Jesus told His followers to expect suffering. What happened to Jesus would happen to them (John 15:18-25). God's justice makes suffering worthwhile and punishes persecutors. Further, the rewards of Heaven would more than compensate for the pain suffered in this world. Thus, as Heschel (1955) noted, "At the end of days, evil will be conquered by the One; in historic times, evils must be conquered one by one" (p. 377).

The Gospel of Matthew

Paul's interpretation mirrors one found in the Gospels, particularly in that section known as "The Beatitudes." The Beatitudes were Jesus' commandments, something that made him comparable to Moses. Instead of commandments, he offered promises of hope for pain and suffering. People's suffering is not in vain, their lives are not without purpose. He gave hope to the hopeless.

Leavell (1962, p. 36) noted that the Beatitudes "give the secret of inner happiness that is superior to circumstances." "Happiness must always work from the heart," he added, "it cannot depend on outward circumstances." Of particular importance is one specific beatitude: "Blessed are those who are persecuted for righteousness sake." The statement was probably startling to his disciples, who had trouble associating persecution and blessedness. But, as Leavell (1962) noted, Jesus meant it. "In persecutions Christians often find their supreme opportunity to witness for Christ. Possibly the King needs a martyr or two today to advance his kingdom" (p. 38).

The Book of Job

The sacrifice of Isaac only raised the issue of the problem of evil. It made no effort to resolve the problem, focusing instead on other themes in the story. Instead, the most common biblical answer to the problem of evil is provided in the Book of Job, but it offers no answers. The only suggested answers come from the villains of the story—the neighbors who blame Job's problems on something he has done. God never told Job why he suffered. He merely spoke to him from the whirlwind by asking a series of rhetorical questions (e.g., "Knowest thou the ordinances of heaven?" (38:33), "Shall he that contendeth with the Almighty instruct Him" (40:2) and never told him it was a wager with Satan. In addition, Job never learned why. He merely learned to accept it.

Overall, Job lived up to God's expectations. At one point though—toward the end of the book, Job complained bitterly to God at the injustice of his suffering. As Davis (1969) noted, it was a simple answer: "I am infinitely superior to you in all ways. Trust me that I know what I'm doing" (p. 37).

An answer, in a word, is Yes.

To most people, this is probably not totally acceptable.

Such is the Problem of Evil.

SECTION III

THEOLOGICAL QUESTIONS

Chapter 10:
A Question of Time

The ability to predict the future is one of those possibilities that have always intrigued mankind. The most famous and prolific of all secular prophets is Nostradamus, who continues to be credited by many with predicting such events as Napoleon's rise to power and subsequent defeat and Hitler's reign in Germany. During the twentieth century, psychic Jean Dixon gained fame for predicting the assassination of President John F. Kennedy. Sidewalk vendors offer to read palms and divine the future of those seeking their fates. Recently, television commercials have touted the ability of a Jamaican psychic who claims to read tarot cards and predict the futures of individuals who will call their 900 numbers. There is, it seems, enough interest in the knowing the future to make it a commercial enterprise.

Religions also take an interest in the topic. The Bible records that Jesus had such ability, predicting the destruction of the Temple in Jerusalem (Mark 13:1-2). He also told Peter that the disciple would "this day, even in this night, before the cock crow twice, thou shall deny me thrice" (Mark 14:30). Similarly, nearly all of the Hebrew prophets had the ability to predict the future. Predictions of the future were regular features of such Old Testament figures as Isaiah and Jeremiah.

The typical religious interpretation of such prophecies is that they came from God, not from the men themselves. God in his wisdom revealed portions of the future to the prophets. They, in turn, articulated these views for the rest of the world. In other words, man's ability to see into the future may be limited, but God faces no such limitation. He is, after all, omniscient. An omniscient, all-knowing entity, must by definition know everything, and "knowing everything" would include knowing the future—all the future.

The problem with such a conclusion is twofold. First, it raises questions about the doctrine of free will. If God knows that something is going to happen, then it has to happen. If it must happen, then humans do not really have free will. If God knows what decision they will freely choose, then they are not really free to choose it. They have to choose it, or God would be wrong.

The second problem is apparent in the story of Abraham and Isaac, as well as other biblical passages. Specifically, there are plenty of indications in the Bible that God does not always know the future. The Bible is full of indirect references to this concept. Numerous references indicate that God is frequently disappointed with the behavior of his creatures. Disappointment, though, implies higher expectations. Expectations are based on hope for the future, not knowledge.

The most obvious biblical passage that indicates God lacks foreknowledge, though, is in the *akedah*. As Abraham raises his hand to slay his child, the spokesmen for God intervenes and say, "Now I know that thou fearest God."

Notice the first three words: "Now I know." This phrase seems to imply that God did not know whether Abraham would pass the test or not. Traditional Christian theologians, particularly those who believe in a literal interpretation of the Bible, often try to rationalize away this statement. They have some inventive ways of doing so. Ultimately, though, they are stymied by the first three words of God's statement—"Now I know." Thus the need to look at this issue in more detail.

Foreknowledge and Omniscience

Sailhamer (1998, p. 27) identified four attributes of God that are time-related—eternality, infinity, immutability, and knowledge. Eternality relates to the nature of God's existence in that He "has no beginning and will have no end" (p. 27). The psalmist, for example, wrote that God's "years shall have not end" (Psalms 102:27) and "The glory of the Lord shall endure for ever" (Psalms 104:31). Both statements emphasize the endless nature of God. Similarly, the concept of infinity asserts that there are no time limits on God's existence, while the attribute of immutability assumes that God does not change over time.

Thus, traditional Christian theology views God as a Being whose relationship with time is different from those of humans. However, as Sailhamer (1998) noted, "That does not mean . . . that he is ignorant of time. He knows of every moment of time because, since the first moment, he has existed eternally present" (p. 27).

Similarly, God's knowledge is viewed as limitless and all knowing. As Ewing (1962) noted, "God must be conceived as completely omnipotent if the religious consciousness is to attain satisfaction. God seems to be intuited not only as good but as absolutely supreme" (p. 264). Further, if he "knows of every moment of time," then he must also know about the past, the present, and the future. Sailhamer (1998) summarized the concept in this manner:

His knowledge of the past is analogous to our memory, through which we can relive the past. God's knowledge of the *present* is similar to our knowledge of the world, which is limited to our senses of sight, sound, smell, taste, and hearing. We have some understanding of what it means for God to have knowledge of the present. But when it comes to God's knowledge of the *future*, we cannot understand it fully. Thus, opinions differ widely on the exact nature of God's knowledge of the future. (p. 27)

Sailhamer (1998) may have understated the controversy when he wrote, "opinions differ widely." To what extent does God know about the future? As Sailhamer noted, "Most answers to this question end up either limiting human free will or limiting the extent of God's knowledge . . . . If God knows what those choices will be, then is not our free will determined by that knowledge?" (p. 29). How do most Christians answer that dilemma? Sailhamer gives a typical response: "Perhaps the best way to express it is to say that God's knowledge of the future is a knowledge of what we will, in fact, choose to do. In his foreknowledge, God already knows what we will freely choose in the course of time" (p. 29). As Dershowitz (2000) noted, this is a common interpretation of the *akedah*. Other commentators try to have it both ways, i.e., "that God knew what Abraham would do even though he had complete free will" (p. 115). As such, the test was merely to build Abraham's character rather than to verify his obedience. McGee (1991), for example, wrote that "Abraham believed God, and he went far enough to let you and me know—God already knew—and to let the created universe know that he was willing to give his son" (p. 74).

Maybe, but philosophers generally consider this a cop-out. If God knows what "we will freely choose . . . ," then we are not actually free to choose it. It merely raises the entire free will versus determinism issue discussed elsewhere. Further, it is directly counter to the text itself. After all, God did not say, "Now, Abraham you know that you fear God."

Free Will vs. Determinism

With few exceptions, free will is a central component of the world's religions. It is of particular importance in Christianity, which typically works under the assumption that people have some influence over their own destinies. Those who choose to repent of their sins and to place their trust in Jesus Christ will be born again. By doing so, people can change their lives and alter their eternal fate. However, if God knows what we are going to do, are we really free to do otherwise? Apparently, we are not. As Davis (1968) noted, "assumptions about the fore-knowledge of God almost inevitably lead to a philosophical view known as 'determinism'. If God knows that something is going to happen, then it is bound to happen. Nothing can be done to change this destiny" (p. 63).

Although traces of deterministic philosophy have existed for ages, Davis (1968) traces its modern-day roots to the scientific view of matter resulting from Sir Isaac Newton's discovery of the laws of motion. Newton's laws of gravity and motion seemed to account for the movement of all physical matter in the universe, and did so in such a manner that any specific movement seemed inevitable. That scientific view of matter was eventually expanded to a philosophical view of humanity. Humans, the argument goes are composed of physical matter and controlled by brains that must conform to Newton's laws of physics. Therefore, human behavior must be mechanistic in nature, i.e., humans are merely complex machines with an inevitable destiny.

Scientifically, that notion was put to rest in the first half of the 20th century. Scientific studies into a branch of physics known as Quantum Mechanics, combined with the discoveries of Albert Einstein, demonstrated that Newton's laws of motion are not nearly as deterministic as once thought. Specifically, quantum mechanics demonstrated that the behavior of individual atomic particles could not be exactly predicted based on the laws of physics. Instead, the behavior of atomic matter seems to contain an element of spontaneity, or "free play," that cannot be predicted. As Davis (1968, p. 63) noted, "We can predict what a given particle will *probably* do, but never *exactly* what it *will* do." That does not mean that philosophers have resolved the issue, but only that 20th and 21st Centuries science has re-opened a debate that 19th Century philosophers thought had been settled.

The Nature of Time

The very issue of foreknowledge is based upon a traditional interpretation of time. Our concept of time is so ingrained in modern society that it is easy to overlook the fact that our view of time has changed dramatically since, well, time began. McLuhan (1964) noted that "great cultural changes occurred in the West when it was found possible to fix time as something that happened between two points. From this . . . came our Western feeling for time as duration" (p. 135). Before the development of measuring time in intervals, primitive man approached time not as duration but in terms of "the uniqueness of private experience" (McLuhan, 1964, p. 135).

The important idea here is that our conception of time has changed over history. Further, it is in the process of changing again. Modern physics has demonstrated that the space-time continuum is considerably more complex than we traditionally assumed. The behavior of time gets particularly complex as we approach the speed of light, altering the length of durations. Consequently, increased speed in space literally changes the space and pace of time, making time travel theoretically possible.

Physicist Stephen Hawking (1998) examined this concept in detail. His discussion included a look at "string" theories in which time can lap back around upon itself, returning to a previous point in the past. Such ideas create the possibility of time travel (pp. 159-169). In fact, it has already occurred. Several astronauts have spent so much time in high-speed space travel that their time in space moved at a slower pace than did time on earth. Consequently, when they finally returned to earth, they returned to an earth that was a few seconds in the future of the world they left. Long-term space travel provides the potential for even longer jumps into the future. There has also been some discussion about the possibility of traveling backwards in time to the past, although the viability of that concept is still merely speculative in nature. Nevertheless, there is support for unusual behavior in the continuum of time and its relationship to the past. Hawking noted that NASA's Cosmic Background Explorer satellite (COBE) was able to aim its camera back to within 300,000 years of the beginning of the universe. The resulting photographs revealed wrinkles in the space-time fabric. Time, it seems, does not always act in the same manner.

This concept is not entirely foreign to theologians either. C. S. Lewis, in his classic work *The Screwtape Letters*, offers a fictional conversation between a demon (Screwtape) and an apprentice demon (Wormwood) who is trying to understand theology and the human psyche. This devil calls God "The Enemy," and talks of time as one of those concepts that humans don't understand. "The humans live in time but our Enemy destines them to eternity," Screwtape wrote.

> He therefore, I believe, wants them to attend chiefly to two things, to eternity itself, and to that point of time which they call the Present. For the Present is the point at which time touches eternity. Of the present moment, and of it only, humans have an experience which our Enemy has of reality as a whole; in it alone freedom and actuality are offered them. (p. 75)

The goal of the Devil, Screwtape added, "is to get them away from the eternal, and from the Present" (p. 76).

Screwtape also has some insight on the future and the human preoccupation with it. The future, he wrote, is "the thing *least like* eternity. It is the most completely temporal part of time—for the Past is frozen and no longer flows, and the Present is all lit up with eternal rays" (p. 76). Further, he added, "nearly all vices are rooted in the future. Gratitude looks to the past and love to the present; fear, avarice, lust and ambition look ahead" (p. 76). The Devil helps, he said, by giving false cues about time: "We have trained them to think of the Future as a promised land which favoured heroes attain—not as something which everyone reaches at the rate of sixty minutes an hour, whatever he does, whoever he is" (p. 139). Such preoccupation with the future is a futile effort, he continued, because "The man can neither make, nor retain, one moment of time; it all comes to him by pure gift" (p. 112).

This view of time also affected Lewis' interpretation of God's foreknowledge:

> [Man] takes Time for an ultimate reality. He supposes that the Enemy [God], like himself, sees some things as present, remembers others as past, and anticipates others as future; . . . for the Enemy does not *foresee* the humans making their free contributions in a future, but *sees* them doing so in His unbounded Now. And obviously to watch a man doing something is not to make him do it. (pp. 149-150)

The Growth of God

One way of reading and interpreting the Hebrew Bible is to view it as a developmental narrative in which mankind learns about God while God learns about mankind. Fromm (1966) argued that Abraham's relationship with God was part of a developmental process, noting "There is a growth and evolution in the concept of God that accompanies the growth and evolution of a nation" (p. 21). As part of this developmental process, foreknowledge seems to be a characteristic that God has not yet developed. Indeed, there are other instances in the Old Testament when God seems unable or unwilling to fully predict the future. As mentioned earlier, there are several instances in which God expresses disappoint with humans, indicating that he expected more from them. Similarly, Kirsch (1998) argued that the Passover that preceded the exodus from Egypt also represented a lack of total knowledge on God's part—particularly the requirement that the Israelites smear blood on their doorposts so that their children will be spared His wrath (Exodus 12:13). As Kirsch wrote, "God seems to know himself well enough to realize that he is not likely to distinguish between the Egyptians and the Chosen People once he has begun to kill" (p. 178).

Such an interpretation may spark disagreement from more traditional commentators, but the text seems perfectly clear when it comes to the *akedah*. God seems to have no idea what Abraham would have done until the deed is almost executed. Indeed, Bodoff (1993) argued that God's uncertainty was an essential reason for the test because Abraham's "decision could not be known— even by God—until he actually made it by bringing down the knife on his son's body" (p. 80). Dershowitz (2000) agreed, noting God did not know how human beings with their post-tree-of-life free will would behave. This may cause some theologians, who believe in literal predestination, to disagree. However, predestination is not the real issue here—man's relationship with and understanding of one true God is at the core of what we are trying to answer ultimately.

The Job Analogy

The most comforting explanation for God's reference to and foreknowledge in this passage might be called the Job Analogy. In the book of Job, Satan makes a wager with God that Job will not be faithful to the Lord if he is subjected to terrible trials. Consequently, Job was indeed tested by Satan, and passed the tests with his faith in God intact. Some scholars have argued that a similar test was perhaps being conducted on Abraham.

In this view, the phrase—"Now I know that you fear the Lord"—is merely an improper translation, particularly of the Hebrew word "*yd'ty.*" That word is usually translated as "I know". However, in some contexts, it can also be translated as, "I have made known." Thus, in this view, the purpose of the test was to prove Abraham's faithfulness to Satan or to the world—not to God or to Abraham. Abraham has passed the test and—by doing so—God has "made it known" to Satan and everyone else that Abraham's faith is unwavering. Indeed, Latin translations of the Hebrew typically use a similar translation (Kugel, 1997, p. 172). In doing so, most of the controversy generated by this statement is eliminated.

Summary

The relationship between God, foreknowledge, and time is a complex one that will continue to perplex philosophers and theologians. Time travel is theoretical possible, at least in terms of the future, because some astronauts have already accomplished that on a minor scale. Still, the entire issue is bound up with other controversies, including the free-will/determinism debate and the problem of evil controversy. More germane to this study, however, is the impact that certainty about the future has on the rhetoric of sacrifice. Those who feel their religion offers them insight into the future may be more prepared to die for that future.

Chapter 11
A Test of Obedience

While the focus of the *akedah* story is on the act of sacrifice, its most popular theological theme is that the entire episode was a test—either of obedience or of his devotion to God. McGee (1991) called it Abraham's "supreme test" and "the fourth great crisis in his life" (p. 72). Armstrong (1996 a) described it as "God's temptation of Abraham" (p. 28).

Ackland (1964) noted that Abraham's test was one of the Bible's early efforts to expand upon the theology of obedience.

> From God's perspective, His early attempts to apply rules had met with mixed results. He places Adam and Eve into the Garden of Eden with only one rule— to not eat of the fruit from the tree of knowledge; naturally, they soon disobeyed that one." (p. 61)

Ackland went on to add:

> Obedience was still being developed as a theological doctrine, and there were few ethical "rules" for the godly to follow. The first codified set of ethical standards for the Nation—the Ten Commandments—had not yet been established. No set of religious precepts explaining the theology of the Jewish nation is known to have existed in written form. If they did exist, there is no reference in Genesis to Abraham having referred to them. Followers of God were largely left to their own devices and to their individual relationship with God to figure out the differences between right and wrong. (p. 51)

The most common interpretation of the test is that Abraham passed. Keller (1980) noted that this is one of the most obvious interpretations of the passage because "The author [sic] of this chapter in the Bible himself suggests this when he writes at the beginning of his account: 'God did tempt Abraham.'" Fox (1995) called the story "The Great Test" and "one of the masterpieces of biblical literature" (p. 92). Spiegel (1993) called it "The Last Trial" because it was the final test that sealed the covenant between God and Abraham. McGee (1991) said that "Abraham believed God, and he went far enough to let you and me know" (p. 74).

Gibson (1999) concluded that, "This was a test of how much Abraham would obey God's word" (p. 177). Baldwin (1986) noted that it was a "personal test for Abraham who was called by name" (p. 90). He continued that Abraham passed the test because "He had proved beyond doubt that he feared God, because he had not withheld his only son from him" (p. 91). MacArtney (1997) called it a "terrible test" but that it "was the end of Abraham's probation. He had been tried and not found wanting" (p. 61). Cahill (1998) said Abraham passed the test because "His faith—his belief in God—is stronger than his fear" (p. 86). Guinness (1988) described it as Abraham's "final and most hardest test," adding that "Abraham's final test is exactly that—a trial of his devotion to God" (pp. 54-55). The conclusion seems simple: God placed a test in front of Abraham, and the Patriarch passed. However, as with practically everything else about the *akedah,* this conclusion is not universally accepted. When looked at from other perspectives, the issue of "the test" becomes considerably more complex.

Alternative Interpretations
The Test as a Rhetorical Device. Rhetorical theory, in particular, comes into play. One possibility is that the concept of the test is merely a rhetorical device to prepare the reader for the rest of the story. Although Cahill (1998) is a supporter of the traditional test interpretation, he also noted that the narrator tells us this will be a test in the first verse "so we know that Yitzhak (Isaac) will not actually be sacrificed, however difficult it is to keep that in mind during the ensuing action" (p. 86). The concept is similar to that of Telushkin's (1997) contention, as noted in Chapter 1, that "without the explanation, the chapter will be too painful to read" (pp. 37-38). By doing so, the narrator provided the reader with information that was not available to Abraham, but it made the story more palpable. Knowing it is a test, we at least read the story, although we do it by peeking to the end to make sure that everything comes out okay. Like a young child at a horror movie, we watch with our eyes only partially opened, ready to close them if the scene becomes too scary.

The Test as a Pseudo-Test. Would God really have commanded that someone sacrifice his own son? Many theologians say no. Gibson (1999) argued that, "God never intended that Abraham would actually sacrifice Isaac. He let Abraham make the preparation, and then He intervened" (p. 179). Indeed, God's original command to Abraham is somewhat ambiguous. Perhaps Abraham simply misunderstood God and mistakenly thought he was supposed to sacrifice his son. Alternatively, perhaps God was deliberately ambiguous, misleading Abraham enough to ensure that the test was a tough one.

Such interpretations have their critics though. Kirsch (1998), for example, described this approach as the work of "apologetic theologians [who] have struggled to explain away the Binding of Isaac" (p. 176). The problem is that this is not the apparent message of the passage. As Dershowitz (2000) noted, "Both the text and general principles of law make it more likely that Abraham intended to kill his son" (p. 123).

The Test as a Learning Experience. This approach argues that God was not really testing Abraham so much as teaching him (Shubert, 2000). Gibson (1999), for example, argued that "God assures us that he will never tempt us, but he does test us. His tests are intended to be learning experiences through which we can grow stronger" (p. 179). Cahill (1998) noted that God was developing a strong relationship with Abraham. If the relationship between the Lord and the Patriarch is to last, then Abraham "requires education" which "he receives in a series of manifestations in which 'the god' gradually reveals himself as God—not just a divinity but the only God that counts" (pp. 84-85).

The problem with these interpretations, though, is that they imply that God lied to Abraham. Could a Supreme Being such as God be guilty of such duplicitous behavior? Would God lie to man? The question, though repugnant to countless believers, merits consideration. After all, that was the serpent's argument when he enticed Eve to eat the fruit from the Tree of Knowledge. Perhaps God would lie to man if the ultimate purpose were to benefit man. Still, that takes some theological maneuvering to make it acceptable to many believers. It requires that readers accept the premise that God applied utilitarian moral reasoning. That is, God deemed it acceptable to mislead Abraham for the greater good of Abraham's progeny and the human race. The realistic flaw in utilitarian philosophy is that people cannot always know what type or amount of otherwise wrongful conduct will actually result in more good than bad (i.e., people cannot always accurately predict all of the consequences of their actions). However, an omnipotent God would have such knowledge. Hence, the utilitarian conduct is fine for God, but it remains unreliable and often dangerous for humans. Regardless, these interpretations require the assumption that God intended the lessons to be learned from this aborted sacrifice as a goal that would justify His misrepresentation, if not a lie.

The Failing Test Interpretations

If we had been the subjects of such a test, would we have passed? Many people know that they would have failed, for understandable human-nature reasons. They simply would not have sacrificed their own child, and they probably question Abraham's decision in some way. As Badoff (1993) did, we might question Abraham's moral backbone for being willing to sacrifice his beloved son. Not surprisingly, then, several theologians have suggested that if this were a test, then Abraham failed it.

Failing the Moral Test. One view is that Abraham may have passed God's test of obedience, but he failed his own test of morality. As Dershowitz (2000) noted, Abraham had done an excellent job of articulating a moral contention for justice when he negotiated with God over the condemnation of Sodom. There he asserted, "that it is always wrong to kill the innocent, even if God commands it" (p. 110). Yet, that is precisely what Abraham later planned to do when he bound Isaac on the sacrificial altar.

Why would Abraham violate a moral imperative that he had demonstrated he understood and believed? Perhaps it was because he was literally afraid to do otherwise. After all, the text states that God recognized that Abraham "feared" Him. While "fear" is often interpreted as being "in awe of" God, what if the literal meaning actually applied to Abraham and was the rationale for his willingness to sacrifice his son? Between the time God began communicating with Abraham and the time he was told to sacrifice his beloved son, Abraham had learned some things about how God dealt with disobedience. For example, he knew God "rained upon Sodom and Gomorrah brimstone and fire" (Gen. 19:24). This alone, had to make Abraham perceive God differently and very seriously. While Sodom and Gomorrah were still smoking, God instantly changed Lot's wife into "a pillar of salt" (Gen. 19:26) because she disobeyed God's instruction regarding which direction she should look.

Abraham knew God had dealt harshly with disobedience, some of which severely punished members of his own family. Lot was Abraham's nephew and they had shared the same family unit after Lot's father died (Gen. 11:26-31), until their shared land would not support both men's great herds, flocks, tents, and employees (Gen. 13:1-12). Even if Abraham was literally terrified, of God, it appears that he still failed the test. Dershowitz (2000) asked rhetorically, "what kind of moral test is that? Acceding to an immoral command out of fear does not show much courage or virtue" (p. 109). More specifically, killing a loved one to avoid punishment does not appear noble or holy—it seems weak and cowardly, at best.

Failing the Contemporary Test. It is probably unfair to judge Abraham by modern standards, but we tend to do it anyway. We operate in our modern realities, which grow more divergent each day from the world in which Abraham lived. While it is certain that Abraham's *past* and our *present* are unimaginably different, his story will always be relevant, regardless of how technologically advanced humans become.

By contemporary standards, Abraham failed miserably. As Dershowtiz (2000) noted, "No one today would justify killing a child because God commanded it" (p. 110). In fact, most cultures' legal systems or their equivalents imprison or institutionalize people who use personal instructions from God as their legal defenses to homicide charges. With few exceptions, modern societies do not even accept such an argument as a legal or moral basis for justifying child abuse, much less, killing the child. There are some religious cults that use the Bible to justify strong physical punishment of disrespectful children, but our courts do not allow biblical interpretations to justify child abuse (Dershowitz, 1988).

A Duplicitous Abraham. Some scholars argue that not only was the test a pseudo-test, one that God never intended to carry out, but also that Abraham recognized the fake nature of the trial from the beginning. Since Abraham knew that God was really testing him, and would never require him to actually kill his son, he willingly went along with the command (Dershowitz, 2000,). The basis of this interpretation is the ambiguity of the instructions, which command

Abraham to "offer" his son but does not specifically say that Abraham should kill him. Supporters of this theory argue that Abraham recognized the vagueness of the command and realized in advance that God would not accept the "offer" and that Isaac would be safe. They also point to verse 5 in which Abraham confidently says that he and Isaac "will come again" as proof that Abraham recognized the pseudo-nature of the test. The problem with this interpretation, though, is that if Abraham knew that Isaac would be spared, it was not much of a test. As Dershowitz (2000) noted:

> One who knows the answer to a test in advance is a cheat. Moreover, based on God's past behavior, why would Abraham trust that his son would survive? After all, this is the same God who destroyed the world in the flood and was prepared to sweep away the innocent along with the guilty in Sodom. (p. 106)

This argument may have a weakness, though. Specifically, those are two different stories written by two different narrators. Friedman (1987) noted that the Sodom and Gomorrah story was written by the Genesis narrator known by scholars as the "I author," while most of the *akedah* was written by the "E author." The two different behaviors may simply be two different interpretations of the Patriarch by two different authors (p. 247). Similarly Bean (2000) argued that if Abraham knew God did not require that he kill Abraham, then "the whole account was simply a drama, not a test of his faith" (p. 78).

Self-Serving Behavior. We should remember that, despite his relationship with God, Abraham had a record of self-serving behavior. On two occasions, he lied about his relationship with his own wife in order to protect himself. No wonder then that Dershowitz (2000) noted, "There is, of course, the possibility that Abraham went along with God's command for entirely self-serving reasons" (p. 106). What possible motive would he have? Abraham could have complied to save his own life. God had commanded him to sacrifice Isaac, and he knew what had happened previously after a failure to comply with a direct command from God. The memory of Lot's wife's fate provided a fresh example. Could the same thing happen to him? He had to consider it as a possibility. Arguably, this could have been his primary motive for obeying the command.

Satan as the Source of Temptation. One interpretation is that Abraham's trial truly was a temptation, but one that came from Satan. The text pointedly states that the command comes from God, not Satan, but supporters of this approach conclude that Satan provoked God into testing Abraham using arguments similar to those that were used with Job (Dershowitz, 2000). While this possibility is accepted by some, it requires the reader to supplement the actual text. We will consider how supplementing and then adulterating scriptural texts can empower rhetors of sacrifice to motivate others to extremes that are the antithesis of the actual intent of the biblical and Koran texts.

The Deterministic Argument. Some theologians disregard the angel's comments in verse 12 that "now I know that thou fearest God." That statement indicates that neither God nor the angel knew for a certainty what Abraham would do. Deterministic theologians, though, simply do not accept that verse as legitimate or they re-interpret it to support their belief in a deterministic God. Feiler (2001) noted that some Jewish theologians believe "God tested Abraham precisely because he knew that Abraham would pass the test" (p. 90). One common version of this approach is to argue that God knew what Abraham would do, but the test was necessary to prove Abraham's faith to himself and to provide God with a reason to reward him. "In other words," Dershowitz (2000) noted, "God rewards good actions more than good intentions" (p. 115). Fox (1995) wrote, "we are left to ponder the difficulties of being a chosen one, subject to such an incredible test" (p. 92).

Did Abraham Fail the Test? Bodoff (1993) suggested that God hoped that Abraham would refuse His command to murder Isaac. This response would send a message "that God does not want even his God-fearing adherents to go so far as to murder in God's name or even at God's command" (p. 71). Shlomo Rishkin (1997), an Orthodox rabbi, agreed, suggesting that Abraham should have argued for Isaac's life (p. 13). In other words, the command was a test, but not a test of obedience. Dershowitz (2000) also agreed, concluding that, "Abraham passed the test of obedience but failed the test of moral self-determination" (p. 125). Instead, it was a test of whether Abraham "would remain loyal to God's revealed moral law, even if ordered to abandon it" (p. 76). If so, then Abraham failed the test. Bodoff noted that if Abraham had actually killed Isaac and received praise for that act, we would have a religion that few modern believers could accept. To pass the test, Bodoff argued, Abraham should have told God that he could not do it because it violated God's moral law to protect the innocent. Dershowitz (2000) noted that Abraham's argument with God over the fate of Sodom and Gomorrah had established a precedent for such a response. Interestingly, the argument by Abraham was one based on his concept of morality versus the concept of morality of the omnipresent, omnipotent God. Did God set this confrontation up so Abraham would feel comfortable arguing his case when told to sacrifice—kill—Isaac? If so, this was the genius of God setting up the Father of many nations to make the right a moral a moral argument at the appointed time. Alternatively, the Sodom and Gomorrah argument could have emboldened Abraham, yet he subordinated his personal morality to that of God's. After all, Abraham saw the results of his winning arguments about Sodom and Gomorrah—two cities with their inhabitants in ashes Lott's wife turned into a lifeless pillar of salt, looking back toward past sins and the smoldering cities Abraham had spared for a brief time.

Some philosophers have argued that Abraham should have not only refused the command, but should have used the command to question whether the voice was actually that of God. This response would be along the lines of, "That I ought not to kill my son is certain beyond a shadow of a doubt; that you, as you appear to be, are God, I am not convinced" (Schulweis, 1994, p. 81). Kant (1960) also questioned Abraham's behavior when he wrote the following:

Was he this strongly enough assured of such a revealed doctrine, and of this interpretation of it, to venture, on this basis, to destroy a human life? . . . After all, the revelation has reached the inquisitor only through men and has been interpreted by men, and even did it appear to have come from God Himself (like the command delivered to Abraham to slaughter his own son like a sheep) it is at least possible that in this instance a mistake has prevailed. (p. 175)

Why even the suggestion that Abraham failed this supreme test in his life? After all, God rewarded him with his promise and the covenant. He has many children and becomes a great man among great people. It is noteworthy that there is also an apparent punishment following the test. The Bible does not record that God ever spoke to Abraham again. In fact, He does not even speak directly to him at the end of the test, but instead sends an angel to be his surrogate. Armstrong (1996a) noted that, "After the supreme test, God never spoke to Abraham again, withdrawing, outwardly at least, from Abraham's life. But he was true to the Promise" (p. 69). Dershowitz (2000) added, "If Abraham had passed God's test with flying colors, we might expect God Himself to come down and praise Abraham. Instead, God sends a mere messenger" (p. 124). The promise of making his seed a great nation is indeed a great promise. But does it compensate for being separated from God? As Dershowitz (2000) noted, "Abraham is rewarded—long life, wealth, new wife, more children, father of a nation, . . . but in some respects all this seems like a consolation prize for doing his best, but not quite enough in God's eyes" (p. 125).

Some observers see support for this interpretation by comparing verses 2, 12 and 16. In verse 2, when God first gave His command to Abraham, He referred to Isaac as his only son, "whom thou lovest." After the test, the angel referred twice to Isaac as Abraham's "only son" (Gen. 22:12, 16), but made no reference to him loving the child. As attorney Alan Dershowitz (2000) concluded, "This suggests that the angel does not believe that a father who was willing to sacrifice his son can be said to love him" (p. 124). The story is remembered, though, because it used the incident as an object lesson about human sacrifice. A later theologian, Soren Kierkegaard (1968) agreed, noting that, "though Abraham arouses my admiration, he at the same time appalls me. He who has explained this riddle has explained my life" (p. 90). Similarly, Armstrong (1996a) concluded that, "The incident leaves us with difficult questions about both Abraham and God. A deity who asks for such an extreme demonstration of devotion can seem cruel and sadistic" (pp. 67-68).

Others have noted that Abraham's behavior was similar to that of parents in nearby cultures whom worshiped pagan gods. Molech, the ancient Canaanite god of fire, would be an apt example. Worship of this heathen god required the sacrifice of children. The ritual required that the feelings of the parents had to be ignored while cruelty toward the children was an integral part of the worship ritual. As noted earlier, Dershowitz (2000), argued that there is little distinction between the pagan ritual and what Abraham was asked to do.

Opponents of this interpretation note that, unlike his Canaanite neighbors, Abraham did not actually kill his son. While this is true, his compliance, albeit interrupted, has never been a serious source of debate. Further, the angel praised the Patriarch for his willingness to do just that. Dershowitz (2000) noted that this raises questions about the nature of God. Would we really want to worship a God who praises Abraham "for his willingness to obey God's immoral command" (p. 119). Further, it raises doubts about God's true intent. If God really wanted Abraham to refuse the command, why praise his willingness to comply (p. 121). Such questions led Elie Wiesel (1981), recipient of the 1986 Nobel Peace Prize and a man familiar with killing via soldiers following orders, to argue that both Abraham and God failed the test. Wiesel reasoned that God should never have asked a father to kill his child, and the father should never have agreed to do so. Since both happened, both behaved immorally.

Others, however, believe that modern commentators are being too tough on Abraham. He lived during a different time and in a different culture. Telushkin (1997) contended :

> Abraham's readiness to obey God's command shows him to be ethically deficient by later standards, but not by those of his age. True, God had revealed Himself to Abraham, but He had not made known to him the full ethical implications of monotheism. Since other contemporary religious believers sacrificed sons to their gods, God, in essence, was asking Abraham if he was as devoted to his God as the pagan idolaters were to theirs. (pp. 38-39)

Similarly, Dumont (1971) had a positive view of Abraham and his behavior. "Abraham stands to gain nothing by sacrificing his son Isaac," Dumont wrote. "God promises him no favors. Faith carries Abraham to Mount Moriah; hope sustains him. Faith makes him heroic; hope makes him human" (p. 38).

Lessons from the Test

If God meant this incident to be a rhetorical lesson for humans, exactly what else can be gleaned from the story? Quite a lot, it appears. Indeed the *akedah* has served as the foundation of a number of rhetorical arguments. These include:

God's Rejection of Human Sacrifice. This is the most common rhetorical interpretation of the *akedah.* It was discussed in more detail in chapter 6.

Daat Torah. "Daat Torah" is a Jewish concept that is used to describe the behavior of believers in religious cults. It refers to those situations in which individuals sacrifice their own behavior, will and opinion and subjugate those to the blind obedience to a charismatic leader or rabbi (Dershowitz, 2000, p. 126). Armstrong (1996a) considered the following possibility: "Perhaps, seeing the consequences inflicted by his 'test' upon Isaac, God came to realize that too relentless a faith can lead to fanaticism and to a lack of humanity that has permanent and damaging effects upon others" (p. 73). This is a view with which Wiesel (1981) would have probably concurred, considering his first-hand experience with the Nazis and the bases of their crimes against humanity. This is not to assert that the Nazi murderous regime would not have manifested without the existence if the akedah. Rather, it is intended to demonstrate that the concept of "Daat Torah" is more than a theory—it is a temptation and trap that human beings should be educated on and guard against. The need for such education and vigilance continues, as fanatics carry out suicide attacks and mass murder in the name of their God—the same God that stopped the murder of Isaac, and sent Jesus to serve as the final sacrifice.

It is difficult to derive the actual message of the akedah without oversimplifying the problem or turning it into a circuitous complex theological and political conundrum. As this book has and will demonstrate, the Devil is in the details—the ones people read between the lines. There is much room for the enemies of the truth about sacrifice to operate between these two extremes. Evil, personified by Satan, has used this to his advantage. Yet, humans were given more intellect than details—words—to work with on this task. The practitioners of the rhetoric of sacrifice possess the intellectual abilities to persuade others to kill and be killed. Both are good in the world of the rhetoric of sacrifice. Only continuing to live and doubting the rhetoric of sacrifice is absolutely wrong in the rhetor' views. Never mind that the ones doing the dying are almost unanimously illiterate and cannot read and interpret their Holy books for themselves. The rhetors will do that for them, and so the sorrow will continue. The mourners take comfort in the "absolute fact" that their lost loved ones are in paradise—information provided, at least initially by the rhetors of sacrifice. At some point, after most families have lost a son or daughter, the rhetoric of the supreme sacrifice and its appealing and eternal rewards becomes a part of life—reality. So, it' not so bad—not once the masses buy into the rhetoric of sacrifice. It is when they pay—when paradise time arrives, that the trouble starts. This is beyond the jurisdiction of the rhetoric of sacrifice. The enemy's enemy is no longer the "infidels of the day," they are the dogs of doom—the fires and features of the abyss.

The Tough Road Theory. This interpretation is related to the problem of evil. As Dershowitz (2000) described it, "by commanding Abraham to sacrifice Isaac, God was telling Abraham that in accepting the covenant, he was not receiving any assurances that life would be perfect . . . . The history of the Jewish people has certainly borne that out" (p. 126). Similarly, Fox (1995) wrote, "The Patriarch passes the test, and we know that the fulfillment of the divine promise is assured. Yet there is an ominous note: love, which occurs here by name for the first time, leads almost to heartbreak" (p. 92).

The Need for Individual Sacrifices. Strom (1998) argued that Abraham's willingness to sacrifice his son should inspire others to commit to God's service. "Any commitment on our part to give God our talents seems to pale in comparison to Abraham's offering of Isaac, but we can at least start there," Strom wrote. "I believe that giving him our talents simply means making them available for his ends" (p. 281).

Separation from Family. Looked at individually, the *akedah* may be viewed as an object lesson on obedience and sacrifice. As part of a larger story, though, it was but one more incident in which Abraham is separated from his family. The chapter before, for example, refers to the exile of Ishmael and Hagar from the family. Further, the entire story of Abraham began with God commanding Abram to leave his family and migrate to a new country. Fromm (1966) noted "a peculiar parallel" between that command to leave his father's land and the command to sacrifice Isaac—a command "to cut the ties of blood to the son" (p. 72). Thus Fromm concluded, "The command to sacrifice Isaac, then, would mean man must be completely free from all ties of blood—not only with father and mother, but also with his most beloved son" (p. 72).

Conclusion

Despite all of the alternative interpretations, the popular view of this passage is that God used the *akedah* as a test of Abraham's obedience. There was always the chance that Abraham could have refused—thus changing the course of Hebrew history. As Ackland (1964) noted, "Obedience can be expressed only when the possibility of disobedience exists" (p. 51). We tend to return to the question of why the test had to be so horrible. Because, wrote Wiersbe (1991), "Our faith is not really tested until God asks us to bear what seems unbearable, to do what seems unreasonable, and expect what seems impossible" (pp. 109-110). The ultimate message, argued Hall (2000) is that Abraham's willingness to kill his own child demonstrates that "We don't belong to each other but to our maker" (p. 61).

Still, with so many interpretations by different theologians, what do they have in common? In each case, the interpretations represent justifications—people who interpret the passage in such manners as to make them consistent with their other beliefs about God. Since God is the embodiment of good, he could not have lied to Abraham; thus he simply changed his mind or gave a vague command that Abraham misinterpreted. Using this rationale, since God is all-knowing, He already knew that Abraham would pass the test; therefore, it was not really a test so much as a learning experience for Abraham.

This assumes that the all-powerful God cannot shield Himself from certain aspects of the future. It is possible that God chose not to employ His omnipotence in this aspect of Abraham's life. Certainly an all-knowing God and an all-powerful God can look away from the future and concentrate on the present, if He desires. A crude, but effective way to think of this possibility is that God has the equivalent to billions of light switches. We ordinarily think of God as having them all placed in the "on" position, but this puts God in a man-made box—a box that limits Him. This is perhaps one of the most common of all human traits. This trait could also be a flaw. It ranges from atheists, who deny the existence of God to theologians, who parse biblical passages, looking for ambiguities to explain or to support their interpretations. Though their conscious motives are contrary, their results are similar. The former build fences to keep God out of their worlds, while the latter build boxes—sometimes extremely large boxes—to keep God inside. When we consider this perspective, the possibilities appear to be numerous, but limited in the context of the *akedah*. After all, the passage is so controversial that at some point it brings into question nearly every single theological question about the nature of God. As each of those passages raises questions, the easiest way to cope is to re-interpret the passage to justify our desired positions.

We conclude this chapter with the admission that we have quoted many box builders through this point. However, that was necessary to demonstrate reality concerning man's quest for understanding God and His relationship with Abraham, during a finite period. This lengthy exercise was essential to set the stage for our ultimate purpose—explicating the rhetoric of sacrifice that has grown and mutated from Abraham's binding of Isaac (or killing of Ishmael, according to Islamic tradition). Without the preceding chapters, we would have invited seductive counter arguments, which would have used one-sided interpretations of the personalities and verses that we have striven to present comprehensively and objectively.

We can judge Abraham as ultra obedient, immoral, or in numerous other ways, most of which are hybrids of the two. Regardless, we are very close to our purpose—understanding sacrifice and differentiating it from actions that result from the rhetoric of sacrifice.

Chapter 12
The Role of Faith

Perhaps the ultimate answer to the questions raised by the *akedah* comes from the role of faith. Faith can be used to explain both Abraham's behavior and our interpretations.

Even those who view the episode as a test often view it as a test of faith, not one of obedience (Keller, 1980). Trimiew (1999) called Abraham "The Bible's most outstanding example of faith" (p. 277). Earle (1963) noted that the reason Abraham is called the "father of the faith" is that "Abraham interpreted God's will as requiring the sacrifice of his son Isaac" and that he "then proceeded to carry out that will" (p. 74). Dershowitz (2000) concluded, "God receives Abraham's attitude of faith, his persistence in Him, as proving true, to the deep valley," as the decisive factor in judging the Patriarch (p. 47). MacArtney (1997) described the time on Mount Moriah as Abraham's "supreme hour" (p. 57), adding that "In this supreme moment of his life Abraham shows us what faith can accomplish, to how much it can submit" (p. 62).

Dimont (1962) wrote that "Without a firm conviction in his preordained role as the progenitor of the Chosen People, Abraham would have been a tragic figure. His faith makes him heroic" (p. 450). Similarly, Keller (1980) noted that Abraham's faith is the distinctive treatment of the *akedah*. MacArtney (1998) wrote that, when God called upon Abraham to sacrifice Isaac, "his faith did not waver" (p. 26). Armstrong (1996a) was less certain, but considered the possibility that "Perhaps he had such faith that he knew that God would intervene at the last moment, as, indeed, he did" (p. 68). MacArtney (1998) added that, "At that time, his faith did not waver, but he immediately began to obey God's command . . . . God honored his faith by sparing Isaac and providing a substitute sacrifice" (p. 26).

The emphasis here is a faith that has no room for doubt. As Davis (1999) wrote, "There is nothing that Abraham does in the story to suggest that he had any second thoughts about this divine request" (p. 77). Similarly, Trimiew (1999) noted that, "Abraham discovered that he was prepared to trust God absolutely" (p. 71). Gruen (1997) called it "an extreme demonstration of his faith" (p. 22).

Baldwin (1986) interpreted Abraham's statement that he and the lad "will come back" as a statement of faith. He added that the source of Abraham's faith came from God's promise in Genesis 21:12 that "through Isaac shall your descendants be named" (p. 90). Thus, as Colson and Dean (1972) noted, "The promise to Abraham is basic to all of God's dealing with the human race" (p. 50). Further, Abraham's faith was justified, for God honored his faithfulness by sparing Isaac's life. At this point, it is reasonable to ask, just what kind of faith did Abraham have? Was it simple faith in God? Could it have been faith in the Future? Perhaps, it was faith in God's promise. Could Abraham have carried out his inhumane task without possessing all of the foregoing types of faith?

Does faith in God mean to "trust" God? Martin Buber (1961) argued that the Bible talks about faith from two different perspectives. In the Old Testament, faith is viewed as trusting someone without being able to give sufficient reasons for the trust. In the New Testament, faith is viewed as acknowledging something to be true without sufficient reason. Buber (1961) contended that the first type of faith arose in the early period of Israel as the Israelites defined themselves as a community of faith. Thus he wrote, "all through the Old Testament to believe means to follow the will of God" (p. 22). Hall (2000) submitted that Abraham was convicted by and indebted to God. Grodis (1995) wrote that, "When the Torah says of Abraham he'emin, it means 'he put his trust in the Lord' (Genesis 15:6). Trust, relationship, feeling—and not proof—are what Judaism and Jews seek as they search for God on their spiritual journeys" (p. 55). Barclay (1977) summarized this view by saying, "faith is the certainty that God is indeed like that" (p. 68). Dershowitz (2000) explained the Jewish interpretation of this view in the following manner: "Fulfillment of the divine commandment is valid when it takes place in conformity with the full capacity of the person and from the whole intention of faith" (p. 56).

The second perspective arose in the early period of Christianity, following the death of Jesus (Buber, 1961, p. 9). New Testament faith, he added, is defined

> in a double aspect and in such a manner that its two aspects stand unconnected beside each other, the 'assurance of what is hoped for' and the 'conviction of things unseen.' Here in a remarkable way a Jewish and a Greek concept of faith are joined together. (p. 37)

Others have described these as "moral faith" and "empirical faith." At first glance, Abraham's faith would seem to be the epitome of Old Testament moral faith, i.e., that if God asked him to sacrifice his son, then sacrificing his son was the right and moral thing to do. However, Baldwin's interpretation of Abraham saying that both he and the lad "will come back" as an example of empirical faith, i.e., that God would not allow Isaac to die in the ritual. The problem, as Dershowitz (2000) noted, is that it's "not clear in which sense trust is used in the context of the akeidah [sic]" (p. 113). There are possible arguments from both perspectives.

MacArtney (1997) argued that Abraham faced a test of both empirical and moral faith. "When Abraham heard the voice of God, how did he know it was the voice of God? . . . If that sometimes troubles us, certainly that natural and free relationship ought to have been true at the beginning of man's history" (p. 58).

A common interpretation among Christian theologians is the possibility that Abraham had faith that God could raise Isaac from the dead. Baldwin (1986) for example, argued that Abraham had faith that God could raise Isaac from the dead (p. 90). Macarthur (1998) noted that such faith is particularly impressive because "While there is no mention in the Bible of Abraham observing any miracles, he was still convinced that God could raise Isaac from the dead" (p. 31). As Barclay (1977) said, "The essence of Abraham's faith . . . was that he believed that God could make the impossible possible" (p. 71). "There is no doubt in Abraham's mind—Isaac would be returning with him," Gibson (1999) wrote. "Abraham did not know what God would do, but he knew God would keep his promise that the covenant blessings would come through Isaac" (p. 178-179).

Others have noted that Abraham faith was not triggered by the command, but the command merely created a situation in which Abraham was able to express a faith that already existed. In other words, Abraham's faith preceded the event. In Genesis 15:6, for example, we find that Abraham "believed the Lord; and he reckoned it to him as righteousness." However, the *akedah* brought his faith to its fullest expression. As Baldwin (1986) wrote, "Already the testing has brought Abraham's faith to full expression, and having put that faith into words, he will expect to see the Lord uphold his testimony, and by some means bring the two of them back to their base" (pp. 90-91).

Faith as a relationship. The concepts of moral faith or empirical faith both base faith as a factor related to a specific belief. A third view of faith is that the operating principle in faith is not a belief, but a relationship. As Buber (1961) noted, "The relationship of trust depends upon a state of contact, a contact of my entire being with the one in whom I trust" (p. 8). If faith is viewed as a relationship between an individual and God, then that approach certainly describes the series of dialogues between Abraham and God. For some, faith is a vehicle for believing in God and trusting that He is watching out for you. For others—particularly Jews—faith provides a sense of connection to their history. Grodis (1995) argued that

> Abraham's and Elijah's models of building a relationship with God without waiting for philosophic or rational proof are important correctives to modern Jews . . . . Abraham's and Elijah's models urge modern Jews to set aside the quest for proof, and to begin the search for relationship. (p. 57)

Cahill (1998) also took a relational view of Abraham's faith. His argument is based on Abraham's cultural background. The Sumerians, who surrounded him, all believed in multiple gods. Abraham's transformation to a belief in one true God would have been gradual and the Patriarch would have retained some residual attitudes from his past. Thus, Cahill argued, "It is highly unlikely that [Abraham] became during the course of his life a strict monotheist, but what we can say is that [Abraham's] relationship to God became the matrix of his life, the great shaping experience" (p. 85).

Huxley (1957) argued that the relational view of faith is the central element of a true religious faith. "Religion . . . is a way of life," he wrote. "It is a way of life which follows necessarily from a man's holding certain things in reverence, from his feeling and believing them to be sacred" (p. 20). Kierkegaard (1968) agreed, arguing that one's faith in God is a perpetual relationship that must be addressed as a constant task. Rollo May (1992) argued that faith in God was not the same as "belief in the existence of God."

> The tendency to make that issue central—as though God were an object . . . whose existence can be proved or disproved as we prove or disprove a mathematical proposition or a scientific fact—shows our modern tendency to split up reality . . . . To make God an entity . . . to argue for the existence of God implies as much atheism as to argue against it. (p. 180)

Faith as Sacrifice. One approach to faith in the episode is to link faith with the act of sacrifice. Grodis (1995) wrote "Abraham's willingness to give up that which he loved most as service to God represents the ideal form of faith for which Jews can strive as they begin prayer each morning" (p. 87). Similarly, Levenson (1998) focused on the act of sacrifice as something that required both "radical obedience to the divine commandments" (p. 274) and "complete trust" (p. 268) in God. Armstrong (1993), though, questioned why sacrifice was the central element of the story.

> There was no reason for the sacrifice, no need to replenish the divine energy. Indeed, the sacrifice would make nonsense of Abraham's entire life, which had been based on the promise that he would be the father of a great nation. This god was already beginning to be conceived differently from most other deities in the ancient world. He did not share the human predicament; he did not require an input of energy from men and women. He was in a different league and could make whatever demands he chose. Abraham decided to trust his god. (p.18)

Kierkegaard's Philosophy of the Absurd

One of the most interesting analyses of the *akedah* was provided by European theologian and philosopher Soren Kierkegaard. Kierkegaard (1968) focused on Abraham's faith and argued that he suspended his own ethical principles in demonstrating his faith. He called this view of faith as the philosophy of the absurd. Faith is an answer to the absurd, for all of life is absurd (Hall, 1995). Thus, Edie (1963) wrote that "a Kierkegaardian view of human experience, of history, of thought, has been a perennial element in the religious experience of the world and that it has been attested to by persons of very diverse historical periods" (p. 14). Belief in God provides meaning to our absurd situation. "The absurdity of human order reveals . . . more than a problem: it reveals a mystery. The absurd cannot be conquered by reason; it can only be answered by faith" (Edie, 1963, p. 14). Earle (1963) concluded that "The religious life is inherently absurd both to the esthetic and the moral lives; it is beyond both, living not in pleasure or in the natural reason of morality but in faith" (pp. 73-74).

Armstrong (1993) provided the following contextual information:

> Today we tend to define faith as an intellectual assent to a creed, but, as we have seen, the biblical writers did not view faith in God as an abstract or metaphysical belief. When they praise the "faith" of Abraham, they are not commending his orthodoxy (the acceptance of a correct theological opinion about God) but his trust, in rather the same way as when we say that we have faith in a person or an ideal. In the Bible, Abraham is a man of faith because he trusts that God would make good his promises, even though they seem absurd. (p. 17)

Davis (1999) noted that part of the absurd is the "fear" of God mentioned in the passage. The Hebrew verb for 'fear' is used in two ways in the Bible. In addition to his traditional meaning of a state of being afraid of something, it was also used in the Bible to represent a psychological sense of experiencing awe or reverence for someone in an exalted position. However, Cahill (1998) argued that the "fear" of God mentioned in the text should be interpreted literally in the former sense. After all, the task he had been commanded to do was a fearful one. But Abraham passed the test anyway, because "His faith . . . is stronger than his fear" (p. 86). As Bonhoeffer (1963) argued, "Discipleship is not limited to what you can comprehend—it must transcend all comprehension . . . . Bewilderment is the true comprehension" (p. 103).

Part of Kierkegaard's (1968) interpretation focused on the sacrificial element. Kierkegaard was particularly impressed by Abraham's willingness to separate himself from his child. The willingness to accept the loss of the child, he argued, was more impressive than the way in which the loss would occur (the sacrifice). "The great thing was that he loved God so much that he was willing to sacrifice to Him the best" (p. 65). Kierkegaard subsequently interpreted the episode to mean that we do not belong to each other, but to our Creator.

Faith then emerges with two elements. First, each person is ultimately and individually accountable to God, and second, we only receive back our beloved as an undeserved gift from God. The first element was crucial. According to Kierkegaard (1968), faith made "made single individual . . . higher than the universal. Abraham represents faith [and] he acts on the strength of the absurd; for it is precisely the absurd that as a single individual he is higher than the universal" (p. 83). Because his faith was so strong, though, he also had empirical faith. "All along he had faith, he believed that God would not demand Isaac of him, while still he was willing to offer him if that was indeed what was demanded" (Kierkegaard, 1968, p. 65). Earle (1963) noted that "The faith in question is a trust in God 'for whom all things are possible': to take seriously such an Absolute Person is indeed to take lightly human reason and its morality. Faith 'suspends the ethical'" (p. 75).

Kierkegaard (1968) also questioned whether modern believers should have doubts about Abraham, noting that he lived in a different time and different culture. "Perhaps in the context of his times, what [Abraham] did was something quite different" (p. 60). "Where is the man with a soul so bewildered that he would have the presumption to weep for Abraham? . . . for how could Abraham do anything but what is great and glorious" (p. 65)?

Such statements trouble some critics. One of the most vocal is Alan Dershowitz (1988, 2000). Dershowitz (1988) rejected Kierkegaard's "context of the times" argument, saying that such an argument also invalidates the message of the story. If Abraham must be viewed in the context of his time, then Dershowitz argued, we must forget about him entirely because "why bother remembering a past that cannot be made into a present" (p. 113)? Dershowitz also argued that "Kierkegaard too is unclear whether he means faith that God would not require Abraham actually to sacrifice Isaac [empirical faith] or that if He did, it would be the right thing to do [moral faith]" (p. 113). Such an approach, he continued "turns Abraham's great test into a simple cost-benefit decision" (p. 107). The biggest criticism, though, is that Kierkegaard is sanctioning the killing of the child. As Dershowitz (2000) concluded, "Kierkegaard fails to provide a persuasive argument for why we should praise faith over parental responsibility" (pp. 113-114).

For Kierkegaard, though, faith is more than just the fulfillment of one task or the passing of one test. It remains, he argued, a perpetual task. Accordingly, it is our only task. Therefore, individuals constantly face faith issues.

Another essential component of Kierkegaard's (1998) view of faith is its relational nature. People stand before God as individuals, not as members of any group. As such, only individuals can stand before God based upon their singular relationship with God. Thus, in one sense, people can only become themselves in that relationship with God. As Earle (1963) noted, in Kierkegaard's view, God "is not a principle or law. Rather, He is an absolute person; the tensions of faith are those between a finite individual and an absolute individual" (p. 75). Kierkegaard's "Knight of Faith" is at peace internally—spiritually. "Outwardly he looks like everyone else, dressing, eating, doing his work like the rest of workaday mankind; inwardly, he has at last found freedom, is rid of despair and resignation; but his freedom in incommunicable and beyond reason" (p. 75).

Earle (1963) also argued that the focus of the faith in the story must be on the act of sacrifice, even if the act was never done. To emphasize his argument, Earle provided the following rationale:

> That it was not finally consummated is nothing to the point; the point is that Abraham was prepared to sacrifice his only son. We must try to understand him at this moment. And Kierkegaard finds quite simply that it is not understandable; to kill one's son is neither esthetic entertainment nor moral conduct. What moral law could ever tolerate such an act? Could there be a moral law that would even admit the possibility of such a "sacrifice" of another without branding it as frankly the most hideous murder conceivable? Yet it was for precisely this faith that Abraham was called the father of the faith. What are

we to make of it? Could any preacher advise the fathers in his flock to kill their sons whenever they heard such a thing from God? How did Abraham know it was God he heard and not the voice of Satan? It might even be more comprehensible if Abraham sacrificed himself, but it was his son; who is permitted to "sacrifice" another? Kierkegaard exhausts the possibilities of understanding the faith of Abraham, but it remains beyond comprehension. And yet that is what faith must be. To trust God is to abandon any ultimate trust in reason, common sense, prudence, moralities of principle, most of all, the detached excitements of the esthete. Faith to these other attitudes is pure madness; and yet, Kierkegaard urges, it is a madness which is the only sanity. (pp. 74-75)

The New Testament Interpretation

Buber (1961) claimed that the three critical elements of Christianity were (1) acknowledgment of Jesus' kingship, (2) Faithfulness to Jesus, and (3) faith in the Jesus. He further submitted "the conception includes the two aspects of reciprocity of permanence: the active, 'fidelity,' and the receptive 'trust.'" (p. 29). This approach implies both faith in the "miracle story" (p. 97) of Jesus and faith "in the resurrection of Christ" (p. 98).

"The difference between this 'It is true' and the other 'We believe and know' is not that of two expressions of faith, but of two kinds of faith," Buber (1961) wrote. "For the first, faith is a position in which one stands, for the second it is an event which has occurred to one, or an act which one has effected or effects, or rather both at once" (p. 35).

Galatians. In the New Testament, the person who most frequently interpreted the *akedah* for the followers of Christ was Paul (formerly known as Saul of Tarsus). Paul, raised as a conservative Jew, was quite familiar with the story of Abraham and Isaac. He also knew the traditional Jewish ways of interpreting the story. However, instead of focusing on the *akedah* as a test of Abraham, his interpretation emphasized Abraham as a man of faith. For example, he talked of faith and grace while using Abraham as an example (Galatians, 3:6-9). Colson and Dean (1972) called this passage "the gospel in preview" (p. 47).

As Colson and Dean (1972) noted, "The Jews naturally took great pride in the fact that they were children of Abraham" (p. 47). Knowing this, Paul used that belief as the premise of his argument for distinguishing between Christianity and conventional Jewish beliefs. His basic argument was that Abraham was justified by his willingness to obey God, not by his specific actions. Therefore, Abraham was justified by faith and not by his works. By extending the analogy, Paul then argued that the true children of Abraham are also justified by faith—faith in Jesus. Thus, "Abraham was . . . the father of the faithful, that is, of those who exercise faith in the promises of God" (Colson & Dean, 1972, p. 47). Thus Allan (1951) concluded, "God's gracious dealing with Abraham by way of promise and answering faith involved the principles of the Christian Gospel and was a real preliminary evangelical proclamation" (p. 60).

Since faith is the way to know God, Paul also concluded that God could be known by Gentiles, i.e., non-Jews. In Galatians 3:8 he argued that Gentiles as well as Jews may inherit the blessing promised to Abraham and his descendants.

Colson and Dean (1972) noted that "In the Epistle to the Galatians (3:6) he repeats first the reference to Abraham: all who have faith share in the blessing bestowed upon him, whereas the doers of the law 'stand under the curse'" (p. 48). Colson and Dean provided a contextual caveat, when they wrote, "The faith, which Paul indicates in his distinction between it and the law, is not one which could have been held in the pre-Christian era" (p. 51).

The Rhetorical Implications. As Colson and Dean (1972) noted, "the early Christian preachers proclaimed the gospel from the Old Testament . . . . In it they found the basis of all the great realities of the Christian faith" (p. 48). There are, however, critics of this view of faith. Dershowitz (2000) argued that Paul's interpretation of faith is a unidirectional, because in Paul's writings, he does not dwell on man's love for God. He added the thought-provoking possibility espoused by Spinoza, " for whom the love of man for God is in truth nothing but God's love for himself." (p. 136).

Further, Paul's emphasis on faith comes at the expense of obedience to the law. While this is acceptable to many Christian theologians, it creates problems for their Jewish counterparts. It also creates problems for some Christians, such as James, the half-brother of Jesus. As Dershowitz (2000) noted, Paul's reliance on faith at the expense of deeds de-emphasizes the need for believers to help others. "Here not merely the Old Testament belief and the living faith of post-Biblical Judaism are opposed to Paul, but also the Jesus of the Sermon on the Mount" (Dershowitz, 2000, p. 55).

James. A quick reading of the New Testament epistles of Paul and the Book of James, of the, indicate a theological distinction between the two. Paul's letters consistently focus on the importance of faith and the outdated nature of the Jewish Law as a means of attaining salvation. James, though, seems to see virtue in the good deeds that are inspired by obedience to God's laws. Not surprisingly, then, James' interpretation of the *akedah* differs from Paul's. James focuses on the deed as a symbol of faith, not the faith itself. "Was not Abraham our father justified by works, when he had offered Isaac his son upon the altar?" he wrote (James 2:21). Paul, though, directly disagrees. In the Book of Romans, he wrote:

> What shall we say then that Abraham our father, as pertaining to the flesh, hath found? For if Abraham were justified by works, he hath whereof to glory; but not before God. For what saith the scripture? Abraham believed God, and it was counted unto him for righteousness. (Rom. 4:1-3)

In an attempt to reconcile James' and Paul's divergent messages, MeGee (1991), maintained that the apparent contradictions in the passages are merely two views of the same concept. He offered resolution in the following manner:

James is talking about the works of faith, not the works of law. Paul is talking about justification before God, quoting the fifteenth chapter of Genesis, way back when Abraham was just getting under way in a walk of faith. (p. 67)

Romans. Are these two arguments really two sides of the same coin, or two divergent theological views by these early Christians? Barclay (1977) argued that Paul's goal in the Book or Romans (Romans 4:1-8) is to demonstrate that the key component in man's relationship with God "is not the performance of the works that the law lays down, but the simple trust of complete yieldedness which takes God at his word" (p. 62). In such an interpretation, Abraham makes for a good rhetorical example for he yielded totally to God's command in this story. Abraham, Barclay could argue, "is the father of those who made the same act of faith in God as he made" (p. 64). Thus Howard (1983) looked at this passage and said, "Abraham's true children, whether they were Jews or Gentiles, were those who had faith like Abraham's" (p. 83).

Abraham had more going for him than just this one incident though. Paul may not have had the advantage of stylistic scholars who attribute the *akedah* to a different author, but he had a full understanding of the earlier stories about Abraham and his faith. Scratch the sacrifice of Isaac from the Bible, and you still have the story of a man who had a unique relationship with God and who had demonstrated a supreme faith in God. As Barclay (1977) noted:

To Paul the essence of his greatness was this God had come to Abraham and bidden him leave home and friends and kindred and livelihood . . . . Thereupon Abraham had taken God at his word. He had not argued: he had not hesitated; he went out not knowing where he was to go (Hebrews 11:8). (p. 63)

Marks (1983) saw Abraham's "fear" of God as reflecting a New Testament theology, particularly Paul's writings in Romans 4. "Abraham's fear of God is revealed in his steadfast obedience, whether or not it results in his son's death. Isaac's deliverance neither invalidates Abraham's act nor serves as his reward for risking everything" (p. 88).

Ellen Gunderson Traylor's *Song of Abraham* (1988) is a novel designed as a biography of the Patriarch. She depicted Abraham as first sensing God's presence in the wind before he heard God's voice. She had God asking Abraham, "How much do you love me, Friend Abraham?" before proceeding to the instructions. She records Abraham's response as, "Have I not given all for You?" (p. 422-424). "He knew the answer," she added, "yet never had he dreamed he still withheld anything from his Master, nor would he have dreamed it important that he had" (p. 425).

Is such faith rational in modern society? Harpur (2001) believed so. Harpur could be described as a rational theologian. He raised questions about the concept of the Trinity and the Virgin birth, but he also argued that emotional components of religion are essential to a well-rounded religious experience. In essence, he argued that faith is intellectually valid—more so, even, than lack of faith.

Smith (1979) concluded that faith is an essential human quality. "It is an orientation of the personality, to oneself, to one's neighbor, to the universe . . . a capacity to live at a more than mundane level; to see, to feel, to act in terms of, a transcendent dimension" (p. 169). Later he added,

> At its best it has taken the form of serenity and courage and loyalty and service: a quiet confidence and joy which enable one to feel at home in the universe and to find meaning in the world and in one's own life. (p. 170)

Earle (1963) went even further. "If men have an eternal destiny," he wrote, ". . .then they have it as individuals as counted to God" (pp. 76-77). Dershowitz (2000) noted that Abraham:

> got brownie points for following God's command and he got his son back. But for the purpose of evaluating the morality of Abraham's actions, we should judge him as if he actually plunged the knife into Isaac's throat. Would that story have appeared in the Bible? (p. 115)

The problem raised by that question is that few modern believers may be capable of living up to the standard of faith established by Abraham. As MacArtney (1997) noted, "It is easier, of course, to talk about Abraham and to praise him than to emulate him, to do as Abraham did, to trust in God as he trusted God" (p. 62).

Wiersbe (1991) agreed: "Our faith is not really tested until God asks us to bear what seems unbearable, do what seems unreasonable, and expect what seems impossible" (pp. 109-110).

Still, there are those who disagree. As Burton Visotzky said, "I'm not sure I want to be involved with a God Who makes these kinds of demands on me . . . . I prefer to think that God demands a faith that calls for the intellect to be engaged rather than one that just says, 'Yes, Sir'" (quoted by Moyers, 1996, p. 231).

Chapter 13
Life after Death

One issue triggered by this story is that of personal views regarding life after death. Did Abraham believe in a life after death—in the possibility of a resurrection of Isaac? Some commentators believe so. Most others, though disagree, simply because there is no reference to the concept in the story. There is no documented evidence that Abraham had belief or perception in an afterlife as conceptualized by modern religions.

Why, then, should this be such an issue? There are two reasons. First, if the issue of life after death is added to the story, it changes some of the interpretations of Abraham's actions and of our interpretations of the story's intent. Dershowitz (2000), for example, argued that such an interpretation "turns Abraham's great test into a simple cost-benefit decision" (p. 107), while, if Abraham had no concept of an after-life, "the stakes were even higher" (p. 109). Second, the possibility of adding the life-after-death element is something that some scholars have still not resolved. Both Jewish and Christian theologians disagree among themselves about its role in the story.

Plato's View

As far as we can determine, the great Greek philosopher Plato should receive the credit for the paradigm shift toward belief in an immortal soul. The idea was a simple extension of his mind-body dichotomy, another concept for which he originated. Plato's philosophical universe was built around the existence of a universal ideal that was in constant juxtaposition to an inherently imperfect world. Using that premise, he was the first to argue that the mind and body were two distinct entities. The body, he argued, was part of the inherently limited world in which we live. Like all mortal things, it would someday die. He viewed the mind, however, as part of an eternal and idealistic part of the universe. He argued that while the body would die, the mind could not die because it was part of the ideal. It would, thus, live forever. In essence, he argued that one's soul was immortal (Hick, 1990).

Such ideas don't surface often in the Old Testament, but they are central components of many beliefs in the New Testament. While the Old Testament was largely written in Hebrew, the language of the New Testament is Greek.

New Testament writers would have been at least exposed to the teachings of Plato on this topic, especially the most educated writers, such as Paul. Thus Paul wrote in his Letter to the Romans, "With the mind I myself serve the law of God; but with the flesh the law of sin" (Romans 7:25), later adding, "For they that are after the flesh do mind the things of the flesh; but they that are after the Spirit the things of the spirit" (Romans 8:5) and "For if ye live after the flesh, ye shall die: but if ye through the Spirit do mortify the deeds of the body, ye shall live" (Romans 8:13). To the Corinthians, he is more direct about the ultimate end of the physical self. He admonished them that "flesh and blood cannot inherit the kingdom of God" (I Corinthians 15:50).

A similar idea, one that closely parallels Plato's thoughts, is found in the first epistle of John:

> Love not the world, neither the things that are in the world . . . . For all that is in the world, the lust of the flesh . . . and the pride of life, is not of the Father, but is of the world. And the world passeth away, and the lust thereof; but he that doeth the will of God abideth forever . . . . And this is the promise that he hath promised us, even eternal life. (I John 2:15-17, 25)

The Traditional Jewish View

Since Christian theology has a strong emphasis on the role of Heaven, some Christians are often surprised by the general disregard of this topic among many contemporary Jewish believers. It is tempting for the amateur to assume that the Jewish religion simply does not believe in an afterlife. This assumption may exist because the topic is rarely mentioned in Jewish theological discussions.

Such a conclusion would not be an accurate assessment of modern Jewish theologians. There is a role for the afterlife in Jewish theology—just not as much as Christians are used to hearing in typical Sunday-morning sermons.

While the views of the after-life differ from group to group, a trend is apparent among most groups. Generally, Jewish theologians view life-after-death as an unanswerable question. Since it cannot be answered, the question is rarely raised. Thus, most Jewish theologians do not disbelieve in an afterlife. Quite to the contrary, the concept of an afterlife is an assumption accepted by many Jewish theologians. However, they typically do not try to understand it. Since the topic is viewed as unanswerable, it follows that it is not something to be discussed and debated. This helps explain the dearth in modern Jewish dialogue and literature regarding a prevalent Christian subject.

That does not mean that the question of an afterlife is dismissed as unimportant. The issue is important. But why speculate, perhaps erroneously, on an important subject that is beyond the capabilities of humans to correctly comprehend? Thus, the general approach of many Jewish theologians could be summarized with this statement: *What happens to us after we die is God's business. What we do while we're here on Earth is our business.*

This thesis simultaneously accomplishes two purposes. First, it eliminates the topic of an afterlife as a theological issue. The afterlife is God's business—

not something that we can understand. Believers who have questions about the afterlife, they contend, must simply put their faith in God. God, in His goodness and judgment, will handle that matter as He sees fit.

Second, the latter part of the statement places the onus on individuals for accepting responsibility for their own lives. We can't control what happens after death, but we can control how we live our lives. That, according to the Jewish view, is our religious obligation—to live a life befitting our God. Ultimately, this sends the believer back to the center of most Jewish theological thought—to the Torah and obedience to the Law—God's Laws.

Thus, for this line of thought, the question of a life after death is an irrelevant question for the *akedah*. The theme of the *akedah*, they would argue, is not immortality but obedience. Any attempt to place the issue on the story distorts its meaning, transforming it into a simple "cost-benefit" decision as described by Dershowitz. (2000).

Alternative Jewish Views

Some Jewish theologians do address life-after-death as a theological issue. Weissman (1980, p. 205) argued that the only reason Abraham would have agreed to sacrifice Isaac would have been if believed in a world to come. Among those who believe the afterlife was crucial to Abraham's decision, some argue that Abraham completed the deed, i.e., that Isaac actually died on the altar, and was subsequently brought back to life (Ginzberg, 1938, p. 282). They point to verse 19 that clearly reports that only Abraham returned from the mountain as justification for this conclusion. These interpretations have been summarized by Spiegel (1993). Goldstein (1998) added that some 12th century commentaries believe that Abraham would have insisted on the sacrifice, even when God intervened, because of his desire to be faithful and obedient (pp. 20-21). Some Jewish sources mention that Isaac was cut and lost one-fourth of his blood during the partially completed ceremony (Spiegel, 1993, p. 47). If so, then Abraham may have indeed killed his own son. These sources suggest, though, that God subsequently resurrected Isaac from the dead.

Those whose conjectures run along this line also have questions about verse 13 and the meaning of the Hebrew word *abar*. The common interpretation of the term is "after." Thus the verse reads, "And behold a ram after." However, as Spiegel (1993) asked, "What is the meaning of 'after' (p. 60). Does it mean that the ram was spotted after everything else was done? Another possibility is that it could denote, "After Isaac was sacrificed?" One may argue with authority that the latter is not accurate. After all, the biblical story clearly states that Abraham sacrificed the ram "in place of" his son. Certainty proves to be evasive; however, as the interpretation is not as clear as one might image. For example, Spiegel noted, the Hebrew word that is interpreted as "in place of" is *tabat*, and that particular word has two different interpretations, depending upon whether its context within a sentence is a spatial reference or a temporal reference (pp. 60-61). Here it is commonly interpreted from the spatial perspective (i.e., "in place of"). In the temporal sense, though, it would be interpreted as "after," i.e., that Abraham sacrificed the ram *after* he sacrificed Isaac. Thus the dilemma. According to one possible translation of the text, Abraham might have actually killed Isaac as part of the ritual.

Isaac would have had to be subsequently resurrected to complete God's miracle, if he had actually been killed. After all, we know that Isaac went on to marry, have children, and live to an old age as part of God's promise. A lingering question resurfaces when we consider this topic—if Isaac was resurrected, why did he not come down from the mountain with Abraham? One familiar argument is that Isaac's resurrection occurred three days later.

Christians, of course, are quite familiar with the concept of a resurrection that occurred on the third day after the death of Jesus. According to Spiegel (1993, p. 110), though, a similar concept existed among many societies during the time of Abraham. Indeed, many pagan religions had a resurrection myth such as the Phoenix that died and arose from his own ashes. The Babylonian god Tammuz and the Egyptian Osiris both are the main character in legends in which they visit the land of the dead and return in three days (p. 112).

Why the consistency of the three-day post-death interval? Spiegel attributed that to the length of the mourning period in ancient societies. For three days after death, the face of the deceased is still recognizable. Thus Spiegel concluded, "that at least as early as the eighth century before the Christian era and the birth of Christianity, pagan conceptions of gods dying and returning to life in countless cycles of death and life were widely known among the people" (p. 113).

The problem with this entire analysis, though, is threefold. First, while the concept of life after death may have been common around the 8th century B.C., that is still several centuries after the time to which this story refers.

Second, even if such a concept existed earlier, there appears no direct reference to it in any of the stories of Abraham. As a theologian, Abraham appears to be oblivious to the concept of life after death. The closest that he can come to thinking about immortality is the idea of his seed being carried on for future generations. Keller (1980) noted that "Abraham laments the fact that he will die without a son" (p. 52). As Armstrong (1996a) observed, "In Genesis we find no belief in the afterlife on which many religious people today base their hopes. The only immortality a man or woman could expect lay in progeny" (p. 65). Dimont (1962) noted that it was God who proposed the covenant in which he promised to "make the descendants of Abraham His Chosen People and place them under His protection" (p. 31). However, nowhere in the covenant is there a mention of life after death, but merely the continuation of one's lines through children. This continuation of one's line was the early concept of immortality.

Some Christians disagree. They see the covenant as providing faith in a future life. Baldwin (1986), for example, argued that "Abraham sustained himself by counting on the Lord's statement, 'through Isaac shall your descendants be names' (21:12), believing 'that God was able to raise men even from the dead' (Heb. 11:19)" (p. 90). That attitude was also one of the biggest sources of stress in the story—the fear that the loss of Isaac will also entail the loss of promised seed. Simply put, the idea of life after death seems to be either an irrelevant concern or an idea that is beyond Abraham's conception.

Finally, if indeed Isaac was sacrificed and raised from the dead, why didn't Abraham ever tell that to someone? Granted, his neighbors might have considered him crazy for telling such a story, and Sarah would likely have been upset that he had actually killed his son. Surely, somewhere in subsequent Bible stories there would have been some reference to his miracle. At the very least, Isaac would have been expected to pass on the story to others, perhaps telling about his three days in Heaven. But no such tales are reported. The closest that Genesis comes to such a reference is at Abraham's death, when we are told he was "gathered to his people" (Gen. 25:8). At best, this can be interpreted as an indirect reference to his soul journeying to a place where his dead ancestors had already gone. In the final analysis, then, most theologians view this interpretation with skepticism. As Dershowitz (2000) concluded, "there is no textual support that the Patriarch believed in a world to come" (p. 107). The closest that scripture comes to acknowledging that Isaac may have died are from Jewish sources outside of the Bible. Armstrong (1993, p. 173) noted that some 13th century Jewish chants refer to God's power to restore the dead; these works identify the first recitation of those chants as coming from Isaac and the angels as Isaac lay bound on the altar.

Reincarnation

Reincarnation—the belief that we have all lived many lives before this one and will live others after we die—is a central component of the Hindu and Buddhist religions. As Hick (1990) noted, those religions assume "that we have all lived before and that the conditions of our present life are a direct consequence of our previous lives" (p. 132). In this view, our souls or essential selves move from life to life, being repeatedly reborn into different forms. Whether the next life is better or worse than the previous depends upon the quality of one's current life.

Jewish and Christian theologians have generally dismissed this idea, but there have been exceptions. When Jesus asked his disciples, "Who do people say that I am?," one suggested answer was that he was the reincarnation of a former prophet such as Elijah. Later, after Herod had John the Baptist beheaded, he feared that Jesus was the reincarnation of the prophet he had killed—perhaps returning to Earth to seek his revenge. Further, the Book of John implies that Jesus' soul was an immortal one that not only continued to live after his crucifixion, but also lived in Heaven before his birth. This idea comes from the opening of the Book, which tells us that "In the beginning was the Word, and the Word was with God, and the Word was God. The same was in the beginning with God" (John 1:1-2).

While we generally scoff at such ideas, modern science as added some substance to the idea. Genetic scientists have already demonstrated that there are a limited number of possible genetic variations for humans. While that limit is rather high, numbering in the billions, it still represents a finite number. Thus, the possibility of two people living at different times with the same DNA structure is not only possible, but also probable. The question remains, though, as to whether those two individuals would have the same soul. That is an entirely different question. Even identical twins, whose DNA structures are essentially identical, are still different people with different souls.

The problem, as Hick (1990) noted, concerns "the criteria by which someone living today is said to be the same person or self as someone who lived, say, 500 years ago of whom one has no knowledge or memory" (p. 133). Specifically, reincarnation assumes that the memory of the self should hypothetically follow the soul to the new body. Supporters of the theory tout any number of individuals who have memories of previous lives. The problem, though, is that 99 out of 100 people have no such memories. Further, the idea seems to have no relevance to the story of Abraham and Isaac. There is no reference anywhere in the story that indicates Abraham believed in reincarnation. All references in the Bible to reincarnation came well after the story.

The Christian Interpretation

Some Christian theologians point to a different verse as indicating Isaac's resurrection—Abraham's steadfast faith that Isaac would survive. Thus Gibson (1999) concluded, "Abraham had no doubt that he and Isaac would both return" (p. 178). Macarthur (1998) agreed, when he wrote, "While there is no mention in the Bible of Abraham observing any miracles, he was still convinced that God could raise Isaac from the dead" (p. 31). Granted, this requires an inferential leap. That verse does not say how Isaac would be returned (i.e., whether Abraham's faith was because he felt Isaac would never be killed or whether—just maybe—he believed that God would raise him from the dead after the ritual was completed). Gibson's conclusion: "Abraham did not know what God would do, but he knew God would keep his promise that the covenant blessings would come through Isaac" (p. 179). This appears to be plausible, as pure and unrestricted faith in God would not require Abraham to know the supernatural mechanism through which God would fulfill the covenant that included Isaac as a necessary character in future events. The most obvious function that Isaac had remaining was biological reproduction.

Others see a prophecy of an afterlife in the story. Typical of this view is McGee's (1991) contention that:

> It took Abraham three days to get there [Moriah], but remember that it was on the third day that Abraham received Isaac alive, back from the dead, as it were. That is the way that Abraham looked at it; Isaac was raised up to him the third day. (p. 75)

Based upon this assumption, McGee saw others elements in the *akedah* that are symbolic of Jesus and the Resurrection:

> We assume that Abraham, Isaac, Jacob and all the Old Testament worthies were great men but that they were not as smart as we are, that they did not know as much as we know. However, I am of the opinion that Abraham knew a great deal more about the coming of Christ and the gospel than you and I give him credit for. In fact, the Lord Jesus said, "Your father Abraham rejoiced to see my day; and he saw it, and was glad." (John 8:56). So he must have known a great deal more than we realize. God had revealed much to Abraham, but the Savior was not yet come . . . . but there on the top of Mount Moriah where Abraham offered Isaac was a picture of the offering and even of the resurrection of Christ! (p. 75)

Generally, the Christian view of death is that the body undergoes the "dust-to-dust" transition mentioned in Genesis 3:19, but that the spirit "returns to God who gave it" (Ecclesiastes 12:7). Thus, for Christian theologians, "death" is defined as "the separation of body and spirit" (Sailhamer, 1998, p. 88). In rare cases, the Bible reports incidences in which that spirit or soul returns to Earth. Some of the disciples saw Jesus speaking with Moses and Elijah (Mark 9:4) long after both of these men had died. Samuel returned to Earth to speak with Saul (I Samuel 28:11-19).

The crucial question is what happens to the spirits and souls (assuming they are ultimately divided) of people when their bodies die. Where do they exist when not making return trips to the living? The common Christian interpretation is that the soul is transported to Heaven, guided or taken there by angels. This view is cryptically mentioned in the parable of the rich man and Lazarus (Luke 16: 19-31, primarily verse 22). Christians' perceptions of Heaven differ greatly. One reason for this is that the Bible does not exhaustively describe Heaven. In addition, various Christian denomination or sects interpret scriptures differently regarding some of the attributes of Heaven. For instance, the King James Version of verse 22, Lazarus "died and was carried by the angles into Abraham's bosom." The remaining verses of the Chapter indicate that "Abraham's bosom" is a stage, phase, or part of Heaven. Without question, Heaven is very comfortable compared to hell, where in verse 24, the rich man's soul is located when he said "for I am tormented in this flame"

Heaven's existence appears to be a common element of most Christian theologies. Further, most Christian views of Heaven identify it as the beginning of either the resurrection of the soul and/or the key to a wonderful eternal life with benefits and blessings that are perhaps too foreign to human to conceptualize. That eternal life is one in which the soul is freed from death— exemplified by the eternal death type of misery that unbelievers like the rich man in the above-referenced verses in the Book of Luke. In Heaven, believers perpetually co-exist in fellowship with God. As Sailhamer (1998) wrote, "The purpose of the resurrection and transformation of the righteous will be to make them fit to dwell with Christ forever" (p. 90). Explanations regarding how that occurs vary, depending upon the beliefs of the individual or of particular churches. Some believe that eternal life with God begins at the point of death. Others believe it is on hold until a future judgment day that is ushered in by the second return of Christ. Even others, based upon their reading of the Book of Revelations 20:4-5, believe there will be a 1,000-year span of time between the return of Christ and the beginning of eternal life. Knowledge regarding the existence of various schools of thought regarding maps to and schedules of when souls arrive in Heaven will be useful to readers. Unfortunately, further analyses of these interesting intra-Christian interpretations are beyond the scope of this book. What is most important, though, is the common belief among most Christians that there is an eternal life after death. Furthermore, the nature of one's existence in that future eternal life is dependent upon one's religious decisions here on Earth.

After learning the foregoing, we can safely proceed from this point by understanding the following concerning Christian beliefs in eternal life. Those who are believers in Christ will be saved from eternal damnation and rewarded with eternal life in Heaven. Those who have rejected Jesus as the Christ will face the eternal damnation of existing—suffering—in Hell.

The Christian View as Rhetorical Critique

The philosopher Pascal was among the first to analyze Christian theology from the cost-benefit approach mentioned by Dershowitz. In Pascal's thinking, any logical person would have to be a Christian. It simply did not make sense to do otherwise. The thought process is elementary. Christians believe that they will go to Heaven after they die, while non-believers will be eternally condemned to Hell. Given such a radical dichotomy of consequences, Pascal argued that the only sensible thing to do would be to become a Christian. If you were right, you would spend eternity in Heaven. If you were wrong, and the Christian theology was wrong about the existence of Hell, then you had still lived an ethical life. You lose nothing by becoming a Christian and have a potential Heavenly reward waiting for you. You risk Hell if you don't believe, with no concomitant long-term reward if you happen to be right.

Logically, a Pascal-type thesis provides a powerful argument—one that has been used by thousands of preachers over the past few centuries. Its extensive presence among the sermons of modern preachers attests to its effectiveness as a rhetorical argument. Still, many preachers may have used the threat of Hell as a religious argument for so long that they may have overlooked the ethical implications of the argument.

Realistically, have preachers really accomplished anything when they convince people to join the church to save their souls? Given the cost-benefit analysis offered by Pascal, are such a converts a true believers? It could be argued that they joined the church for the most selfish of all reasons—fear for their own eternal lives. In laymen's terms, such converts are essentially hedging their long-term bets.

However, many would contend that such converts would place themselves in environments—congregations—where their once-flawed decision grows into a true belief in God and Christ as the way to salvation. Many seasoned Christians could tell of their spiritual journeys from fledgling converts, with little understanding of Christian growth, to maturing spiritual beings with relationships with Christ. Such cases may be rare, as evangelists and even pastors of Christian churches would admit that the after-conversion nurturing environment that encourages post-conversion growth is the exception rather than the rule.

This type of failure to guide new converts from thinking like Pascal to thinking and acting like Jesus could be a cultural phenomenon. In the United States, we tend to be interested in measurable results—especially in business environments. Evangelists often tell of the numbers of people who were saved at their revivals or events. Pastors of many denominations are expected to show growth in membership lists, among other quantitative information regarding their tenures at churches. Churches with 1,000 or more members are common. Generally, such large churches are run by boards of trustees, elders, deacons, or the like, who step out of their spiritual roles as Christians and into their secular roles as business leaders when they meet regarding church matters. The secularization of aspects of Christian churches may manifest in new converts being looked at as customers—the sale has been closed. Other than contribute money, there may be little that they can do for the church quantitatively. It would be up to such new Christian converts to seek whatever is needed to grow out of a Pascal mentality and into a maturing Christian mentality and life.

As a result of these types of "Christians" in the United States, a rhetoric of sacrifice is often developed and utilized by Christian church leadership boards and pastors. This is especially true when building projects have been adopted and when downward trends in monetary contributions are detected.

There are actually companies that perform only one function—devising and assisting in campaigns to obtain large amounts of money for churches. These companies epitomize Christian churches willingness to use the rhetoric of sacrifice. While churches may not link making monetary contributions directly to salvation, the implication exists. Some preachers have gone so far as to state from the pulpit that Christians who do not give at least 10 percent of their incomes to their churches are "stealing from God." Reluctantly giving 10 percent of members' incomes to their churches after motivating—sometimes threatening—sermons and professional campaigns strongly supports the utilization of the cost-benefit analysis. It also provides a literal example to the cost-benefit approach to Christianity. The rhetoric of sacrifice that is sometimes used sometimes resembles extortion.

SECTION IV

CONCLUSIONS

Chapter 14
The Impact

William James, the father of modern pragmatism, argued that the meaning of any event could be determined by its impact. If so, then what rhetorical impact did Abraham's deed have on its participants and on mankind? The immediate results were three-fold—the creation of a new people, the end of a personal relationship, and the apparent destruction of a family. The long-term rhetorical impact has been even more dramatic. The story has become an integral part of the rhetoric in three great religions. The discrepancies and theological contradictions of the story are one reason that the story is so appealing. Some of the discrepancies can be easily dismissed. After all, two different narrators contributed to the story. Some of the discrepancies, such as the disappearance of Isaac in the final verses, may have simply been editing choices or errors that crept into the manuscript as the final editor tried to put the entire story in context. The same reasoning would imply that other elements of the story were lost to history, forgotten, and omitted at unknown points as the story passed to subsequent generations through the oral history of the region. The story does not pretend to provide the comprehensive post-covenant history of the lives of Abraham, Sarah, Ishmael, Isaac, and Hagar. To understand it thoroughly, we must utilize knowledge of the culture, use previously and subsequently provided biblical information, and not ignore human nature—we must read between the lines—without taking advantage of the liberties that it allows. Even after using such methods, our explanations account for only a few of the many questions raised by the story. Some believers may see those discrepancies and questions as minor items that were perhaps consciously omitted by the writers. We must remember that recording matters in writing was difficult and costly for thousands of years after Abraham lived. Brevity was not just a general goal or a characteristic of good writing, as it is today. It was essential and probably affected most, if not all, Old Testament stories.

For others, though, the discrepancies and apparent contradictions constitute an important rhetorical statement about the simplicity of faith and the complexity of religious belief. To reconcile both goals in a single story is indeed a remarkable rhetorical and theological achievement. The story is simultaneously engaging and repulsive—a dramatic story of faith and obedience with a vicious and unpleasant plot. Its theme triggers discussions and debates on complex theological and philosophical issues. Meanwhile, adherents interpret and rationalize elements of the story as justifications for their own beliefs and arguments that are used to address others. Believers, particularly those who do not dwell on theological implications, find in it a multitude of messages that are supportive of beliefs that are inherent within their views of God and religion. In doing so, though, they often overlook the immediate impact that the story had on Abraham, his family, and the Jewish nation.

The Immediate Impact

The Covenant

The meaning of the word "covenant" in the Bible may be apparent from the context. Although this is true, a brief explanation of the term's general meaning may be useful to some readers. Most readers of this book have been a party to some type of covenant. Sometimes the word covenant is used as an equivalent term for "contract." Leases and deeds are covenants, in and of themselves. Leases and deeds typically contain covenants, especially the latter. Deeds often contain covenants against encumbrances. This merely means that sellers of real property guarantee buyers that the sellers hold full and complete packages of rights concerning the real estate (i.e., that there are no unpaid mortgages, liens, or other types of current claims by third parties regarding the property). A contract is an agreement, so it follows that a covenant is a contract. There is nothing uncommon about contracts, which are covenants, having clauses that are referred to as "covenants." This is just a way of documenting all of the terms of an agreement. Some contemporary contracts and covenants must be in writing to be legally enforceable. This was not the case when God and Abraham's covenant was formed. Although much more could be written about the meaning of "covenant," this is essentially all of the information that readers might need to resolve any questions about the meaning of related terms when they are used later in this book.

We should not underestimate Abraham's achievements for mankind. As Kirsch (1998) wrote, "The whole of Jewish history might have turned out differently . . . if Abraham had just said, 'No'" (p. 176). Indeed, as Barclay (1977) noted, Abraham was the founder of the Jewish people "and the pattern of all that a man should be" (p. 62).

Kelley (1977, p. 92-93) noted that the Hebrew word for covenant, *berith*, meant "bond" or "fetter" and referred to a contract or treaty between individuals or parties. It is a popular concept in the Old Testament, appearing a total of 286 times (Kelley, p. 92). Some of those references were to covenants between individuals, such as the agreement between David and Jonathan that is recorded in the book of I Samuel (18:1-4). Others were national treaties, such as the one between the Israelites and the Gideonites, which is recorded in the ninth chapter of the Old Testament Book of Joshua.

The term typically used for "making a covenant" is literally translated as "cutting a covenant" (or, in modern terminology, "cutting a deal"), a phrase that could be associated with making a blood sacrifice. If so, the *akedah* would be a final sacrificial ritual that would have sealed the covenant. Of course, in Abraham's instance, it could also be a reference to the ritual of circumcision, with Abraham cutting the skin from his own penis and those of his children. Kelley (1977) believed the "cutting" terms had a different reference.

> The term apparently arose from the custom of slaying a sacrificial animal, cutting it into pieces, arranging the pieces in two parallel rows, and requiring those entering into the covenant to pass between the two rows (see Gen. 15:9-21; Jer. 34:18-20). This arrangement seems to have been symbolic; if either party should break the covenant or fail to fulfill its obligations, he would suffer a fate similar to that of the sacrificial animal. (p.93)

Kelley (1977) also distinguished between two types of covenants—parity covenants and vassal (or ruler) covenants. Parity covenants were those agreements established between equals; they imposed mutual obligations on each party to the agreement. The contract between God and Abraham, though, was more similar to a vassal covenant—contracts between parties of unequal status. The inequality in status could affect the obligations of each party. The ruler was typically expected to provide protection to the subjects, while the vassals were expected to justify that protection with their portion of the agreement. The subject's obligation in such an arrangement was represented by the Hebrew word *hesed*. As Kelley noted, this term is "a word which cannot be translated adequately by any single word in English. It combines the ideas of love, loyalty, and ready response to need" (p. 93).

God's covenant with Abraham falls within this second type of biblical covenant. God, as the ruler of Earth, promised to watch over Abraham's people. In return, Abraham was expected to provide *hesed*—love, loyalty, and a willingness to obey. Cahill (1998) noted that God wanted a covenant with Abraham "just as chieftains covenant with one another" (p. 71). "To us this covenant may appear barbaric," Cahill added. "But within the rigid simplicities of Canaan and Mesopotamia, this 'covenant in your flesh,' this permanent reminder, makes perfect sense" (p. 72).

One somewhat surprising aspect of this covenant is that the idea for it originates with God. As Dimont (1962) wrote:

> It is God who proposes a covenant to the Patriarch . . . . If Abraham will follow the commandments of God, then He, in His turn will make the descendants of Abraham His Chosen People and place them under His protection. (p. 31)

The interesting aspect of this, from the viewpoint of a vassal contract, is that the ruler made the first step toward reaching the agreement. Typically, in most negotiation interactions, the weaker party is the one who must first approach the other party about an agreement. The party in the weakest position is, after all, the one most in need of a treaty. Here, though, the Almighty God makes the first step.

God's covenant with Abraham was His second agreement with a human being. His first covenant was made with Noah (Gen. 6:18; 9:8-17). In that instance, God's covenant was a unilateral promise that he would not destroy the world by water again. When the agreement was reached, Noah had to do nothing to fulfill his part of the contract. Instead, God counted his obedience in building the ark as meeting the requirements of *hesed*. Noah had believed God, was loyal to his instructions, and was ready to take on a strange task at the request of his God.

Fromm (1966) argued that Abraham's commitment to the covenant required a sense of obedience from the beginning that was unusual for the Mid-Eastern culture in which he lived. "Abraham is told by God to cut the ties with his father's house, to leave it, and to go into a country which God will show him" (p. 58). Later, Fromm (1966) added:

> There is a peculiar parallel to God's ordering Abraham to leave his father's house, and that is God's order to sacrifice Isaac. This command is interpreted as implying a test of Abraham's obedience, or an attempt to show, though indirectly, that God does not approve of the heathen ritual of child sacrifice. While these interpretations are probably correct, the text suggests still another: namely, the command to cut the ties of blood to the son . . . . The command to sacrifice Isaac (Gen. 22:2-3) parallels the former command. The command to sacrifice Isaac, then, would mean man must be completely free from all ties of blood—not only with father and mother, but also with his most beloved son. But "free" does not mean that man does not love his family; it means that he is not "tied" in the sense of incestuous fixation. (p. 72)

Marks (1983) agreed, noting that Abraham had to cut himself off from his entire past when he left his father's family. The *akedah* intensified the separation by asking Abraham to surrender his future.

The level of devotion required by God is also high. As Feiler (2001) concluded, "If nothing else, God . . . seems to want the process of inheritance to involve testing and perseverance. God insists on testing the Patriarchs, but he requires something akin to total devotion in return" (pp. 90-91). Feiler added that the *akedah* provides a model for God's view of the vassal covenant.

> Just as God is the father figure who requires the total submission of this favored son Abraham, so Abraham is the father figure who requires the same from his favored son Isaac . . . . The biblical story thus becomes a perfect looking glass: Look at it from Isaac's point of view, and one soon sees Abraham's point of view, and one soon sees God's point of view, for both are fathers in the story. This may be the story's greatest gift. Abraham, by binding his son on God's orders, binds himself forever to God. Both are creators who almost destroy. (p. 91)

As several commentators have noticed, though, God's covenant is not one of total reassurance. Dimont (1962) noted that when God promised Abraham that his seed would multiply and spread across the land, he did not say that their lives "shall be better—merely that they shall exist as a separate and distinct entity and be His people" (p. 31). Fox (1995) aptly concluded that after the events on Mount Moriah,

> We can breathe easier, knowing that God will come to the rescue of his chosen ones in the direst of circumstances. At the same time we are left to ponder the difficulties of being a chosen one, subject to such an incredible test. . . . [Further] . . . we know that the fulfillment of the divine promise is assured. Yet there is an ominous note: love, which occurs here by name for the first time, leads almost to heartbreak. (p. 92)

Riskin (1997, p. 17) agreed, and noted that the *akedah* was God's way of warning Abraham that the covenant might require God's people to make sacrifices in the future. Dershowitz (2000) summarized this position by arguing that the *akedah* made it clear to Abraham and other Jews that having a covenant with God did not mean "life would be perfect" for them (p.126).

The End of a Relationship

Despite the various points of contention discussed previously, we can at least agree that Abraham's actions did not breach the covenant with God. While Abraham's performance, whatever precise chain of events it actually consisted of, sealed the covenant with God, it also apparently ended his close interpersonal relationship with God. True, Abraham's faith probably remained strong. Further, his devotion, dedication and worship of God surely continued. Nevertheless, he lost the opportunity to speak with God on an interpersonal basis.

Believers may counter that Abraham could always pray to God, any time he wanted to do so. That is true, but God would never again answer in the same manner as he had in the past. As Armstrong (1996a) noted, after Abraham departed from Moriah, "God never speaks to Abraham again" (p. 69). The decision appears to be God's—not Abraham's. It is God who chooses to withdraw his communication from Abraham.

Why did God remain silent? Three explanations have been presented. The first is that there was no need for further communication. Abraham had passed the final test, the covenant would be honored, and a new nation of monotheists would be developed. With man's religious destiny set, there was no further need for God to have one-on-one conversations with his human protégé.

The second possibility is that God was disappointed with Abraham. In this view, Abraham failed the test of morality, although he passed the test of obedience. Dershowitz (2000) supported this possibility when he wrote:

> Abraham's special status as a covenantal partner is a double-edged sword: It gives him special rights in relation to God (he may argue with Him), but it also imposes extraordinary obligations in relation to God—he may not refuse a

direct, individualized order from God, even if it is in conflict with God's general rules for the rest of humankind. (p. 211)

Did Abraham meet God's expectations? It is quite possible that he did not. Abraham was rewarded with riches, which were different from but not novel to him. He was a wealthy man before the binding of Isaac. He continued an already long life, but was this actually a blessing when we consider his exalted place in the afterlife? Abraham was given a new wife, and more children, but were any like the son he "loved" and bound? His earthly blessings were limited, as he was not made the ruler of many nations. He did not have Isaac around. Reasonable men, in his place, would have longed to explain his actions and repair his relationship with Isaac. Thus, God may have praised Abraham for his obedience, while being disappointed with the Patriarch in some ways. After such a disappointment, perhaps God could not face Abraham again. However, when we consider that for a period after death, many Christians believe that their souls rest in the bosom of Abraham, it could be argued that his ultimate reward came after he died. Being rewarded after death for living a Godly life is a concept that is not foreign to any of the three great religions that revere Abraham. We can only hypothesize about whether Abraham's actions during his test fully satisfied God. However, we can be sure that Abraham's behavior did not invoke the wrath of God.

The final suggested explanation is that God was disappointed in Himself. This approach posits that God's personality, when He dealt with Abraham, was the result of a developmental process—one that was still in its formative stages at that time. For example, Fromm (1966) noted that, "There is a growth and evolution in the concept of God that accompanies the growth and evolution of a nation" (p. 21). When God created the world, His first experiences with humans were with the creation of Adam and Eve. Since He created these new creatures with free will, he could hardly be sure what they would do or how He would react to their unusual behavior. The rest of the chapter of Genesis becomes, from this perspective, a series of trials in which God learns about humans while learning more about His reaction to them. In this perspective, then, what God learned was not particularly pleasant. He could have regretted what He had asked Abraham to do, and thus was ashamed to face him again. After all, God does not even deliver Isaac's pardon in person, and instead uses an angel to deliver the message. In fact, the last time that God spoke to Abraham directly was when he gave the command to make the sacrifice. All subsequent conversations on the topic are between Abraham and Isaac, Abraham and his servants, or Abraham and the angel. God chooses not to speak to Abraham even at the moment of delivery.

The Destruction of a Family

Abraham never had much of a reputation as a family man, nor did many of his descendants in the generations that followed. As Armstrong (1996a) wrote, "the Patriarchs were not family men. Whatever their other achievements, their domestic lives left much to be desired" (p. 62). Further, what little family life Abraham might have enjoyed in the past was shattered by the *akedah*.

Traditional interpretations of the *akedah* focus on its transcendent meanings, not its practical consequences for the participants. As Kirsch (1998) noted:

> The terror visited upon Abraham, Sarah, and Isaac by the Almighty during the ordeal—and the prospect of what would have happened to Isaac if his father had failed the "test of faith" by refusing to slay his son—is mostly ignored in the more pious readings of the Binding of Isaac. (p. 176)

Indeed, the *akedah* may have created a nation, but it practically destroyed a family. None of the principals—Abraham, Isaac, or Sarah—appeared to recover fully from the ordeal. Abraham, as noted, lost his ability to commune directly with God, but the psychological damage to Sarah and Isaac may have been, at least in earthly terms, even worse. Armstrong thus concluded that the entire incident "dealt a mortal blow to God's chosen family" (p. 71).

Sarah died soon after the story is completed. Some Jewish traditions believe that she died of grief and stress when she realized that her husband had been ready to kill their only son (Ginzberg, 1938, p. 286). After all, Sarah would not have had the reassurance that this command came from God; apparently, Abraham had not shared the promise of the covenant with her (Cahill, 1998, p. 75). As Armstrong (1996a) noted, "In the very next chapter we read of Sarah's death. It is almost as though the shock killed her" (p. 71). Not surprisingly, then, Abraham and Sarah were apparently living apart at the time of her death. Abraham was living in Beersheba, while Sarah died in Hebron. Abraham had to travel there for the funeral, buying his first piece of property in Canaan so that she would have a secure tomb. Abraham was blessed with more children, but only because he married again. His new wife, Keturah, came from the Midianites (Gen. 25:2-6) and presented him with six children. Abraham, though, seemed upset by their arrival. As Armstrong (1996a) noted:

> This time Abraham did not need God to tell him what to do. With his customary ruthlessness, he sent all his sons away, lest they jeopardize the position of Isaac, the son of the Promise. They were all dispatched far from the divine presence, to the godless realm of the east (25:6). (p. 69)

Isaac remained to carry on the family seed, but he apparently had a miserable life. Armstrong (1996a) called him "The primary casualty of Mount Moriah" (p. 70). Abraham never speaks to him again (Grodis, 1995, p. 88). Armstrong (1996a) observed the following:

> After Mount Moriah, it was impossible for father and son to have any kind of normal relationship. We are told that Isaac grieved for his mother long after her death (24:67), but, though he dutifully buried his father when the time came, we are given no clue about his feelings for Abraham. Isaac did not die

physically on Mount Moriah, but in some deeper sense his life came to an end there. (p. 72)

Indeed, the details of Isaac's life are withheld from most of the remainder of the story. Armstrong (1996a), for example, noted that Isaac's life after the binding is "a blank" (p. 71). His disappearance from much of the Bible has prompted many observers to conclude that he suffered severe psychological damage because of the experience. Dershowitz (2000), for example, viewed Isaac, after the binding by his father, as "a shattered person, who rarely speaks until his deathbed" (p. 124). Armstrong (1996a) observed that "There are virtually no stories about Isaac in his prime: one of these is simply another version of the tale of Abraham and Pharaoh and may have been included by the editors at this point because of a dearth of Isaac material" (p. 70). "God may have eventually saved Isaac *physically*," Dershowitz added, "but He crippled him emotionally" (p. 125).

In retrospect, such an effect is not surprising. After all, "How can you cope with the fact that your father was prepared to kill you in cold blood?" (Armstrong, 1996a, p. 70) asked. Modern psychologists are aware that the impact of the Vietnam War on American soldiers taught us the long-lasting effects that post traumatic stress disorder can trigger. In fact, Post traumatic stress disorder can manifest after any unexpected and potentially fatal experience. Once PTSD occurs, it may disturb one for a lifetime. Few people have faced the psychological trauma that Isaac faced—bound and stretched out on an altar with his father poised to slit his throat with a knife. Armstrong wrote that, "Freud spoke of the murderous rage that some parents feel toward their offspring. Isaac was one of those damaged children who have experienced this parental hostility to the full" (p. 71). Perhaps, as Armstrong added, "It is . . . not surprising that he called God 'the Fear' (31:42, 53)" (p. 71).

For whatever reason—whether Isaac suffered from a shattered personality or endured a mental defect from birth—God seems to ignore the Patriarch of the Hebrews' second generation. Armstrong explained the miniscule amount of specific information in the Bible about Isaac after he was bound.

> God did not relate easily to Isaac, who seemed to live in ignorance of his intentions. Instead, God chose to communicate with a woman in the generation after Abraham. Rebekah, Isaac's wife and the most powerful of the matriarchs of Israel. (Armstrong, 1996a, p. 73)

We have documented the worldly impact of the *akedah* on the principal characters, but we cannot reveal the eternal and heavenly impact of this captivating story. However, we have provided ample evidence to provide readers with the impact of sacrifice. The history of the world has been profoundly affected by the ideal of sacrifice. In many cases, the three great religions that arose from Abraham have used and abused the construct of sacrifice for worldly reasons, while clothing it in pious rhetoric. True sacrifice and the rhetoric of sacrifice often conflict. In fact, in the following chapter, we will attempt to explain how true sacrifice has been adulterated, yielding the rhetoric of sacrifice and its problematic illicit offspring.

Chapter 15
The Rhetoric of Sacrifice

The title of this chapter could be misleading. However, it will deal with many aspects of rhetoric that have been and are used to motivate others to sacrifice themselves and/or others. Perhaps most importantly, this chapter will describe the use of the rhetoric of sacrifice in the 21st Century. The construct of sacrifice is broad, as many acts and omissions qualify as sacrifices. The rhetoric of sacrifice is designed to result in people, other than the rhetor (who induces the sacrifice) to willingly give, or surrender tangible and intangible matter of extremely diverse value. Sometimes this type of sacrifice may be characterized as martyrdom.

The rhetoric that motivates the most disturbing types of sacrifices— suicides, murders, and mass murders committed in the name of sacrifice, a purported supreme being, or ideal that is claimed to call for sacrifice. Contemporary instances of human sacrifices—murders—differ from what we simply have referred to as "sacrifice" in two poignant ways. In the case of human sacrifice, something is given that does not belong to the giver—a life or lives of one or more fellow human beings. This disturbing type of sacrifice is akin to a Robin Hood-type rationale. The sacrifice amounts to a theft of life from the perceived undeserving people and essentially presenting the shocking results to the rhetor of sacrifice, who is believed to be worthy of perverted reward (e.g., a representative of a god, etc.). The fact that many deadly results of the rhetoric of sacrifice today are shocking and available almost immediately through videotape footage, satellite links, or other new technologies provide maximum value, as such atrocities are more likely to receive free wide-scale publicity via news coverage. Secondly, human sacrifices through mass-murders are often coupled with suicides. Neither would occur, nor would either be considered anything other than criminal behavior if they were not inspired by the rhetoric of sacrifice. This factor adds impact on some or all of the audience, drama, the unusual occurrence, conflict, and currency (i.e., it is topical) as news values, making the stories extremely newsworthy.

Murders in the name of sacrifice, regardless of whether suicide is involved, are often presented as idealistic or tests of obedience, but they are actually functional in nature. They empower rhetors of sacrifice, and they convey strong messages to both internal and external audiences. Power and fear are two common functions of communications delivered by news coverage of modern human sacrifices to the two audiences, respectively. Hence, the stage has been set for deadly acts of terrorism, clothed as the obedient performances of sacrifices. Sacrifices that require murder or suicide coupled with murder are capable of delivering double dividends. With each deadly attack, an agenda-setting function is achieved, without which great power would not be perceived by the rhetors of sacrifice, and widespread fear would not grip their enemies.

Sacrifice and Martyrdom

The rhetoric of sacrifice often precedes sacrifices or acts of martyrdom. However, when the rhetoric of sacrifice is used to procure them, there is often an agenda that encourages the sacrificing of others human beings. At the least, the rhetoric of sacrifice usually seeks to impose pain, suffering, and/or death on third parties. Sacrifice and martyrdom, in their consummate and purist forms, require little, if any, motivating rhetoric.

No burning of politicians in effigy, no burning of nations' flags, no incendiary speeches by politicians, or use of religious positions to gain political power are necessary to convince one not to buy products made in certain other countries or to fill one's car with explosives and drive it into a group from another sect, religion, or nation. However, such hate speech in the form of the rhetoric of sacrifice should increase the chances of a corrupted sacrificial act.

Perhaps the most effective tool to convince another to sacrifice is the trading of something desired for the sacrifice—the promise of a quid pro quo for acts of sacrifice and perhaps martyrdom converts them into an intangible genre that can only be understood by closely examining the rhetoric of sacrifice. The following diagram differentiates three key terms—sacrifice, martyrdom, and the rhetoric of sacrifice. Essentially, it reveals that almost all sacrifices made with no expectation of a quid pro quo need no rhetorical prompting, although some sacrifices may require a spiritual or secular request. Further, it shows that few acts of martyrdom are motivated by the rhetoric of sacrifice, although that possibility exists. The rhetoric of sacrifice is particularly well suited for manipulation and exploitation—two possibilities that are not philosophically inconsistent with compulsion, intimidation, destruction, violence, suffering,, and human sacrifice.

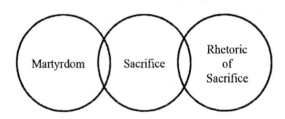

Sacrifice

Sacrifice could be thought of as institutionalized in some cases. Although no English translation can present the impressive prose of the Koran, Islam scholars have provided the world with much of the substance of the Koran. For example, during the month of Ramadan, which is the ninth month of the Muslim year, believers fast by not eating, drinking, or engaging in any sexual act during the daylight hours. This type of sacrifice is set forth in the Koran. It could be thought of as a Thanksgiving sacrifice, as the 27th day of Ramadan marks the time when the "gates of Paradise are open, the gates of Hell shut and the devils in chains" (The World's Great Religions, 1957, p. 114).

The Koran emphasizes submission. To be truly submissive, Muslims must sacrifice regularly in many ways. For instance, Muslims are directed to face Mecca on their prayer rugs and pray five times per day. This requirement, alone, is a sacrifice in today's frantic Western culture and certainly in other parts of the world also. Muslims also contribute (i.e., almsgiving—monetarily or perhaps otherwise) to Allah. Pursuant to the Koran, Muslims are also directed not to gamble, eat pork, or practice usury (The World's Great Religions, 1957). These are just some of the Islamic practices that could be considered as sacrifices—things that they do regularly or refrain from doing, in a spirit of submission.

Certainly, Christians and members of the Jewish faith practice various forms of sacrifice in the process of living by the principles of their religions. Judaism has a multitude of dietary rules that if followed, impose sacrifices upon its followers. Additionally, Jews have the Ten Commandments that proscribe many tempting activities. Christianity has a similar version of the Ten Commandments, and they were instructed by Jesus to love their neighbors, as they love themselves. This may be Christianity's most challenging method to sacrifice.

Martyrdom

Unabashed Muslims who live in the United States have endured a different milieu after the terrorist attacks that occurred on September 11, 2001. Although reports of outright physical persecution of Muslims in the United States merely for the sake of their religions have been relatively rare, acts of violence against people who were assumed to be Muslims have occurred.

Consider a hypothetical example of a male Muslim living in North America who might be confronted by a group of angry Americans and beaten severely or killed, merely because of his religious and ethnic background. He might have avoided what appeared to be certain suffering if he had answered that he was a Christian, but he elected to tell the truth due to his commitment to Islam. This victim is a martyr, as he chose to suffer or even die rather than to renounce his religion. Furthermore, under such circumstances he may not have attempted to defend himself or harm any of the attackers. He had only the hope of an afterlife, which he had long before the attack. Untold numbers of Muslims have been martyrs. For example, during the Crusades, many Muslim civilians were murdered merely because they lived in places where their enemies wanted to claim or reclaim. In fact, the first time that Jerusalem was captured, the city was an excellent example of multiculturalism, with Christians, Jews, and Muslims living together within the city walls. Whether the inhabitants were martyred or simply murdered in a blood-lusted conquering, we do not know. There is evidence that the Christian crusaders considered all inhabitants to be the same, regardless of their religion. They were all marked for death. There were many other Crusades, during which Christians martyred inhabitants of the Holy Land; however, none were blessed with long-term success, and all made martyrs by the thousands.

Christians have also endured persecutions and had numerous martyrs Some of the most notable martyrs of the Christian religion were Jesus' disciples Stephen and Peter, both of whom were brutally killed. Perhaps the most interesting Christian martyr was Paul, a former Roman and Jewish persecutor—or martyr maker—of Christians, until his dramatic conversion. Paul, formerly known as Saul, was not trusted immediately by Christians. In the Ninth chapter of the New Testament book of Acts, readers are told of a story with similarities to some of Abraham's conversations with God. A disciple named Ananias was told by God in a vision, among other things, to go to a house in Damascus and ask for a man named Saul of Tarsus. Ananias, perhaps thinking that God had not heard of the notorious Saul, replied to God that he had information about how much evil Saul had done to Christians in Jerusalem. God was not persuaded by the news. Ananias submitted to God and acted as the intermediary by which Saul regained his eyesight. The text implies that Ananias considered the possibility that he would be Saul's next martyr when he was able to see him. However, Saul was a changed man, and he became a Christian rather than continuing to persecute them. Ultimately, Paul was jailed and put to death because of his Christian beliefs.

Adolph Hitler had millions of Jews, among many other members of races and religions, exterminated in death camps. Their crimes were being Jews, Catholics, Gypsies, among other unwanted races and religions. Even before the formal beginning of the "Final Solution," Jews were targeted by Nazis and subjected to assaults, discrimination, and death because of their religion or race. In the United States, the Ku Klux Klan carried out what are now known as "hate crimes" against Jews, among other religious and racial minorities. These examples of hate and persecution based on beliefs, among other things paint portraits of martyrs suffering and dying. It took little or no rhetoric to convince these victims to suffer.

The rhetoric of sacrifice was flowing from the people imposing the suffering and death. That is what makes this chapter salient to sacrifice. It takes rhetors—masters of rhetoric—to draw and motivate others to sacrifice dissimilar human beings and their property. The rhetors sometimes have to first convince their followers to sacrifice their existing beliefs before the followers become willing to engage in human sacrifice. Joseph Goebbels, possibly the Nazi Party's "only intellectual" was a "prize-pupil of a Jesuit Seminary" before dedicating himself to Adolph Hitler (Roper, 1947, p. 16). Goebbels"created a system of propaganda, ironically styled 'public enlightenment,' which successfully persuaded people to believe that black was white" (p. 17). He was able to maintain German hopes and to support the notion that the Jews were Germany's real problem. With the use of the radio medium, Goebbels became a master rhetor of sacrifice. His effectiveness can be seen in records of sacrifices made by the German people. Unfortunately, his rhetoric also served to justify human sacrifice—cold blooded murder and slow starvation—on a massive scale. In his final act in Hitler's bunker, Goebbels poisoned his six children before having a soldier shoot his wife and him, whereupon their bodies were burned.

Some who do not follow or believe in any religion, might think of the rhetoric of sacrifice as just another way of getting things done. It is the "things" that make this topic worth thoroughly investigating. The three religions of which Abraham is the Patriarch clearly require certain rudimentary activities that result in either a work ethic or a responsibility to support oneself. Additionally, the three religions address giving money, aid, or the equivalent to the religion and/or to the needy. Followers of the three great religions started by Abraham's descendants have obligations to use their blessings in a generous and positive way. For some, this may be the most difficult part of following the teachings of one of the religions.

Sacrifice as a Construct

People tend to use the word sacrifice as if there were no need to provide the social science justification for referring to this predominant term as a "construct." In fact, there is not only a reason to refer to sacrifice as a construct, but it would be improper to imply that it is a "concept" or a term that has relatively few agreed-upon meanings.

Wimmer & Dominick (1997) explained that a construct is an abstract combination of concepts, "that because of its abstraction usually cannot be directly observed" and "its exact meaning relates only to the context in which it is found." (p. 40). Sacrifice is not a concept, because "A concept is a term that expresses an abstract idea formed by generalizing related observations" (p. 40).

The task when dealing with some constructs like "sacrifice" is complex and requires objectivity. Aids in such endeavors, such as definitions carry assumptions that may create one meaning to one receiver and diverse meanings to other receivers of the same message (construct). The possible meanings are so diverse that the making of meaning may depend on intangibles, such as the sender's ultimate goal, prominence, persuasive abilities, shared philosophy and religion, context, and a cornucopia of other factors.

"Sacrifice" is a complex term and ambiguity is one of its most universal characteristics. This is one reason that it can be used so effectively by masters of rhetoric, whose motives and agendas are hidden or deliberately misrepresented. Sacrifice is a word that can evoke positive and negative emotions and reactions. It can also be used in innocuous messages, providing little or no emotion or reaction. It is a loaded word that needs the open ranges of meaning that constructs can provide. It could mean that one will have a small, bland, and inexpensive dinner at home to save money, that one is going to give up one's next three regular golf Saturdays in order to afford to treat one's spouse to a very expensive dinner at the best restaurant in town, or that one will be the dinner for a hungry group of cannibals. The rhetoric of sacrifice can be used repeatedly by ambitious cult leaders in their sermons and/or messages to followers and recruits. One reason that manipulative leaders can develop such extreme sacrifices is that the construct of sacrifice can mean so many things to so many people.

Sacrifice, an Essentially Contested Term?

In an edition of *Ethical Issues in Social Science Research*, Terry Pinkard (1982, p. 261) examined the term "privacy" in the social science research setting. He observed that philosophers, social scientists, and other scholars from various disciplines interpreted "privacy" in very different terms. He considered whether a search for the meaning of privacy was prudent because of the possibility that privacy had no "core meaning" (Self, 1997, p. 91). With the rapid rise in terrorism in the form of suicide bombings (also called homicide bombings) the same question could be asked regarding the construct of "sacrifice."

Pinkard (1982) noted that "If a concept is essentially contested, then dispute (the "contest") about its meaning is not an accidental feature but is a necessary ("essential") feature because of the *kind* of concept that it is" (p. 262). He identified four elements associated with essentially contested concepts.

> A concept belongs to the class of essentially contested concepts if it satisfies the following conditions: (1) it must be appraisive in character, i.e., its use must involve the evaluation of some human achievement (e.g., in art, politics, or religion); (2) the achievement to which the concept refers must be internally complex, i.e., it cannot be understood simply by translation into a set of synonyms but must be analyzed into a complex set of properties and conditions; (3) the worth of the achievement must admit of different descriptions, or, to put it another way, how its parts contribute to its worth is variously describable; and (4) the description of the relevant achievement must be capable of (perhaps unpredictable) modification in light of changed circumstances. (p. 262)

Perhaps 15 years ago, sacrifice would not have been a candidate for Pinkard's test for an essentially contested term. However, over the past decade and a half, sacrifice has taken on meanings ranging from contributing to disaster relief funds to the acts of suicide bombers out to kill and maim as many people as possible. For this reason, a new term to the family of words relating sacrifice is needed. Rather than inserting an adjective or various adjectives immediately before "sacrifice," which may ultimately be the solution, we offer a new concept that describes people who engage in one particular genre of sacrifice. Its use stop "sacrifice" from falling into the abyss of ambiguity that Pinkard (1982) so aptly identified.

The New Construct of the Sacriatic.

The theological problem is trying to distinguish between the rhetoric of sacrifice and sacrifice (i.e. giving things of value, ranging from personal property, to money, to one's life to save or mitigate damages to others).

The term "**sacriatic**" (sac' re-at-tick) is a construct that provides a single term to describe the ultra-faithful followers of the masters of the rhetoric of sacrifice—those who are willing to murder any person, any quantity of people, at any time, and die in the process. The term is the result of combining the word sacrifice and fanatic. Sacriatics must be willing to die when told to do so by the masters of the rhetoric of sacrifice. A sacriatic is much more than a follower of a religion and one of its leaders. Masters of the rhetoric of sacrifice tend to survive, while their sacriatics, do the dying—the ultimate sacrificing. Therefore, if we see a suicide coupled with the attempt to murder and maim people selected by the rhetor of sacrifice, while the rhetor is insolated from danger, we should look further into the incident, as the rhetoric of sacrifice was certainly involved. A negative connotation may equate sacriatics to gullible pawns who may be duped into making their final act a combination of suicide and the intentional murder of targeted enemies of the rhetor of sacrifice.

A sacriatic is a victim of the following logic: "Lets you and them die." Certainly, sacriatics may have strong pre-existing ideas and beliefs about the issues and people that they are convinced to kill. Maybe they have even fantasized about killing some of the people the rhetor of sacrifice wants them to kill, in the process of sacrificing their own lives. If the reason for killing such people is valid, the cause will live on after the master of rhetoric of sacrifice has died in his or her own suicide attack. Valid causes and ideas cannot be killed, but shallow, gullible, young people with little hope for the future can and do die. To use a cliché, their lives are worth "a dime a dozen" to the rhetors of sacrifice.

So many variables, including new ways to kill, have changed over the last 25 years. Rhetors of sacrifice have sharpened their rhetorical skills and trained sacriatics in formerly forgotten and inaccessible places. Technology has reintroduced the old commercial slogan that said, "let your fingers do the walking." With wireless Internet communication, cellular telephones, and satellite reception, this is precisely what has been done in recent terrorist attacks. Additionally, now videotapes, repetitive use of talking points, buzzwords, and the invocation of carefully selected holy scriptures can provide what a pre-1980 military leader once had to provide live or monitor himself. Multiple recruitment and training camps have allowed terrorists leaders—often cultural icons or their close lieutenants—to mass produce future sacriatics, guised as and perhaps thinking they are eager deadly martyrs. They go into assaults with the intent of carrying as many of the perceived enemies into death with them as possible.

Dying in the process of fierce fighting and killing can be inspired by acts of sacrifice—giving of lives for countries, religions, or both in the case of certain theocracies. Such sacrificial behavior may replace pre-existing notions that one should live to do the work of God until death occurs through no self-help.

Regardless, the obedient and self-sacrificial conviction must totally replace any preexisting notions that conflict with the rhetoric of sacrifice. Again, the quid pro quo appears to be a necessary element for the rhetoric of sacrifice coupled with mass murder to succeed. That is, the exchange of the sacriatics' worldly lives, based on a spiritual interpretation or for a spiritual proclamation that promises a reward is preferable to living and continuing to do the will of a god or the rhetor of sacrifice on Earth. The supreme sacrifice and motivation to murder can be provoked by factors other than religion, such as extreme anger, fabricated stories, or mental illnesses.

The Dichotomy of Sacrifice

The general construct of sacrifice must be divided into at least two divergent parts that have substantial differences in meanings. Confusion is generated when one word can have opposing meanings. History and the study of propaganda document the fact that sacrifice has developed diverse and tangled meanings resulting in a communication nightmare. This certainly applies to how scholars may attempt to attune the existing constructs of sacrifice and the rhetoric of sacrifice.

Sacrifice

In addition to the descriptions of sacrifice that we have provided previously, we needed to present a relatively small amount of information about this noble construct. Sacrifice in modern society appears to be relatively rare, but it does exist. Newspapers report numerous instances of parents saving the lives of one or more of their children while risking their own lives—mothers who entered burning buildings in futile efforts to save infants or fathers who can't swim but dove into pools or lakes anyway to try and save drowning children. Military history is also full of stories of soldiers who willingly gave their lives so that their fellow soldiers might live. Several soldiers have been awarded the Medal of Honor for throwing themselves on top of live hand grenades; such selfless acts shielded the rest of the unit from harm, but meant almost certain death for the sacrificing soldiers. Yet, they did it anyway—real sacrifices in which people gave up their lives for others.

The Rhetoric of Sacrifice

Without true sacrifice, today's world would probably exhibit a diminished state of humanity. Bumper stickers and billboards have carried the slogan, "Commit a random act of kindness today." While following this plea may not require sacrifices, it demonstrates a truly sacrificial mindset. The message may reasonably be decoded as encouraging people to do things for people for whom there is no anticipated reward. So, while newsworthy altruistic sacrifices today are infrequent, they do occur and they are encouraged.

The adulteration of sacrifice has yielded the rhetoric of sacrifice, which appears to be more common than sacrifices with no expectation of reward. The accuracy of this statement may be deceptive, as small sacrifices evincing brotherly love lack enough criteria of newsworthiness to be reported by the news media. Additionally, many acts of sacrifice are done anonymously.

Still, without the rhetoric of sacrifice, many treacherous intersections along the human journey would be eliminated. The benefits would reach much further than eliminating suicide-bombing terrorists, who act in good faith based on misrepresentations of facts or promises that essentially result in trading objectivity, respect for human life, and charity for domination, obsession, dehumanization. It seems odd to most Westerners that the rhetoric of sacrifice is so powerful that mass murders and perhaps the followers' deaths must be accomplished before the any proof that an afterlife full of pleasure and ecstasy—the rhetors' half of the bargain is shown or delivered. Thus, the construct of sacrifice is divided into two usually antithetical concepts—true sacrifice and sacrifice resulting from some form of rhetoric of sacrifice.

The rhetoric of sacrifice tends to have several common factors. First, the **target audience** is usually individuals with problems, be they homeless, debt-ridden, or social outcasts. Islamic extremists recruit from young people who see little hope in the future. American cults also seek those on the fringe of society, offering them a chance to join their "family."

Second, **isolation** is an essential factor. The person who tries to convince others to sacrifice their lives for causes invariably tries to isolate that sacrifice candidates from anyone or anything that who might dissuade them. That element of isolation is a common point for suicide cults, Islamic suicide bombers, Japanese kamikaze pilots, and any other type of movement that requires the death of its participants. We also have discovered that isolation of abandoned people at abandoned locations was utilized to motivate and maintain loyalty within the Manson "Family." This group did not mandate suicide, but did require strict loyalty to its leader—Charles Manson. That loyalty eventually required in mass murder of innocent people by several of his followers.

The isolation of the individual allows and simplifies a third factor—**reinforcement** through controlled messages in a controlled environment. Such messages usually contain religious or strong cultural elements. That is, the person is doing the sacrificial act to fulfill the will of God, on behalf of the group, nation, and/or religion. One way of reinforcing candidates/trainees for sacrifice is to keep them very busy in their isolated environments. Lack of free time as a form of reinforcement is intuitive. The cliché "An idle mind is the Devil's workshop," appears to be inapplicable here. In fact, just the opposite is probably accurate. This is because if blocks of free time are provided, the candidates may engage in sincere thought about scriptures that are inconsistent with committing murder/suicides. Free time may allow people's consciences to compete with the repetitious messages of the rhetors of sacrifice. So, it is no surprise that attendees at terrorist training camps engage in exhausting physical exercises, tactical exercises, training with various weapons, attending propaganda sessions, which turns into religious indoctrination, memorizing carefully selected portions of religious legends or books. As if those were not enough, they also must deal with adverse environmental conditions. The camps are generally Spartan and primitive. If trainees are not living in tents, they are sheltered by rooms with little or no furniture, no forms of media entertainment, no plumbing (i.e., privies instead of bathrooms), minimal electricity, which usually must be produced by generators, and they must take measures to avoid contact with poisonous snakes, scorpions, and other wild creatures that threaten humans. After going through this type of intensity together, they develop bonds with their fellows and their trainers. Within just 20 to 30 days of these types of intense reinforcement tools, previously untrained recruits are much more likely to see themselves as a unit, capable of unprecedented murderous feats, all in the process of attaining the paradise rewards available only to martyrs.

Kimball (2000) identified five elements that are usually inherent within the rhetorical arguments of the leader (also called the rhetor or master rhetor herein). Those elements are the following: (1) claims of absolute truth, (2) blind obedience, (3) establishing the "ideal" time, (4) the end justifies the means, and (5) declaring holy war. Some cult leaders use trial suicides to test their followers' commitment—their blind obedience. Jim Jones, who will be discussed later in this chapter, ordered the mass suicide of 914 people in 1978, would sometimes test the loyalty of his followers by directing them to drink a liquid that he said was or could be poison. These harmless trial rituals effectively prepared an unsuspecting congregation for the real thing.

Finally, there is some type of **inducement**—either a reward for committing the act or a punishment for not doing so. In an example provided later in more detail, an Iraqi father, with the help of one son, shot and killed another son. The inducement was a negative one—that the entire family would be killed if the son was not sacrificed. For Islamic extremists who make the transition to terrorists, in the form of suicide bombers inside Israel, the inducement is more positive—a divine reward (e.g., a promise of numerous virgins in paradise) sometimes coupled with a more worldly one (e.g., Cash payments equivalent to $20,000 or more were offered to the suicide bomber's families by Sodom Hussein when he controlled Iraq). Both forms of inducements—positive or negative—infuse the rhetoric of sacrifice with the characteristics of the bartering of goods—life being one side of the bargained-for exchange. None of these arguments, however, appear to be a part of the Abraham and Isaac narrative. We can see that time and artful utilization of the rhetoric of sacrifice have provided extremists with a remarkably potent tool for repeated use in their deadly games. None of the factors or elements discussed above appears to be part of the Abraham and Isaac narrative. Instead, they are components that have been added to the rationale of the story to increase the desired rhetorical impact.

Such an approach can be highly persuasive and offers the rhetor the potential to wield considerable power, both within and outside of organized religion. Organized religions use the rhetoric of sacrifice to seek more devotion and sometimes more financial contributions from their members. Those outside of religion can use the same approach to achieve a variety of military, political, territorial, professional, and social goals. Further, some cultures might be more receptive to the rhetoric of sacrifice. Members of an authoritarian culture, for example, may have less moral dilemmas if faced with orders to kill themselves or a loved one, particularly if the orders are perceived as coming from God.

Understanding such situations helps explain the willingness of *kamikaze* pilots to sacrifice their lives on behalf of their perceived "divine" emperor, and understanding the motivational tools used on *kamikaze* pilots aids our inquiries. In 1946, Emperor Hirohito denied that he was divine, and said that former claims that he was a god were false. It appears that Hirohito was not the person or group that most zealously claimed that he was divine. The Japanese military needed a tool to inspire heroic acts of bravery on the battlefields, in the air, and on the oceans. The desperate *kamikaze* types of aerial attacks, often carried out by young pilots with inferior skills, are particularly illustrative of the recruitment and motivation of modern suicide bombers.

The rhetorical impact of the *akedah* has developed along three different lines (1) the development of religious thought, (2) the triggering of theological and philosophical issues, and (3) alterations of the story to justify individual beliefs and agendas.

The first component is easily identified and was addressed in Chapter 5. The story of Abraham and Isaac has become an integral part of the three great religions. In the Jewish tradition, the binding of Isaac is the culmination of Abraham's story—the event that established the Hebrew nation and the Jewish religion. In the Christian tradition, the sacrifice of Isaac is an event that foreshadows the sacrifice of Jesus—the cornerstone of Christian faith. For Islamic believers, the story represents supreme obedience by both a father and his child, thus capturing the crucial theological element of the Islamic religion. The story's basis in these religions intensifies its rhetorical potential because, as Kimball (2000) noted, "Religion is arguably the most powerful and pervasive force on earth" (p. 1).

But the impact of the story also addresses troubling issues that can trigger a number of theological and philosophical debates about the nature of God, the nature of man, and the nature of the universe. What does it say about a God who would demand such a test? What does it say about the moral nature of a man who would willingly take the test? To what extent does it represent the problem of evil and raise questions about the existence of God? Does it raise questions about the omniscience of God and God's relationship to time? Such questions are just that: questions. As such, the rhetorical impact of the story—from a theological and philosophical perspective—is not to provide answers but merely to trigger discussion and debate for a series of different issues. In that sense, its rhetorical impact has been to keep the discussion going for centuries.

Many religious adherents, however, skip this second rhetorical stage and move directly to the last. They use the story or interpret the story to justify their own existing beliefs or desires. As such, the *akedah* becomes justification for whatever religious belief they may have. In that form, it is not true rhetoric so much as rationalization (Hill & Cheadle, 1996). In its extreme form, fanatics could use it to justify killing their own children. The extremists may also find justification for the work of suicide bombers, terrorists, or other violent religious fanatics. In a more moderate form, it could provide justification for increased funding for education in the political arena. In fact, given the moral ambiguities and ethical dilemmas posed by the story, it could theoretically be interpreted to support practically any behavior or position. As Stephen Carter (2000) wrote, "God's name becomes a tool, . . . a ticket to get us where we want to go" (p. 17). Sadly, in the case of Abraham and Isaac, the story often becomes a tool to manipulate others into mass murder and suicide.

Either approach, however, oversimplifies the story. In the story of Abraham and Isaac, the rhetoric of sacrifice raises questions that should trigger thought-provoking debate and discussion. It makes little attempt to provide answers to those questions. That's why the story bothers us and why it has provoked readers for thousands of years. And that may be its major rhetorical impact. Establishing a relationship with God may involve a simple step of faith by the believer, but the God who is revealed in that relationship is a complex One who is not easily understood by human standards.

One element that distinguishes the modern approach to the rhetoric of sacrifice from its historical predecessors is that the power of the mass media has increased its potential for abuse. Contemporary weaponry allows mass destruction from the sacrifices of a relatively small number of people. Further, the mass media quickly spread word of the destruction to almost the entire world, thus multiplying the potential impact of the act. The relative ease with which the process occurs and succeeds, in turn, makes it easier for terrorists to recruit others for their suicide missions. For Islamic terrorists, the main vehicle for their communication has been the Kuwait television station *"Al Jezera." Al Jezera* is known for televising the terrorists' videotapes made shortly before they committed suicide bombings, beheadings, and desecration of bodies. Such airings add to the glorification of the suicide bombers and other terrorists, making the mass media both a justification and recruitment tool for the rhetoric of sacrifice.

Such approaches can be highly successful. The March 2004 train bombings in Spain, for example, occurred just a few days before national elections, received extensive news coverage, and may have contributed to the election outcome. Further, in true sacrificial mode, when confronted the suspects in the bombings blew themselves up rather than face capture (Roman, 2004). Meanwhile, the newly elected leaders quickly followed predictions of media pundits and announced that they would withdraw their portion of the coalition forces stationed in Iraq.

It could be argued that by calling instances of murder and mass murder less disturbing terms, the act of murder may have gained a measure of legitimacy. Television news media, and other news media, through oversimplified reporting have antisepticized murders by labeling them "suicide attacks," "terrorist attacks," and other terms, such as simply a "roadside bomb" or "roadside explosive devices."

Sometimes the news media use military terms in reports of civilian mass murders. However, the use of military jargon is no excuse for substituting such technical language exclusively when describing the surroundings of mass murder scenes caused by a suicide bombers or roadside bombs (also referred to as "roadside detonated units [RDUs]" or similar military terms, which are known for their cryptic, technical, and unfamiliar characteristics).

Human sacrifices are not merely things of the past. Both voluntary and involuntary human sacrifices are occurring with some regularity during the 21st Century. It is the rhetoric of sacrifice that has changed. In fact, the rhetoric of sacrifice has changed so much that we have very limited access to state of the art rhetorical tools that are being used to recruit suicide bombers and other terrorists. Certainly, isolation and the traditional characteristics are utilized, but there are indications of a well-organized support system in place to provide messages that are consistent with the specific themes of the rhetoric of sacrifice that they have previously been subjected. Occasionally, television news shows portions of the final videotapes made by suicide bombers who have recently sacrificed their lives in the process of killing and maiming many others. Those tapes may contain repetition of some of the rhetoric used to convince them that suicide and murder were their callings in life.

Historians hundreds of years from now, when trying to explain the late 20th and early 21st Century phenomena of terrorist attacks, will find many of today's uses of sacrifice. They will not have to fight the elements to uncover layers of fossilized drawings on buildings. Rather, they will be attempting to extract the truth from today's newspapers and other surviving news reports.

Broadcast television news provided Americans first, and then the world, with splendid video of tragedies, like the 9-11 attacks—the effect of an extreme kind of sacrifice, and then predictably a glancing view of some of evidence of the cause or causes of the attacks—sacrifice and martyrdom.

Regardless of the advances in technology that could educate modern people about the danger built into the rhetoric of sacrifice, we remain relatively ignorant about the threats that continue because of it. In general, many reporters and North American people do not recognize the existence or consequences of the rhetoric of sacrifice, as it is not newsworthy until it manifests in horror, which satisfies enough news values to be reported. Even when terrorist events are covered, news entities tend to cover the effects much more than aggressively reporting on the causes. Thus, reporting on terrorist attacks makes people aware of terrorism, but it does not provide emphasis on the cause for terrorist suicide attacks—the rhetoric of sacrifice.

If a functional test is used to determine whether human sacrifice is appropriate, some murders are seen as contemptible and others are seen as valorous, depending on relative factors. Intentional killing—sacrificing humans—is punishable if committed against citizens of associated nations and/or members of sects of the prevailing religions. However, human sacrifice, even by means of suicide attack is encouraged and labeled as glorious if perpetrated against people of perceived enemy nations. Whether sacrificing oneself and other human beings is right or wrong appears to be based on functional reasons. When master rhetors of sacrifice name themselves as the judges of such matters, fundamentally flawed, yet persuasive directives to murder can yield horrible results.

Further ambiguity flowing from divergent interpretations of the lessons of Abraham's ordeal on Mount Moriah set the stage for the rhetoric of sacrifice that has manifested in a burgeoning industry of human sacrifice organizations.

Unfortunately, sacrifice and martyrdom infrequently occur in vacuums. That is, in many documented cases, sacrifices are coupled with murders. More complicated scenarios manifest when sacrifice occurs when one kills during combat or some other more accepted or approved types of official conflicts. In fact, the holy books of the three religions appear to call for certain wars. Certainly, voluntarily participating in war as a soldier involves a multitude of sacrifices, the most disturbing of which are sacrifices of lives.

More Examples

In the summer of 2003, Salem Kerbul and two of his sons walked behind a house where some other people were waiting. Salem, the father, and Salah were armed with AK-47 assault rifles. Sabah Kerbul, the other son, was going to die that day. An unknown number of other people acknowledged their presence and took their places. Their role was to serve as witnesses while the father and one son shot and killed Sabah.

Why was Sabah supposed to die? There had been an accusation that he had worked as an informer for the Americans during the Iraqi war. The punishment was death at the hands of his own family. The witnesses were there to ensure that the punishment was carried out.

Salem Kerbul and Salah both fired their rifles. A problem was noticed by the witnesses—Sabah was not dead. Salah, his brother, finished the execution by firing three more times into his brother's body before he was clearly dead. It was around that time that Salem, their father collapsed.

Later, father Salem moaned that he had no choice. If the family did not kill the son, the witnesses would kill the entire family. Still, he lamented, "I have the heart of a father, and he's my son. Even the prophet Abraham didn't have to kill his son" (quoted by Shadid, 2003, p. A1). So, thousands of years after Abraham bound Isaac, fathers were being told to kill their sons. Unlike Abraham, Salem did not receive his orders from God or Allah. Instead, he obeyed custom, and followed a utilitarian philosophy.

Nevertheless Salem was directed to kill his son Sabah. Moreover, Sabah willingly accepted his fate—never flinching while looking at the guns aimed by his father and brother. Both father and sons, it seems, became modern victims of the rhetoric of sacrifice that has grown wild around the story of Abraham and Isaac or Ishmael (as the case may be, depending on the religion). The term "grown wild" is used metaphorically. More specifically, people who are members of the three great religions attributable to Abraham have taken the story that we have so carefully scrutinized and used it to motivate, require, and call for all kinds of behaviors that would be otherwise unacceptable. The rhetoric of sacrifice was used to accomplish the World Trade Center attacks;

suicide attacks in other countries, and global terrorism. To contend that the sacrifice by Abraham on Mount Moriah is justification for mass murder and indiscriminate mayhem is truly an adulteration of the holy construct of sacrifice regardless of the religion that sanctions such acts. But this statement is merely the conclusions of two academicians—two people from the nation where the World Trade Centers were attacked. To achieve credibility, we must examine the rhetoric of sacrifice, apply what we have learned about sacrifice, and draw conclusions based on all of the applicable variables.

Do not assume that only one group or religion perpetrates extreme violent acts in the name of sacrifice. There is no preconception that adulteration of sacrifice is limited to Islamic regions and religions. For example, consider the murder of Brenda Lafferty and her 15-month-old daughter in Utah. Lafferty and her child met their deaths at the hands of two family members—brothers-in-laws—who said they received a directive from God to kill the two because God said they were barriers to a true faith. It was later discovered that Mrs. Lafferty's husband knew of his brothers' intentions, but he did nothing to stop the act. He did not even warn his wife of a possible threat to her safety (Krakauer, 2003).

Sadly, the Lafferty murders were not isolated incidents. On March 10, 1993, Dr. David Gunn was shot and killed by Michael Griffin outside an abortion clinic in Pensacola, Florida. The following year—on July 29, 1994—Reverend Paul Hill killed two others, a doctor and his bodyguard, at the same clinic. Both men were convicted of murder, and Hill has already been executed, as he would not cooperate with those who attempted to spare his life through the legal system. In many ways, his behavior was similar to that of the modern, Middle East suicide bombers, in that he willingly died for a cause in which he believed. Further, like the modern suicide bombers, he probably believed that he was a martyr who would be rewarded in Heaven (or Paradise) for his illegal and lethal actions. Yet, juries convicted both Hill and Griffin. In each case all 12 jurors unanimously interpreted their actions as murder. If the legal issue had been religious devotion, they would have prevailed, but that was not the issue. Hill appeared to aggressively seek his own "speedy" execution, at the hands of the government that had made abortion legal under certain circumstances.

This provided strong evidence that in his mind, he did the right thing—the godly thing. Hill attempted to argue that he had killed to prevent the murder of another human being. Every state has some version of a law that makes it legal to use deadly force to stop the imminent killing of another person. His position was that human life starts at the moment of conception. Perhaps because he would not allow state-appointed lawyers to defend him in court, his defense was unsuccessful.

Another infamous act of ostensibly religious self-sacrifice had its origins in California, but actually occurred in rural Guyana. The charismatic Reverend Jim Jones led a mass suicide of 914 people in 1978, after some of his followers murdered a group of people. This horrible moment in history is remembered by many as the Jonestown massacre at the People's Temple in Guyana or just the Jonestown massacre.

Jones alleged limitations of freedom of religion in the United States, and used this as his primary rationale for moving his congregation into another nation. Upon arrival at their new home in Guyana, Jones' followers literally had to carve a niche-like camp out of the wilderness in the South American nation. Jones used the rhetoric of sacrifice to lead more than 900 people to their deaths (Stoen, 1997). To add even more pain to a gruesome episode chain of events to come, there was a mass murder before the sacrifices. U.S. Congressman Leo Ryan had just concluded a visit to Jamestown and was preparing to fly back to the United States. Before he and all of his crew could board the plane, a group of Jones' followers appeared with assault rifles. At the crude landing strip, Ryan, the pilot of his plane, a member of the press, and many other innocent people were shot and killed. Much of the carnage was captured on videotape. These shocking murders are beyond normal human understanding. Certainly, Jones felt that the visit had gone poorly. He probably knew that some Jonestown residents had given notes to Ryan and his aids. Although Jones was not present at the airstrip, there has been little doubt that the murders were perpetrated based on his orders.

Jones, however, was not finished killing. His preaching and teaching had stressed governmental persecution. To ultimately win their struggle for religious freedom, he often stressed to his group the possibility of self-sacrifice. He reinforced his rhetorical power to order and carry out the ultimate and fatal sacrifice when he staged several practice sessions. In some or all of these, his followers went through the motions of drinking liquids that could later be laced with cyanide. It is reasonable to conclude that many followers took their final lethal doses unknowingly, as they thought their actions were just another practice session. In an eerie audiotape that survived the mass sacrifice, Jones can be heard announcing instructions over a public-address system to the group during the cataclysmic ceremony. Jones made promises to his followers about what they would gain by going through with his plan. He reassured them as they drank and died.

Some of his followers noticed the agonizing last minutes of fellow-followers' lives. Parents who had noticed the convulsions and last gasps of their children and others must have experienced some of the horror Abraham had when his knife was raised. Their choices were essentially nonexistent. That day, there would be no angel to stop Jones' sacrifice of almost 1,000 followers. His gunmen shot the few who refused to follow his directions. In the name of God, a master rhetor of sacrifice would have his way, except for one thing. We know Jones did not drink the poison—he shot himself. It is probable that Jones desired to survive, but something prevented his escape. We will never know, but we do know that most modern masters rhetors of sacrifice prefer their followers to do the dying—the sacrificing.

The followers of Charles Manson thought he was Jesus. His followers believed him and believed in him. Manson, an uneducated career criminal, used effective rhetoric. Charles D. Watson, better known at the Manson camp as "Tex," found himself around a campfire with Manson and his group. Manson slowly touched a large knife to Watson's neck. "Tex? Would you die for me? Would you let me kill you?" Manson asked seriously (Watson, 1978, p. 12). Watson wrote the following:

> I didn't even have to think about it: "Sure, Charlie, you can kill me." I meant it. Like some mystic, so filled with the love of God that nothing is too great to ask. I was filled with Charlie. He was God to me. (p. 12)

Less than three weeks before that night, Watson and other Manson followers had murdered seven innocent people for Manson. Watson, just over a year after an all-American boyhood, had sacrificed himself for Manson. From prison, Watson explained to a chaplain that he had proved he had already figuratively died for Manson. To perpetrate those murders, he explained,

> To do that I'd had to die. Manson understood that. He realized that once my own life meant nothing, no one else's life would mean anything either. ... I felt no remorse for the murders, no revulsion at the incredible brutality of the killings. I felt nothing at all. ...not even fear of what might happen if I were caught. Because, like the rest of the family, I knew a secret. The next day or the day after that (at least sometime very soon), Los Angeles and all the other pig cities would be in flames). (p. 13)

Through the rhetoric of sacrifice, Manson predicted a race war in the United States. He planned to start it by making the murders he ordered look as if they were based on class envy and race. As he spoke of the specifics of how the murders were to be carried out, using racial slurs, he routinely mixed in some actual biblical passages that many of followers recognized from their childhood and adolescence. Many of them had a Christian background, which gave Manson's pseudo-sermons, sprinkled with real and modified biblical messages. Love was his invocation. The rhetoric of love for Manson was similar in many ways to the rhetoric of sacrifice that is used so successfully by terrorist recruiters and trainers today to sell death without guilt—death as a means to his vision.

Meanwhile, a growing number of religious cults expect the ultimate sacrifice from their own members. Consider the March 1997 mass suicide by 39 members of the Heaven's Gate cult in Rancho Santa Fe, California, where the members—directed by leader Marshall Applewhite—killed themselves in a ritual timed with the appearance of the Hale-Bopp comet (Corelli & Gregor, 1997; Goode & Brownlee, 1997; Streisand, 1997; Taylor, 1997).

Each of the 39 members professed to believe that they were aliens who had been planted on Earth years ago by a spacecraft—what most Americans would call an Unidentified Flying Object (UFO). They also believed that another UFO was hiding behind the comet, ready to take them to another world if they would only dispose of the current "vehicles" for their souls (i.e., their bodies). Each was found dressed in black clothing, on neatly made bunk beds in seven bedrooms of a single house; each member had a $5 bill and some quarters in their shirt pockets, and each had a neatly packed suitcase nearby (Streisand, 1997).

In some instances, their deaths were typical of many suicides brought on by depression where the participants feel death is preferable, because life has nothing to offer while death may bring its own reward. One of the Heaven's Gate members, for example, left a note that read:

> They had a formula of how to get out of the human kingdom to a level above humans . . .. That's what I want. That's what I've been looking for . . .. I've been on this planet for 31 years, and there's nothing here for me. (Good & Brownlee, 1997, p. 32)

Reward is another key factor. Members viewed the suicide ritual as a pathway to rewards in the afterlife. In essence, the cult members responded to "charismatic and self-styled messiahs who claim that group suicide leads to spiritual rewards" (Corelli & Gregor, 1997, p. 44).

Cult members are typically recruited during moments of vulnerability. Given the right situation, one former cult member noted, "almost anybody can get swept away" (Stoen, 1997, p. 45). The victims of the Uganda cult were described as "all simple people looking for a better life" (Hammer, 2000, p. 44). "People join cults in moments of weakness," Stoen added, "when they're angry about something in their personal life or in the world around them . . .. Anything that involves a family—which is what a cult is—can be very appealing" (p. 45).

Once introduced to a new way of thinking, they are then isolated from others who might have different views. One Heaven's Gate member, for example, told his family he could not talk with them because they might hinder the group's goals and "tug at their vibrational level" (Goode & Brownlee, 1997, p. 34). The cult leader thus had total control over the information provided to the members and allowed no exposure to counter persuasion. After that, as Lacayo (1997) noted, "the self-denial and regimentation of cult life will soften up anyone for the kill" (p. 44).

Once indoctrinated, their actions become—from the perspective of outside observers—irrational. For those members, though, that very irrationality is at the core of their belief and faith—much like Abraham had faith in doing an otherwise irrational act. In fact, one justification for their actions was the same as those used by believers to justify Abraham's actions—faith. As one member wrote before dying, "For us to shed our vehicles is totally opposite of somebody committing suicide. It's a final act of trust" (Taylor, 1997, p. 43).

Instead, members are asked for loyalty to cults and their leaders (Barnswell, 1997). For Islamic suicide bombers, a single commitment ensures their death in that "A recruit's pledge to become a martyr is irrevocable . . .. Their belief that hell awaits those who break such a solemn promise" (Kimball, 2000, p. 56). The leader becomes the surrogate father who makes their decisions for them, particularly during times of upheaval within their own lives (Lacayo, 1997). It may sound like a simple concept, but as one former cult member noted, "People want simplicity; a cult provides ready-made answers" (Stoen, 1997, p. 45). The deaths themselves had the markings of a religious ritual, or, as Taylor (1997) noted, "an act staged for the sanctification of the performers" (p. 43). Some of those left out may resent the omission. Some associates of the St. Casimir suicides, for example noted that, "There are still a lot of people who are disappointed not to have been called by the gurus in 1994—to not have been part of the most triumphant voyage" (Branswell, 1997, p. 47).

Taylor (1997) found the suicides particularly disturbing because of their implications for the power of religion and its "fatal power of belief" (p. 40). "Though Americans love the idea of religion, they are frightened of true religion's naked power," he added (p. 41). One year after the suicide, the cult itself continued to exist and was still recruiting new members (Geier, 1998).

The list continues to grow. Indeed, modern society seems to consider Abraham as a role model for dramatic rhetorical statements. The results of the rhetoric of sacrifice are often so extreme that tens of thousands have died and more will die as a result of someone or some groups' motivation of sacriatics via the rhetoric of sacrifice. Suicide bombers and other terrorists are considered martyrs for sacrificing their lives to kill others in a manner that draws extensive news coverage. Terrorists are more learned in manipulating the news media than ever. Four of the seven primary news values are conflict, timeliness, impact, and the unusual. Suicide bombers who kill the most innocent people create the most conflict. Television, the medium of the great masses (both literate and illiterate) prides itself on getting the big stories to their audiences as soon as it is happening. This is what sets television apart from all other media. Terrorism via suicide squads or individuals has impact on people everywhere, as no place is completely safe anymore. Finally, indiscriminate killing by people who would rather murder than live is bizarre and unusual.

Examples are numerous: the March 2000 deaths—in an explosion and fire—of more than 400 members in Uganda of a sect called the Restoration of the Ten Commandments of God (Hammer, 2000; A better world . . ., 2000); the 74 members of the Order of the Solar Temple who committed suicide over a three-year span culminating with the death of five in St. Casimir, Quebec in March 1997 (Branswell, 1997; Lacayo, 1997). Even the September 11, 2001 terrorist attacks were based on the rhetoric of sacrifice; Muhammad Atta, the leader of the squads that flew airplanes into the World Trade Center and the Pentagon, left behind a note justifying his actions on religious ground. As Kimball (2000) noted, "The attacks were carefully planned and skillfully executed by seemingly intelligent people whose level of commitment to their cause included suicidal self-sacrifice" (p. 3).

The *akedah*, it seems, has produced a dramatic impact on the generations that have continued to revere the sacred story. People have used the story for a variety of purposes. Among theologians, philosophers, and other academicians, it has generated a broad range of intellectual questions and theological debates. In this sense, it has been thought provoking, generating questions about the nature of God and about man's relationship to the divine. Papers, journal articles, and books have been written on a myriad of aspects of ethics, philosophy, psychology, and speech communication regarding whether Abraham was right or wrong when he bound Isaac. Since academe is available to the public, unlike research done by corporations and some government projects the rhetors of sacrifice have quarterly, if not monthly scholarly works that they can incorporate into their persuasive appeals. There are some articles that praise true sacrifice, either directly or indirectly. However, such literature is not usually suspenseful or appealing to the masses. It is not intellectually stimulating to argue the positive and negative points of covering a grenade to save one's comrades.

Abraham's dilemma has carried over into the 21st century. We all face questions of what to do when we think we are in total seclusion. Abraham believed that sacrificing his son was the right thing to do, and—in God's eyes— he was correct. The story tells us that doing the right thing is not always the same as doing the easy thing. Further, the many interpretations of the story probably reflect more upon human nature than they do on the nature of God. Many of those interpretations amount to little more than adapting the story to fit a pre-determined view of God. Intellectually, that is the equivalent of creating a god in our own image, rather than in a theological sense.

On the negative side, the *akedah* has also spawned thousands of imitators— people who are willing to die for a cause they consider important or at least willing to let others die for such a cause. The results have sometimes led to acts of murder, mass murder, and war—with many of these violent acts perpetrated in the name of God. Justifications of such acts are often difficult for outsiders to understand, particularly since Isaac's death was not required at the culmination of the act. Still, the story itself has been turned into one in which many religious people justify acts that would otherwise be considered horrific. In fact, other leaders and cultures apparently see their willingness to "out-sacrifice" Americans as an advantage. As Americans reeled from the September 11, 2001 attacks on the World Trade Center, Osama bin Laden contended that he would prevail because his Islamic supporters were more willing to die for a cause than were Americans.

The academic question is how do such acts of suicide/murder compare and contrast with the story of Abraham and Isaac or Ishmael. By seeking similarities, we can perhaps identify those elements of the story that have contributed to a rhetoric of sacrifice. By identifying differences, perhaps we can distinguish between real sacrifice and rhetorical sacrifice.

A Return to Sacrifice

Jesuit priest Patrick Ryan (1991) recalled a colleague who spotted an industrial pipe leaking poisonous material. Shouting for the others nearby to leave the room, this man threw his body over the pipe as the others hurried to safety. He was the only one contaminated, and the only one to die. His sacrifice had saved the others.

Such behavior is rare enough in our society that it is considered heroic. It is common enough that we can find numerous examples of parents who have drowned saving their children, soldiers who have jumped on and covered live hand grenades with their bodies to save the others in the impact area, and strangers who have dashed into burning buildings to attempt to save trapped infants.

These examples represent true self-sacrifice (i.e., people willing to sacrifice their lives with no expectation of rewards). Just the opposite is often the case; while there are some rare instances in which soldiers have survived direct grenade attacks, soldiers who jump on live grenades do so fully aware that they are probably going to die. Ryan (1991) expressed a common theological view when he said that true self-sacrifice is an elevated form of behavior: "Self-sacrificing love (*agape*) goes beyond friendship, even subordinating the lover's personal end to that of the beloved" (p. 479).

Sacrifice as Rhetorical Argument. More frequently, though, self-sacrifice is used as a rhetorical argument at a much less extreme level. Even there, it triggers philosophical and theological debates. Peter Unger (1997), for example, looked at the extent to which a person is morally required to sacrifice for the purpose of helping strangers. Unger also looks at the alternative, i.e., whether there are situations in which one would be morally permitted to harm some people in order to prevent greater harm to others. The first issue addresses the general concept of sacrifice; the second is arguably the issue that Abraham had to face.

Unger's conclusion to the first question was that people should sacrifice to the point that their own lifestyles are diminished, since anything less than that is not a true sacrifice. That conclusion has been considered extreme by his critics (Hooker, 1997a, 1997b), but note that even it only points to the concept of monetary sacrifice. Unger's primary concern is charity donations—the extent to which a person donates money to help those in need. His argument is an extreme version of the "give 'til it hurts" argument, with the added admonition to "keep giving 'til it hurts more."

Unger (1997) also answered the second question in the affirmative—a conclusion that would offer some vindication to Abraham. Although Isaac may have suffered severe emotional trauma from his role in the sacrificial ritual, the role that the event played in establishing three great religions could be argued to be greater than his pain. The problem, as Hooker (1997b) argued, is that "Unger's conclusions conflict with much of our behaviour and many of our ordinary moral beliefs" (p. 26).

Unger does have an important contribution to the rhetoric of sacrifice—a rejection of futility thinking. Those who refuse to donate to charities often cite the futility of the charity's effort as a justification for their behavior. The problems of needy children are too great, always present, and something that cannot be cured by monetary donations. Unger notes that such futility thinking becomes a self-fulfilling prophecy while justifying lack of response from the potential donor. Futility thinking also affects those who use the rhetoric of sacrifice to solicit money for such causes. As Hooker (1997a) wrote, "Many people espouse principles about helping the world's needy that, if rigorously applied, demand far more self-sacrifice than these same people seem to expect from themselves or others" (p. 1). Sacrifice as a rhetorical argument, it seems, is an effective persuasive tool. As medicine for the soul, however, it is preferred only in moderate doses.

Conclusion

No definitive conclusion can be offered for a story that has intrigued scholars for thousands of years. Perhaps that is its intention. Robert Alter (1981), for example, argued precisely that, noting that, "an essential aim of the innovative techniques of fiction worked out by the ancient Hebrew writers was to produce a certain indeterminacy of meaning, especially in regard to motive, moral character, and psychology" (p.12).

If so, the *akedah* achieved its goal. It is a complex tale with broad theological, philosophical, and social implications. Perhaps its greatest contribution is its ability to trigger such discussions, raising questions that make many people re-examine their own belief systems. What is important, though, is to realize that the impact of the story goes well beyond its religious and theological bases. Abraham's actions have generated a rhetoric of sacrifice that continues to exert a powerful influence on modern society. The rhetoric of sacrifice was born when the first person used the story of the *akedah* to inspire another to willingly sacrifice on his or her behalf. Since then, a multitude of religious leaders and religious imposters have used the rhetoric of sacrifice to do their bidding. History has demonstrated that those who master the rhetoric of sacrifice can and do persuade others to commit a wide range of actions, some of which stand out in history as among man's most inhumane moments. After decades of refinement, the *akedah* has proven to be an all-purpose tool that can be used for good or evil. As Kimball (2000) wrote, "In their origins and their core teachings, religions may be noble, but how they develop almost invariably falls short of the ideal. Adherents too often make their religious leaders, doctrines, and the need to defend institutional structures the vehicle and justification for unacceptable behavior" (pp. 32-33).

Phyllis Trible summarized the problems with using the *akedah* for rhetorical purposes, saying:

> It's not a good idea to make this into an ethical story, a 'should' story. But it is very much alive as a descriptive story. This is the human predicament, and this is how God is perceived. There is a terror in God's mysteriousness and inscrutability. (quoted by Moyers, 1996, p. 236)

God's "mysteriousness and inscrutability" creates a wall that hinders full understanding of the divine nature. One lesson from the rhetoric of sacrifice, though, is that perhaps we should be suspicious of those who try to persuade us with claims that they can see beyond that wall.

References

A better world, they were told (2000, March 25). *Economist, 354(8163)*, 46.

Abramovitch, H. (1994). The relations between fathers and sons in biblical narrative: Toward a new interpretation of the akedah. *Proceedings of the Eleventh World Congress of Jewish Studies*, 31-36.

Ackland, D. F. (1964). *Studies in Deuteronomy*. Nashville: Convention Press.

Aldred, C. (1991). *Akhenaten: King of Egypt*. New York: Convention Press.

Allan, J. J. (1951). *Galatians*. London: SCM Press.

Alston, W. P. (1963). *Religious belief and philosophical thought*. New York: Harcourt, Brace & World.

Alter, R. (1981). *The art of biblical narrative*. New York: Basic Books.

Alter, R. (1996). *Genesis*. New York: W.W. Norton.

Armstrong, K. (1993). *A History of God*. New York: Ballantine.

Armstrong, K. (1996a). *In the beginning*. New York: Alfred A. Knopf.

Armstrong, K. (1996b). *Jerusalem: One city, three faiths*. New York: Ballantine.

Baldwin, J. G. (1986). *The Message of Genesis 12-50*. Leicester, England: Inter-Varsity Press.

Barclay, W. (1977). *The Letter to the Romans*. Philadelphia: Westminster.

Bark, E. (2000, March 5). NBC ready to try its luck with new animation show. *Birmingham News Punch*, 30T.

Batson, J. W. (2000, November, 2). An everlasting promise. *Alabama Baptist*, p. 15

Bean, A. (2000, Fall). Being part of a covenant people. *Family Bible study: Ventures and pathways leader guide* (72-81). Nashville: Southern Baptist Convention.

Beilby, J. (1996). Does the empirical problem of evil prove that theism is improbable. *Religious Studies, 32*, 315-323.

Ben-Dov, M. (1986). Herod's mighty Temple Mount. *Biblical Archaeological Review, 12(6)*, 40-49.

Beyer, L. (2001, Dec. 3). The women of Islam. *Time*, 50-59.

Bodoff, L. (1993). The real test of the Akedah: Blind obedience versus moral choice. *Judaism, 42*, 71-92

Boling, R. G. (1975). *Judges*. Garden City, NJ: Doubleday.

Bonhoeffer, D. (1963). *The cost of discipleship*. New York: Macmillan.

Borg, M. J. (1987). *Jesus: A new vision*. San Francisco: HarpersSanFrancisco.

Boyd, G. A. (1997). *God at war: The Bible and spiritual conflict*. Downers Grove, IL: Intervarsity Press.

Boyd, G. A. (2000). *God of the possible: A biblical introduction to the open view of God*. Grand Rapids, MI: Baker Book House.

Boyd, G. A. (2001). *Satan & the problem of evil: Constructing a trinitarian warfare theodicy*. Downers Grove, IL: Intervarsity Press.

Branswell, B. (1997, April 7). Deadly voyages. *Maclean's, 110(14)*, 46-47.

Brown, C. A. (1992). *No longer be silent*. Louisville, KY: Westminster-John Knox Press.

Buber, M. (1961). *Two types of faith*. New York: Harper.

Buber, M. (1982). *On the Bible*. New York: Schocken

Burgoon, J. K., & Saine, T. (1978). *The unspoken dialogue*. Boston: Houghton Mifflin.

Butler, A. (1999, October 19). Lottery failure proves Alabamians flock of sheep. *Kaleidoscope*, 4.

Cahill, T. (1998). *The gifts of the Jews*. New York: Nan A. Talse-Doubleday.

Carter, S. L. (2000). *God's name in vain: The wrongs and rights of religion in politics*. New York: Basic Books.

Colson, H. P., & Dean, R. J. (1972). *Galatians: Freedom through Christ*. Nashville: Convention Press.

Cooper, D. A. (1997). *God is a verb*. New York: Riverhead.

Corelli, R., & Gregor, A. (1997, April 7). Killer cults. *Maclean's, 110(14)*, 2-4.

Cornforth, M. (1954). *The Theory of Knowledge*. London: Lawrence & Wishart.

Davis, J. M. (1989). On the idea of covenant. *Conservative Judaism, 41(4)*, 20-34.

Davis, K.C. (1999). *Don't know much about the Bible*. New York: Avon.

Davis, W. H. (1968). *Science and Christian faith*. Abilene, Texas: Biblical Research Press.

Davis, W. H. (1969). *Philosophy of Religion*. Abilene, Texas: Biblical Research Press.

Dawood, N. J. (trans.) (1997). *The Koran*. New York: Penguin.

Day, P. L. (1989).*Gender and difference in ancient Israel*. Minneapolis, MN: Fortress Press.

Dershowitz, A. (1988). *Taking liberties*. New York: Contemporary Books.

Dershowitz, A. M. (2000). *The Genesis of justice*. New York: Warner Books.

Dimont, M. I. (1962). *Jews, God and history*. New York: Penguin.

Doctorow, E. L. (2000). *City of God*. New York: Random House

Dodson, J. (1993). *When God doesn't make sense*. Wheaton, IL: Tyndale House

Donin, H. H. (1991). *To be a Jew*. New York: HarperCollins.

Dumont, M. I. (1971). *The indestructible Jews*. New York: Signet.

Earle, W. (1963). The paradox and death of God. In W. Earle, J. M. Edie, & J. Wild (eds.), *Christianity and existentialism* (66-87). Evanston, IL: Northwestern University Press.

Edie, J. M. (1963). Faith as existential choice. In W. Earle, J. M. Edie, & J. Wild (eds.), *Christianity and existentialism* (3-39). Evanston, IL: Northwestern University Press.

Eisen, R. (2000). The education of Abraham: The encounter between Abraham and God over the fate of Sodom and Gomorrah. *Jewish Bible Quarterly, 28(2)*, 80-86.

Eliade, M. (1957). *The sacred & the profane*. New York: Harcourt Brace.

Everett, S. (1991). *The mystery of Melchisedec*. Shippensberg, PA: Destiny Image.

Ewing, A. C. (1962). *The fundamental questions of philosophy*. New York: Collier.

Exum, J. C. (1989). The tragic vision and biblical narrative. In J. C. Exum (Ed.), *Signs and wonders* (pp. 59-84). Semeia Sudies: Society of Biblical Literature.

Exum, J. C. (1993). On Judges 11. In A. Brenner (ed.) *A feminist companion to judges* (131-144). Sheffield, England: Sheffield Academic Press.

Feiler, B. (2001). *Walking through the Bible*. New York: William Morrow.

Forsyth, N. (1987). *The old enemy: Satan and the combat myth*. Princeton: Princeton University Press.

Fox, E. (1995). *The five book of Moses*. New York: Schocken.

Freud, S. (1961). *The Future of an Illusion*. New York: Liveright. (Trans. by W.D. Robson-Scott

Freud, S. (1987). *Moses and monotheism*. New York: Random House.

Friedman, R. E. (1987). *Who wrote the Bible?* New York: Harper & Row.

Fritsch, C. T. (1983). The second book of the Chronicles. In C.M. Laymon (Ed.), *Old Testament History*, (pp. 258-272). Nashville: Abingdon Press.

Fromm, E. (1966). *You shall be as gods.* Greenwich, CN.: Fawcett.

Frye, N. (1982). *The great code.* New York: Harcourt Brace Jovanovich.

Fuchs, E. (1989). Marginalization, ambiguity, silencing: The story of Jephthah's daughter. *Journal of Feminist Studies in Religion, 5,* 35-45.

Geier, T. (1998, March 30). Is there life after death for Heaven's Gate. *U.S. News & World Report, 124(12),* 32.

Ghazali, M. (1994). The problem of evil: An Islamic approach. In *Evil and the response of world religion* (pp. 70-79). New York: Paragon House.

Gibson, J. L. (1999). *Genesis.* Lancaster, PA: Starbord

Ginzberg, L. (1938). *The legend of the Jews* (vol. 4). Philadelphia: Jewish Publication Society.

Girard, R. (1977). *Violence and the sacred.* Baltimore: Johns Hopkins University Press.

Goldstein, E. (1998). *ReVisions: Seeing Torah through a feminist's lens.* Woodstock, VT: Jewish Light Publishing.

Gomes, P. J. (1996). *The good book.* New York: Avon.

Goode, E., & Brownlee, S. (1997, April 7). The eternal quest for a new age. *U.S. News & World Report, 122(13),* 32-34.

Gottwald, N. K. (1983). The book of Deuteronomy. In C.M. Laymon (Ed.), *The Pentateuch* (276-340). Nashville: Abingdon Press.

Grodis, D. (1995). *God was not in the fire.* New York: Touchstone.

Gruen, D. (Ed.) (1997). *Who's who in the Bible.* Lincolnwood, IL: Publications International.

Guinness, A. E. (1988). *Mysteries of the Bible.* Pleasantville, N.Y.: Reader's Digest.

Haley, J. W. (1992). *Alleged discrepancies of the Bible.* Springdale, PA: Whitaker House.

Hall, R. L. (1995). Kierkegaard and the paradoxical logic of worldly faith. *Faith and Philosophy, 12,* 40-53.

Hall, R. L. (2000). Self-deception, confusion, and solution in Fear and Trembling with Works of Love. *Journal of Religious Ethics, 28,* 37-61.

Hamada, L. B. (1990). *Understanding the Arab world.* Nashville: Thomas Nelson.

Hammer, J. (2000, April 3). An apocalyptic mystery. *Newsweek, 135(14),* 46-47.

Hammer, R. (1994). *Entering Jewish prayer.* New York: Shocken Books.

Hanusa, R. L. (1999). Killing the daughter: Judges' Jephthah and The Jew of Malta's Barabas. *Notes & Queries, 46(2),* 199-200.

Harpur, T. (2001). *Would you believe? Finding God without losing your mind.* Toronto: McClelland & Stewart.

Hawking, S. (1998). *A brief history of time.* New York: Bantam Doubleday.

Hertz, J. H. (1981). *The Pentateuch and Haftorahs* (2nd ed). London: Soncino Press.

Heschel, A. J. (1955). *God in search of man: A philosophy of Judaism.* New York: Farrar, Staus, & Giroux.

Heschel, A. J. (1969). *The prophets.* New York: Harper.

Heesterman, J. C. *The broken world of sacrifice.* Chicago: University of Chicago Press.

Hick, J. (1957). *Faith and Knowledge.* Ithaca, NY: Cornell University Press.

Hick, J. H. (1990). *Philosophy of religion* (4th ed.). Englewood Cliffs, NJ: Prentice Hall.

Hill, J., & Cheadle, R. (1996). *The Bible tells me so: Uses and abuses of holy scripture.* New York: Doubleday.

Hooker, B. (1997). Sacrificing for the good of strangers—repeatedly. *Philosophy and Phenomenological Research, 59(1)*, 1-6.

Hornung, E. (2001). *Akhenaten and the religion of light.* Ithaca, NY: Cornell University Press.

Howard, D. M., Jr. (1999). *Fascinating Bible facts.* Lincolnwood, IL: Publications International.

Howard, F. D. (1983). *1 Corinthians: Guidelines for God's people.* Nashville: Convention Press.

Hume, D. (1779). *Dialogues concerning natural religion.* London.

Humphreys, W. L. (1998). Where's Sarah? Echoes of a silent voice in the akedah. *Soundings, 81,* 491-512.

Hunt, D. P. (2001). Evil and theistic minimalism. *International Journal for Philosophy of Religion, 49(3),* 133-154.

Huxley, J. (1957). *Religion without revelation.* New York: New American Library.

Jensen, R. M. (1993). Isaac as a Christological symbol in early Christian art. *ARTS: The Arts in Religious and Theological Studies, 5 (Winter),* 6-12.

Johnson, L. D. (1971). *Out of the whirlwind: The major message of Job.* Nashville: Broadman.

Jones, E. S. (1975). *The divine yes.* Nashville, TN: Abingdon.

Jung, C. S. (1954). *Answer to Job.* London: Routledge and Kegan Paul.

Kant, I. (1960). *Religion within the limits of reason alone.* New York: Harper & Row.

Keller, J. A. (1995). The hiddenness of God and the problem of evil. *International Journal for Philosophy of Religion, 37(1),* 11-22.

Keller, W. (1980). *The Bible as history.* New York: Bantam.

Kelley, P. H. (1977). *Exodus: Call for redemptive mission.* Nashville: Convention Press.

Kierkegaard, S. (1968). *Fear and trembling.* Princeton: Princeton University Press.

Kimball, C. (2000). *When religion becomes evil.* New York: HarperCollins.

Kirsch, J. (1997). *The harlot by the side of the road.* New York: Ballantine.

Krakauer, J. (2003). *Under the banner of Heaven.* New York: Doubleday.

Kugel, J. L. (1997). *The Bible as it was.* Cambridge, MA: Belknap Press/Harvard University Press.

Lacayo, R. (1997, April 7). The lure of the cult. *Time, 149(14),* 44-46.

Landers, S. (1991). Did Jephthah kill his daughter. *Bible Review, 7(Aug.),* 28-31, 42.

Landsburg, A., & Landsburg, S. (1974). *In search of ancient mysteries.* New York: Bantam.

Laperrousaz, E. M. (1987). King Solomon's wall still supports the Temple Mount. *Biblical Archaeological Review, 13(3),* 34-44.

Laytner, A. (1900). *Arguing with God: A Jewish tradition.* New Jersey: Aronson

Leavell, R. Q. (1962). *Studies in Matthew: The King and the Kingdom.* Nashville: Convention Press.

Lerch, D. (1950). *Isaaks opferung christlich gedeutet: Eine auslegungsgeschichliche untersuchung.* Turbingen: J. C. B. Mohr.

Lerch, D. (1950). *Isaaks Opferung.* Turbingen: J.C.B. Mohr.

Levenson, J. D. (1998). Abusing Abraham: Traditions, religious histories and modern misinterpretations. *Judaism, 47,* 259-277.

Levine, M. P. (1994). Pantheism, theism and the problem of evil. *International Journal for Philosophy of Religion, 35(3),* 129-151.

Lewis, C. S. (1996). *The problem of pain.* New York: Touchstone.

Lewis, C. S. (2001). *The Screwtape letters.* San Francisco: Harper.

Lyman, L. M., & Scott, M. G. (1967). Territoriality: A neglected sociological dimension. *Social Problems, 15,* 236-249.

MacArthur, J. F. (1998). *In the footsteps of faith.* Wheaton, IL: Crossway.

MacArtney, C. E. (1997). *The greatest men in the Bible.* Grand Rapids, MI: Kregel.

Marcus, D. (1986). *Jephthah and his vow.* Lubbock: Texas Tech University Press.

Marcus, D. (1989). The bargaining between Jephthah and the elders. *Journal of the Ancient Near Eastern Society, 19,* 95-100.

Marcus, D. (1990). The legal dispute between Jephthah and the elders. *Hebrew Annual Review, 12,* 105-114.

Marks, J. H. (1983). The book of Genesis. In C.M. Laymon (Ed.), *The Pentateuch,* 1-88. Nashville: Abingdon Press.

May, R. (1992). *Man's search for himself.* New York: Delacorte Press.

McGee, J. V. (1991). *Genesis: Chapters 16-33.* Nashville: Thomas Nelson.

McLuhan, M. (1964). *Understanding media: The extensions of man.* New York: Signet.

Mendelsohn, I. (1953). The disinheritance of Jephthah in the light of paragraph 27 of the Lipit-Ishtar Code. *Israel Exploration Journal, 4(2),* 116-119.

Miles, J. (1996). *God: A biography.* New York: Vintage Books.

Mill, J. S. (1874). *Three essays on religion.* London.

Miller, M. S., & Miller, J. L. (1996). *Harper's encyclopedia of Bible life.* Edison, NJ: Castle Books.

Moyers, B. (1996). *Genesis: A living conversation.* New York: Doubleday.

Murphy, C. (1998). *The Word according to Eve.* Boston: Houghton Mifflin.

Murphy, F. J. (1995). The problem of evil and a plausible defense. *Religious Studies, 31,* 243-250.

O'Connor, D. (1996). A reformed problem of evil and the free will defense. *International Journal for Philosophy of Religion, 39(1)* 33-63.

Orr, J. E. (1977). *The faith that persuades.* New York: Harper & Row.

Ostriker, A. (2001). Jephthah's daughter: *CrossCurrents, 51(2),* 201-218.

Oz, A. (1981). *Where the jackals howl and other stories.* New York: Harcourt Brace Jovanovich.

Pagels, E. (1996). *The origin of Satan.* New York: Vintage.

Pelikan, J. (1985). *Jesus through the centuries.* New York: Harper & Row.

Penchansky, D. (1992). Staying the night. In D. N. Fewell (ed.) *Reading between texts* (pp. 77-97). Louisville, KY: Westminster-John Knox Press.

Perry, D. (2000, Dec. 30). Temple Mount: Ground zero in Jerusalem. *Birmingham News/Post-Herald,* p. C8.

Pike, N. (Ed.) (1964). *God and evil.* Englewood Cliffs, NJ: Prentice-Hall.

Pilzer, P. Z. (1995). *God wants you to be rich: The theology of economics.* New York: Simon & Schuster.

Pinnock, C. H. (Ed.) (1994). *The openness of God.* Downers Grove, IL: Intervarsity Press.

Price, R. (1997). *The stones cry out.* Eugene, OR: Harvest House.

Provenzo, E. F., Jr., & Provenzo, A. B. (2002). *In the eye of Hurricane Andrews.* Miami: Florida Press.

Rader, D. (2001, Dec. 2). 'I discovered what faith and love are really about.' *Parade,* 4-6.

Ramras-Rauch, G. (1990). Fathers and Daughters. *Bucknell Review, 33(2),* 158-169.

Redford, D. B. (1987). *Akhenaten: The heretic king.* Princeton, NJ: Princeton University Press.

Reeves, C. N., & Reeves, N. (2001). *Akhenaten: Egypt's false prophet.* New York: Thames & Hudson.

Reis, P. T. (1997). Spoiled child: A fresh look at Jephthah's daughter. *Prooftexts, 17(3),* 279-298.

Riskin S. (1997). *Confessions of a biblical commentator.* Ohr Torah Institutions.

Ritmeyer, K., & Ritmeyer, L. (1989). Herod's Temple Mount ☐ Stone by stone. *Biblical Archaeological Review, 15(6),* 23-53.

Ritmeyer, L. (1992). Locating the original temple mount. *Biblical Archaeological Review, 18(2),* 24-45, 64-65.

Roman, M. (2004, April 4). Spain bombing suspects blow themselves up. *The Birmingham News,* 1A, 11A.

Roper, H. R. T. (1947). *The last days of Hitler.* New York: MacMillan.

Russell, J. B. (1970). *The Devil: Perceptions of evil from antiquity and primitive Christianity.* Ithaca, NY: Cornell University Press.

Ryan, P. J. (1991, April 27). Self-sacrifice. *America, 164(16),* 479.

Sailhamer, J. H. (1998). *Christian theology.* Grand Rapids, MI: Zondervan.

Sanders, J. (1999). *The God who risks: A theology of providence.* Downers Grove, IL: Intervarsity Press.

Sarna, N. H. (1970). *Understanding Genesis.* New York: Schocken Books.

Schulweis, H. (1994). *For those who can't believe.* New York: HarperCollins.

Self, W. R. (1997). *A comparative analysis of privacy paradigms: The range of legal and social science conceptualizations.* Unpublished doctoral dissertation, University of Alabama, Tuscaloosa.

Shadid, A. (2003, Aug. 1). For an Iraqi family, no other choice. *Washington Post,* A1.

Shakespeare, W. (1973). *The complete works of Shakespeare.*Glenville, IL: Foresman.

Shakir, M. H. (trans.) (2002). *The Qur'an* (13th ed.). Elmhurst, NY: Tahrike Tarsile Qur'an.

Shubert, S. (2000). Abraham's trials: Tests of strength or learning experience? *Jewish Bible Quarterly, 28(2),* 56-65.

Singleton, W. C., III (2001, Dec. 20). Beliefs a way of life for many. *Birmingham Post-Herald,* A1, A6.

Smith, H. (1965). *The religions of man.* New York: Harper & Row.

Smith, R. H. (1983). The book of Judges. In C. M. Laymon (Ed.), *Old Testament History,* (39-80). Nashville: Abingdon Press.

Smith, W. (1948). *Smith's Bible dictionary.* Grand Rapids, MI: Zondervan.

Smith, W. C. (1979). *Faith and belief.* Princeton, NJ: Princeton University Press.

Spiegel, S. (1993). *The last trial.* Woodstock, VT: Jewish Lights.

Spong, J. S. (1991). *Rescuing the Bible from fundamentalism.* San Francisco: HarperCollins.

Stoen, J. (1997, April 7). The most horrible night of my life. *Newsweek, 129(14),* 44-45.

Strassfeld, M. (1985). *The Jewish holidays.* New York: Harper & Row.

Streisand, B. (1997, April 7). www.masssuicide.com. *U.S. News & World Report, 122(13),* 26-30.

Strom, B. (1998). *More than talk: Communication studies and the Christian faith.* Dubuque, IA: Kendall-Hunt

Tapp, A. M. (1989). An ideology of expendability: Virgin daughter sacrifice in Genesis 19.1-11, Judges 11.30-39, and 19.22-26. In M. Bal (ed.), *Anti-Covenant* (158-174). Sheffield, England: Almond Press.

Taylor, J. (1997, June). Heaven couldn't wait. *Esquire, 127(6),* 40-43.

Telushkin, J. (1997). *Biblical literacy.* New York: William Morrow.

Tennant, F.R. (1930). *Philosophical Theology* (Vo. 2). New York: Cambridge University Press.

The World's Great Religions (1957). New York: Simon & Schuster, Inc.

Thomas, W.H.G. (1985). *The Pentateuch.* Grand Rapids, MI: Kregel.

Tinker, M. (1995). The suffering of man and the sovereignty of God: An examination of the relationship between the problem of evil and the purposes of God. *Churchman, 109(1),* 50-60.

Traylor, E. G. (1988). *Song of Abraham.* Wheaton, IL: Living Books.

Trible, P. (1981). A meditation in mourning: The sacrifice of the daughter of Jephthah. *Union Seminary Quarterly Review, 36,* 59-73.

Trimiew, A. (1999). *Bible almanac.* Lincolnwood, IL: Publications International.

Unger, P. (1997). *Living high and letting die: Our illusion of innocence.* New York: Oxford University Press.

Urban, L. (1995). *A short history of Christian thought.* New York: Oxford University Press.

Von Daniken, E. (1971). *Chariots of the gods?* New York: Bantam.

Watson, C. D. (1978). *Will you die for me?* Old Tappan. New Jersey: Fleming H. Revell.

Webb, B. G. (1986). The theme of the Jephthah story. *The Reformed Theological Review, 45(2),* 34-43.

Weissman, M. (1980). *The Midrash says.* Brooklyn: Bnai Yakov.

Wevers, J. W. (1983a). The first book of the Kings. In C.M. Laymon (Ed.), *Old Testament History,* (169-207). Nashville: Abingdon Press.

Wevers, J. W. (1983b). The second book of the Kings. In C.M. Laymon (Ed.), *Old Testament History,* (208-238). Nashville: Abingdon Press.

Whitmore, J., Jr. (Director). (1999). *The Pretender.* New York: NBC.

Whitney, B. L. (1994). An aesthetic solution to the problem of evil. *International Journal for Philosophy of Religion, 35(1),* 21-37.

Wiegall, A. (2000). *The life and times of Akhnaton.* Lanham, MD: Cooper Square Press.

Wiersbe, W. (1991). *Be obedient.* Colorado Springs: Chariot Victor Publishing

Wiesel, E. (1981). *Night.* (Translator, S. Rodway). Harmondsworth.

Willis, T. M. (1997). The nature of Jephthah's authority. *Catholic Biblical Quarterly, 59(1),* 33-42.

Wooley, C. L., & Moorey, P. R. S. (1982). *Ur of the Chaldes: A revised and updated edition of Sir Leonard Wooley's Excavation at Ur.* Ithaca, NY: Cornell University Press.

Yancey, P. (1999). *The Bible Jesus read.* Grand Rapids, MI: Zondervan.

Younce, D. (2001, Nov. 1). Trust God. *Alabama Baptist,* p. 15.

Zagzebski, L. (1996). An agent-based approach to the problem of evil. *International Journal for Philosophy of Religion, 39(3),* 127-139.

Index